Yeats
and the
Logic of
Formalism

Yeats
and the
Logic of
Formalism

Vereen M. Bell

University of Missouri Press
Columbia and London

Library of Congress Cataloging-in-Publication Data

Bell, Vereen M., 1934–
    Yeats and the logic of formalism / Vereen M. Bell.
        p.   cm.
    Summary: "Attempts to balance traditional and modern criticism of Yeats by
linking formalism and philosophy in the context of Yeats's work and evaluates
its credibility in Yeats's practice in relation to other theoretical discourses and in
the context of the turbulent cultural and historical circumstances under which
Yeats worked"—Provided by publisher.
    Includes bibliographical references and index.
    ISBN-13: 978-0-8262-1612-0 (alk. paper)
    ISBN-10: 0-8262-1612-9 (alk. paper)
    1. Yeats, W. B. (William Butler), 1865–1939—Criticism and interpretation.
2. Formalism (Literary analysis)   3. Philosophy in literature.   I. Title.
    PR5907.B36   2005
    821'.8—dc22   2005026483

Designer: Stephanie Foley
Typesetter: Phoenix Type, Inc.
Printer and binder: Thomson-Shore, Inc.
Typefaces: Adobe Caslon and New Caledonia

For credits, see page 201.

For Jane and our wonderful children:
Mary, Leighton, Eleanor, Julie, and Jonathan;
and for Will, Roy, Jim, Dan, Cliff, Gerald, and Bobby

The use of [poesy] hath been to give some shadow of satisfaction to the mind of man in those points wherein the nature of things doth deny it, the world being in proportion inferior to the soul; by reason whereof there is, agreeable to the spirit of man, a more ample greatness, a more exact goodness, and a more absolute variety, than can be found in the nature of things.... And therefore [poesy] was ever thought to have some participation of divineness, because it doth raise and erect the mind; ... whereas reason doth buckle and bow the mind unto the nature of things.

Francis Bacon, *The Advancement of Learning, Book II*, 96–97

Contents

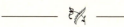

Acknowledgments

———— ❧ ————

I WISH, FIRST of all, to express my thanks to Carolyn Levinson and to Scott Hicks, whose extraordinary care and patience in the preparation of this manuscript have been indispensable. I wish to thank Helen Vendler and Roy Gottfried for carefully reading this manuscript at different stages and for giving invaluable criticism and advice. I wish to thank the Guggenheim Foundation for their generous underwriting of this project at the very beginning. I wish to thank Janis May, Sara Corbitt, Natalie Baggett, Dori Mikus, Paul Burch, and August Johnson for their friendship and support.

And finally I wish to express my gratitude to the staff of Vanderbilt Dining Services, who simply by being themselves and doing their jobs have made their workplace into a second home for others.

Chapter 1 was first published in a different form in *The Southern Review.*

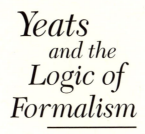

Yeats
and the
Logic of
Formalism

Prologue

———— ❧ ————

WHAT FOLLOWS in this study is yet another "master reading" of Yeats's poems. I express it in this ironic way in order to observe one of the conventions that has persisted in Yeats criticism since the mid-sixties, forced upon us by the energy, subtlety, and the capaciousness of his mind. Amy Stock felt obliged to say in 1961: "There are more ways than one of approaching most poets, and I should be sorry if the hypothetical reader mistook mine for the only one." Thomas R. Whitaker wrote at the beginning of his foundational study in 1964, "We continue to pool our efforts at understanding and judgment," and he cites Allen Tate as having pointed out the obvious, "'that Yeats had a more inclusive mind than any of his critics has had.'" "Yeats's mask-theory," Edward Engelberg says, "seems, when applied to poetic theory, essentially an attempt to escape the tyranny of a single identifiable persona; or to invest the persona with personae that defy a categorical definition or reduction." The capacity Yeats had for reinventing himself and his own ideas was his most distinctively modernist trait, and it kept him from being claimable for any single master-reading or ideology. Richard Ellmann gave this explanation:

> Our backs against the wall, we cannot decide whether reality is adequately described by our intimations of a state of completeness, or whether it is describable only as the opposite of all that we can see or imagine. In either case the artist must be its interpreter. Affirmative capability does not free him from the responsibility of intellectual search or understanding of experience, as negative capability might seem to; rather it forces him to live, as well as to write, in such a way that his consciousness will be inclusive. Any narrowness, any adherence to a given affirmation beyond the moment that it satisfies the whole being, any averting of the eye, destroys the vision.... [Affirmative capability] is suited to a time when man is not regarded as a fixed being with

1

fixed habits, but as a being continually adapting and readapting himself to the changing conditions of his body and mind and of the outside world.[1]

Least of all, on these readings, could Yeats's work ultimately be claimed by such critical philosophies as have the stabilizing schema of Plato and Plotinus as their points of reference. This is not only because in "The Tower" Yeats explicitly rejects such schema as symbols of a now-unserviceable metaphysic but because they seemed to him to discredit the labor of creation that gives the poet and his imagination their reason for being: "I mock Plotinus' thought / And cry in Plato's teeth / Death and life were not / Till man made up the whole, / Made lock, stock and barrel / Out of his bitter soul." That Yeats was closest in "the history of thought" to Plotinus and Diogenes Laertius today seems a strange claim, and it was not even supported in argument by Morton Seiden in the text in which it appeared. Kathleen Raine's combative identification with Blake and Yeats as fellow initiates in the ancient esoteric traditions—and as fellow explorers "of a greater truth than our own complacent yet despicably second-rate materialist ideologies offer"—is plausible in the context she constructs but seems oddly dissonant when the context is Yeats's poems alone. Nor could *A Vision* ever have been thought of as a skeleton key to Yeats's work since he himself spoke so explicitly of its being heuristic and imaginary, "stylistic arrangements of experience" that he unambiguously identified with the abstractions of high modernist art. F. A. C. Wilson argued that a full body of esoteric knowledge was necessary to an understanding of Yeats's poems and that the Platonist and Kabbalist doctrine of obedience to an inflexible, symbolic language—derived from a "central fountainhead"—was one to which Yeats unambivalently subscribed. In Wilson's view, all readings of Yeats are naive that do not trace his symbols back to that "central fountainhead." But even as Wilson advances this argument, specific cases in specific poems eventually begin to contradict and deconstruct it.[2] It is credible that Yeats was attracted to Plotinus as a

1. A. G. Stock, *W. B. Yeats: His Poetry and Thought,* ix; Thomas R. Whitaker, *Swan and Shadow: Yeats's Dialogue with History,* 16; Edward Engelberg, *The Vast Design: Patterns in W. B. Yeats's Aesthetic,* 8; Richard Ellmann, *The Identity of Yeats,* 244.

2. Morton Irving Seiden, *William Butler Yeats: The Poet as a Mythmaker, 1865–1939,* 3; Kathleen Raine, *Yeats the Initiate: Essays on Certain Themes in the Work of*

way, as Wilson observes, to defend himself against the changingness of the world, and classical Neoplatonism would certainly have reinforced Yeats's disposition to think in terms of hierarchies of conditions of being; but to say that Plotinus's thought became a religion for Yeats is to disbelieve in the dynamic interaction of the poems themselves with their passion for transmuting life and history from the rawest of raw materials that life and history cast up. It is also to ignore the poems' reembodiments and celebrations of the things of the world—of conflict and contradiction, of sexuality and the body, of erotic love, of friendship, of war—of "[w]hatever is begotten, born, and dies," in short, or what Yeats himself called "tragic joy." It is not *Presence* but *presences* in "Among School Children" that mock enterprise, and even they are invented, he says—born out of the self.

Yeats processed and co-opted ideas and ideologies eclectically. He was not the sort of "primary" personality who was susceptible to being co-opted *by* them. We are compelled to continue to pool our resources because Yeats was so inexhaustible in pooling his own, a *bricoleur* of the first order. His interests in mystery religions, in Platonism, Neoplatonism, Hinduism, Buddhism, the Kabbalah, occult sciences, Christianity, Irish mythology and folklore—not many of which have very much in common with any of the others—were all mainly aspects of his desire to rescue human life from banality, from science, and from the mechanist, utilitarian philosophies that seemed to him to dominate the nineteenth century.

It makes sense, then, to speak as Patrick J. Keane has done of Yeats's *interactions* with tradition rather than to expound a case for his obedience to *a* tradition, allowing for the fact that Yeats's romanticism was a kind of multicultural tradition of its own. "Yeatsian Romanticism," Keane points out, "becomes increasingly '*antithetical*,' a life-affirming vitalism opposed, in Yeats's dialectical quarrel with himself, to '*primary*' religious transcendence." Keane presses his point by arguing that Yeats's

---

W. B. Yeats, 437–38; F. A. C. Wilson, *W. B. Yeats and Tradition,* 28. In the first chapter Wilson says "Yeats knew that the sea was a traditional symbol for the malevolence of the natural world, and always used it as such" (32–33); in the last part he says, "The symbolic system of Neoplatonism [which Yeats has been shown to draw upon] was fixed and one might even say rigid: the sea, for example, symbolizes always 'the waters of emotion and passion'; or simply life" (199). For a sense of just how *de*-stabilized Yeats's poetry can be shown to be under poststructuralist scrutiny, see Edward Larrisey, *Yeats the Poet: The Measure of Difference.*

interest in the philosophy of Alfred North Whitehead was a continuation itself of what Whitehead had called the romantics' "'protest against the exclusion of value from the essence of matter of fact.'" Yeats had said of Whitehead, "I have now read the greater part of [*Science and the Modern World*] and so far it seems to me my own point of view. [Whitehead] proves, as I think, that the mechanical theory of the world is untrue."[3] The problem is that Yeats also enthusiastically endorsed at different times the philosophies of Kant, Schopenhauer, and Nietzsche, for example, none of whom was endorsed by Whitehead or shared Whitehead's precisely rationalized crypto-Platonic metaphysic. Yeats "interacted" with both modern philosophies and ancient ones in a pragmatic, ad hoc way. The modern philosophies that Yeats did interact with had in common the intellectual strategies committed to what Keane calls "a protest on behalf of value."

Being antithetical in this way entailed imposing the human moral will back upon the otherwise amoral content of mere unmediated life. This attitude, in turn, was forced upon him by his fatalistic reading of history where he saw eternally (and purposelessly) conflicting forces engaged. *A Vision*, Declan Kiberd points out, has an obvious kinship with the historiographical models of Bruno, Hegel, and Marx. (The example of Nietzsche is relevant here, too, though Kiberd does not say so.) What Bruno, Marx, Hegel, and Yeats (and Nietzsche) have in common is a concept of history as what we would now call a "deconstructive" process. Kiberd quotes Yeats on the logic of the gyres: "'[Every] movement in feeling or thought, prepares in the dark by its own increasing identity and confidence, its own execution.'" What is missing in Yeats's version of this dialectic is the third term, *synthesis*, and this means that linearity and progression are missing, also. Without linearity and progression, a logical and ultimately tragic option for the poet is what the generation of Irish critics associated with Kiberd finds most troublesome in Yeats's work, an aesthetic ideology that either mediates or overrides altogether such political considerations as are imagined to lead to material progress. And yet, as Kiberd also points out, even aesthetic ideology, especially for a colonial subject, can be grounded in a mode of political resistance:

3. Patrick J. Keane, *Yeats's Interactions with Tradition*, xvii; W. B. Yeats and T. Sturge Moore, *W. B. Yeats and T. Sturge Moore: Their Correspondence, 1901–1937*, 89.

A writer in a free state works with the easy assurance that literature is but one of the social institutions to project the values which the nation admires, others being the law, the government, the army, and so on. A writer in a colony knows that these values can be fully embodied only in the written word: hence the daunting seriousness with which literature is taken by subject peoples.... Attention is given less to the concrete world ... than to the fertile minds which repeatedly displace it with their own superior alternatives. Art in this context might be seen as man's constant effort to create for himself a different order of reality from that which is given to him: against the ability to imagine things as they are, it counterpoises the capacity to imagine things as they might be. Fictions, though they treat of the non-existent, by that very virtue help people to make sense of the world around them.[4]

The paradoxes embedded in this issue will remain pervasive in Yeats's thought. Writing—appropriately for this context—of the theme of desire in Wallace Stevens's poetry, Helen Vendler observes that "It is not possible for us to live without desire."

[We] cannot help but engage in that process that Freudians call idealization and trace to Oedipal causes. Our common names for idealization are romantic love, religious belief, and political engagement: these do not differ in essence, for Stevens, from the poet's creation of the aesthetic object of desire. All human beings engage in poesis in constituting an imagined world to live in; and the engagement in poesis is coterminous with life. To be alive is to desire.[5]

Among the modernist poets—perhaps of all poets writing in English— it was Yeats who kept the commonalities of this triad—"romantic love, religious belief, and political engagement"—closest to the surface of his poems and made his great theme of their perpetual dialogue with one another.

Thomas R. Whitaker quotes Kierkegaard as arguing that the system builder "is tempted to ignore his own involvement in the world of change and contingency and to find a self-deceptive haven in his nontemporal vision." Yeats was certainly a system builder in one of his vocations. Characteristically, his system was grounded in his repeated engagements

4. Declan Kiberd, *Inventing Ireland: The Literature of the Modern Nation*, 320, 118.

5. Helen Vendler, *Wallace Stevens: Words Chosen out of Desire*, 32.

with authentic temporal history—in his refusal, being Irish, to ignore history—and eventually he made modest gestures toward disclaiming *A Vision*. But the fact of the existence of that system shows a depth and strength in his commitment to impose his own thought and cultural values upon the thoughtlessness of the world and to give the world and history a theme. "All art," he argued, was in some way "the disengaging of a soul from place and history."[6] Dante, Keats, and Synge, he said, had distorted and adapted history to their own purposes, but in doing so they had added not to our knowledge but to our *being*. Adding to our being was Yeats's project, too—political as well as aesthetic. Art was the supplement for him without which there is nothing.

The terms "art" and "soul" are cognate in Yeats's lexicon and interdependent in his thought. "Art delights . . . in the soul expressing itself according to its own laws and arranging the world about it in its own pattern."[7] As a metaphor, the "soul" symbolizes for Yeats the desire in human consciousness to overcome the limitations and contradictions of its own material and political state. At the same time, traditional or conventional connotations of the "soul" lend to art, by association, at least the illusion of transcendent authority. But then art remains nevertheless a human construct—as in "the artifice of eternity"—and its identification with the "soul" in Yeats's vocabulary grounds the idea of the "soul" within contingency so as to make of it an expression of otherwise thwarted existential desire. At the site of this impassable threshold—between "art" and "soul," natural and supernatural—is an aporia of a kind that Yeats would have had no embarrassment in laying claim to. It was his subject, and he struggled throughout his career to give that subject formal definition and identity.

It may not be accurate to claim, as Morton Seiden has, that Yeats felt out of place in the modern world because he hated "democracy, science, and laissez-faire capitalism";[8] but Yeats clearly formed his identity as a poet, as a maker, out of his engagement with those modern forces and out of his desire to transmute and overcome them. Ironically, he was dependent, therefore, upon the world out of which those modern forces emerged and also upon there being no antecedent transcendent Presence that took their place. His instructors for *A Vision* showed him

6. Whitaker, *Swan and Shadow*, 9; W. B. Yeats, *Essays and Introductions*, 339–40.
7. W. B. Yeats, *Explorations*, 168.
8. Seiden, *Poet as a Mythmaker*, 9; W. B. Yeats, *A Vision*, 71; 214.

the double-interlocking cones in order to illustrate for him that "subjectivity and objectivity [are] intersecting states struggling one against the other." They also told him that they "identify consciousness with conflict."

In this struggle Yeats shrewdly adapted and modernized the aesthetic doctrines of nineteenth-century German and English romanticism. He brought forward with these aesthetic doctrines a stern Kantian ethic. These elements visible in his work encouraged major post–World War II critics—doubtless as a reaction to the appalling three decades of human history in which they had matured—to stress the Platonist and Platonized Christian aspects of Yeats's work. Part of the point of the present study is to extend the discussion that has centered around such aesthetic and philosophical ambiguities while focusing, on the other hand, upon what Richard Ellmann called the "Yeats without Analogues." I wish to show how what I have called "formalism" in my title regulates both form and content at all levels in Yeats's work and unifies his thought without ideologically rigidifying it. I use the term *formalism* not in the narrow Russian sense (though the two usages are related) but in an existential one. Frank Lentricchia linked Yeats and Wallace Stevens as co-workers in this kind of formalist project and in the process clearly defined its paradoxical terms: "The impact of symbolist theory on the two poets is clear: it is not epistemological, but aesthetic in the sense that both understand a poem to be a closed system of interrelated verbal effects, whose purpose is to suggest a sense of harmony, wholeness, and unity which is not allowed by the naturalistic and existential sense of reality which they project." Formalism in this aspect may be said to express the desire, as Yeats said of *A Vision,* "to hold in a single thought reality and justice," or as Frank Kermode has expressed it, "a concord between the human mind and things as they are."[9]

⚡

The Yeats who is both a victim and the master of this existential antimony is the Yeats who is in the foreground of this present study. In

9. Richard Ellmann, "Yeats without Analogues," 30–47; Frank Lentricchia, *The Gaiety of Language: An Essay on the Radical Poetics of W. B. Yeats and Wallace Stevens,* 191–92; Frank Kermode, *The Sense of an Ending: Studies in the Theory of Fiction,* 150.

this manifestation he is most recognizable in both the overt and covert strategies of "Sailing to Byzantium." Both the pattern and the logic of this poem's own rhetoric eventually complicate and subvert what appears on the surface of it to be a single-minded assertion of art's power to transcend nature and of the soul's to transcend the body. It is plain enough that the poet in the poem whose heart is sick with desire is not sick with desire for a Neoplatonic eternity but sick with desire for the generative cycle of nature—"eterne in mutabilitie" as Spenser described it,[10] which, in a cruel irony, by its own logic, ensures the very aging and physical decay which now requires that he be excluded from it. Even without overscrupulous decoding, the poem appears to be spoken by one whose primary disposition toward the world is at least as sexual and erotic as it is aesthetic and spiritual. Given the plight of his mortality, but *only* given that plight—his heart "fastened to a dying animal"—his only recourse is art. But art here is also only that, a recourse, a psychological refuge, where desire may be imagined to become sublimated or redirected so that it is no longer born, as the poet expresses it in "Among School Children," "out of its own despair."

In "Sailing to Byzantium" there is a sorrow in the loss required by this essentially alienating process. This is first noticeable in the way in which the ennui of the fanciful Byzantine world of the last stanza (where nature itself has disappeared except to be sung of) contrasts with the undrowsy, indiscriminate, primal animation—"caught in that sensual music"—of the world in stanza one. This depletion is then encoded in the way in which the verbal substantiality of whatever is "begotten, born, and dies" is emptied out in the poem's final line to become the disembodied abstractness of "what is past, or passing, or to come." The change of "whatever is begotten, born, and dies" into "what is past, or passing, or to come" denotes a second parallel narrative line conducted within the poem's language itself. In the first stanza the aged man, who is ostensibly estranged from the exuberant turmoil of generation, seems nevertheless to speak through its creatures to commend *with* them "whatever is begotten, born, and dies," being in the midst of life, even though also necessarily therefore in the midst of death. The tableau of disaffection he imagines himself a part of at the end of his soul's journey is so far out of life and death, being "out of nature," that it does

---

10. From Spenser's "The Garden of Adonis"; see Kermode's discussion of the tradition of the *aevum* in *Sense of an Ending*, 67–81.

not permit the stately affirmation of *commending*, only *singing of,* and even that is first deflected by singing *to.* So there is at least a shadow of a sense of a diminishing of the poet's powers from beginning to end. In this shadow the poet appears to have intuited that in eternity he has stepped out of the role from which his powers derive.

The poet's specifically poetic powers derive from the will both to be of the world and to overcome it. That those powers (as opposed to his sexual powers) are intact is evidenced by the poem itself, and they are still intact because what he imagines happening in the holy city of Byzantium has in fact not yet taken place. Old man or not, he is still among the dying generations and is as caught up as they are in the sensual music. The poem by design loops back upon itself at the end, because of the echo in the phrasing—"begotten, born, and dies"; "past, or passing, or to come"—and brings this stubborn, contraindicated presence in it back to life. The symbol of that life is the commanding formality, the shapedness of the poem itself—a model if there ever was one of "a closed system of verbal effects, whose purpose is to suggest a sense of harmony, wholeness, and unity that is not allowed by the naturalistic and existential sense of reality which [it projects]." To be able to dwell in this paradox without recourse to metaphysical strategies of evasion was for Yeats the point of being a poet: the affirmation of a dialectic in which art and life, without succeeding, struggle eternally to be reconciled.

I accept in advance the criticism of my approach in this study that I fail to discuss at greater length Yeats's artistry as a poet, which, of course, is what makes such a study as this worth preparing in the first place: his subtle, attentive ear for the musical properties of the English (and Anglo-Irish) language and for the expressive possibilities of its idiomatic range; his rhetorical command of the physical properties of words as well as their content as signs ("Passion and conquest, wander where they will, / Attend upon them still"); of his resourceful decorum in the use of metaphor; his creativeness in adapting and modernizing traditional English and European verse forms; his mastery of the rhetorical nuances of syntax. But these extraordinary aesthetic gifts Yeats possessed as a poet were put to the service of his existential project, too. Indeed, in some irreducible way they *are* the project—music and language and form forging their own kind of victory over the irrationality and ordinariness of the world. As Amy Stock said in her preface, "It is true that a poet's ideas cannot be detached from his words, but there is nothing wrong in taking his ideas seriously: to believe that great art does not grow out of flabby thinking is not the same thing as mistaking the 'message' for the greatness of the art."[11]

Citing in that preface studies that had been useful to her, Professor Stock also said, "I have found in them the kind of stimulus that one gets from well-informed discussion, and without consciously echoing any of them must often have said the same things."[12] Anyone who has undertaken to write about Yeats's work understands both the burden and the privilege implied in that deferential remark. And that was more than forty-five years ago, before the contributions of Norman Jeffares, Helen Vendler, Denis Donoghue, Thomas Parkinson, Hazard Adams, Frank Kermode, Donald Torchiana, George Bornstein, Thomas Whitaker, Kathleen Raine, Curtis Bradford, Frank Lentricchia, Harold Bloom, Jon Stallworthy, George Harper, and Edward Engelberg—or, more recently, Elizabeth Cullingford, Phillip Marcus, Terry Eagleton, Seamus Deane, Declan Kiberd, Terence Brown, and Roy Foster. The burden of indebtedness has become greater and, literally, incalculable. The dialogue has become livelier and more global. Yeats, of course, was an animated controversialist himself and was a mischievous and subversive exponent of outrageous views; he would not have wanted it any other way.

11. Stock, *W. B. Yeats*, vii.
12. Ibid.

1

Introduction

———— ✢ ————

Western minds who follow the Eastern way become weak and vapoury because they become unfit for the work forced upon them by Western life. Every symbol is an invocation which produces its equivalent expression in all worlds. The Incarnation involved modern science and modern efficiency and also modern lyric feeling which gives body to the most spiritual emotions. It produced a solidification of all things that grew from the individual will. . . . The historical truth of the Incarnation is indifferent, though the belief in that truth was essential to the power of the evocation. All civilization is held together by a series of suggestions made by an invisible hypnotist, artificially created illusions. The knowledge of reality is always by some means or other a secret knowledge. It is a kind of death.

Memoirs

I N HIS STUDY of Yeats's work, *Out of Ireland,* Dudley Young describes a claim that the imagination has upon identity in such a way as to claim for poetry the power to affect real change in the world by affecting the idiom through which we think ourselves into existence.

As the philosopher and the scientist take over a culture's classification, the poet's assertions become metaphorical; that is, they no longer proclaim *identities* between Man and Nature but only resemblances. For example, when the primitive Greek poet says "An angry man is a roaring lion," this means that the man actually becomes a lion, participates in the Form of leoninity. But when the culture no longer looks to the poet for such definitions, the statement can only mean that an angry man behaves in a similar fashion to a roaring lion. To discover what anger really is we look to the psychologist, and these days he tells us that it is drive-acceleration; and of course the psychologist is right. Henceforth when a man is invaded by the leonine he will feel like a high-revving machine, and we can expect the culture to be modified accordingly. The poet may go on saying that anger is *like* a roaring lion, but we who know it is drive-acceleration can only smile at the pretty epithet and agree that poets are idlers and fantasists.

In short, when the poet must settle for metaphor, his magical powers are in decline. In the case of western culture, this has meant that we have come to experience ourselves and the world as machinery instead of living substance—a cliché of Romanticism but none the less true for that. The implications are serious because the major human experiences, of birth and death, of duty and love and virtue, cannot be registered meaningfully as mechanism; and without them a culture collapses, as ours has.[1]

A point that deserves underscoring in this passage is that the two kinds of discourse, represented by "leonine" on the one hand and "drive-acceleration" on the other, are both metaphorical, but that they represent two different functions of language in its approach to human reality, or to what we refer to as human reality when we speak of what language is about. The metaphor of the lion is intended to be value-laden, and the metaphor of "drive-acceleration" is intended to be neutral, though of course it cannot be. The poet's image is shaped to the purpose of a metaphorical enhancement of reality, the psychologist's to a descriptive representation of it, and since they serve different functions, they are not in any real sense competitive. "Drive-acceleration" is fundamentally a materialistic notion; "leonine" is, too, but it has the rhetorical merit of seeming not to be. The relationship was described concisely in 1877 by the neo-Kantian Friedrich Lange. The assumptions underlying materialism are our most reliable access to reality, Lange argued, but "man needs to supplement reality by an ideal world of his own creation," a world of value "against which neither logic, nor touch of the hand, nor sight of the eye can avail."[2] The difference is analogous to thinking of Lough Gill in County Sligo as a great pool of Giles's nursemaids' tears, as the story of Omra and Romra would have it, and thinking of it as a limestone basin collecting water from sur-

1. Dudley Young, *Out of Ireland: A Reading of Yeats' Poetry*, 16–17.
2. Friedrich Lange, *The History of Materialism and Criticism of Its Present Importance*, 3:342, 347.

rounding watersheds. Inventors of discourse fabricate reality for their audience, and missionary idealists like Yeats (or like Wallace Stevens at a different extreme) aspire by such means to the invention—or reinvention—of human self-consciousness. Given the logic of this enterprise, Dudley Young does not press his point about it far enough. Most people conduct their moral lives in metaphorical, or in what Foucault would call discursive, terms, however driven they may be otherwise by unconscious forces that we can understand only within the limits of a given episteme. Given also that both Yeats's (sometimes perverse) Berkeleyian idealism and modern theoretical physics raise disconcerting, counterintuitive questions not only about the nature of reality but also about whether what we think of as reality is even there, truth claims—even political ones—could be argued to resolve themselves only in the form of paradigms or as cultural texts. One does not have to be a postmodernist to see this, or to infer from it, as Yeats did, that poetry's ontological claims as a discourse could be as competitive as any other's. Yeats's Irish background—especially, as, Declan Kiberd points out, his subject status as an Irishman—richly endowed him for this contest.

T. S. Eliot, Anglo-puritan, could never bring himself to say, "Death and life were not / Till man made up the whole." He would hardly be able to understand what it meant except as an idealist heresy. For Yeats, on the other hand, it was the whole point.

> One feels always that where all must make their living they will live not for life's sake but for the work's, and all be the poorer. My work is very near to life itself and my father's very near to life itself but I am always feeling a lack of life's own values behind my thought. They should have been there before the stream began, before it became necessary to let the work create its values.

The dualism that he implies here corresponds suggestively to the distinction in Schopenhauer between the striving, reasonless will, on the one hand, and the guiding, explanatory principle of sufficient reason on the other. Yeats was to say later that "Schopenhauer can do no wrong in my eyes,"[3] but his Schopenhauer seems to have been mediated through Nietzsche, who had envisioned a heuristic dualism of his own—

3. A. Norman Jeffares, *A New Commentary on the Poems of W. B. Yeats,* 93; Yeats and Moore, *Correspondence,* 117.

between the unintelligible Dionysian other and the Apollonian, shaping illusion of human intelligence. The Yeats that I represent in this study is the Yeats who was among the first modernists by virtue of being the last romantic—a Sophist afflicted with Platonist nostalgia—for whom value and Apollonian subjectivity have become identified and for whom that identification, in the absence of any other extrinsic metaphysical support, is a conscious, deliberated choice. He is both romantic and modern in the way that Sartre was when he made the claim that "existence precedes essence" and that all human value derives from that proposition.

Yeats's work of making value is romantic in the sense that the values themselves are romantic, in obvious ways, but also in the sense that they are idealist in origin on the one hand and put to the service of human life on the other—not narcissism and self-indulgence but cultural and even political work.[4] That work is modern in the sense that it is conducted in a metaphysical vacuum. Yeats managed to make it seem as though he preferred it this way, since the very discontinuity and absurdity of this role made the endeavor the more heroic. Yeats has alone constituted a major segment of our literary history because he is impossible to imagine as existing in any other time.

The existential issue in itself was concisely formalized as early as 1912 in "The Cold Heaven":

> Suddenly I saw the cold and rook-delighting heaven
> That seemed as though ice burned and was but the more ice,
> And thereupon imagination and heart were driven
> So wild that every casual thought of that and this
> Vanished, and left but memories, that should be out of season
> With the hot blood of youth, of love crossed long ago;

---

4. "[F]or Yeats," Seamus Deane has pointed out, "[t]he peasant and the aristocrat, kindred in spirit but not in class, united in the Great Romantic battle against the industrial and utilitarian ethic.... Ireland was not only a special country. It was one where the great battle must be won precisely because it had been so totally lost elsewhere." Yeats's "sense of crisis allowed him to see the archetypal patterns of history emerging out of the complexities of contemporary politics" and "gave Ireland's technological and economic backwardness the benefit of a spiritual glamor which had faded from the rest of Europe, as if it were a vestigial Greece in a sternly Roman world" (*Celtic Revivals: Essays in Modern Irish Literature, 1880–1980*, 39–40).

And I took all the blame out of all sense and reason,
Until I cried and trembled and rocked to and fro,
Riddled with light. Ah! when the ghost begins to quicken,
Confusion of the death-bed over, is it sent
Out naked on the roads, as the books say, and stricken
By the injustice of the skies for punishment?

"The Cold Heaven" is an oxymoronically complex poem in that it presents a deep irrationality in human experience through the medium of an authoritative, cerebrated rhetoric. Its being a sonnet that lacks a final couplet is an odd, accidental symbol of its subject matter; the poem is about partial knowledge and our incompleteness. We are not accustomed to finding such a theme in Yeats, and therefore we may tend to force more articulation between the poem's thoughts than is really there. What at first seems to be a logical progression from beginning to end in this poem is closer to being paratactic. We have only a sequence of events connected by *and*s, not by *because*s, *for*s, or *therefore*s. The poem's most distinctive characteristic is its lack of the spirit of coherence that conjunctive adverbs bring to discourse (as in "Therefore I have sailed the seas and come"). The speaker does not even seem to know why any of what happens in the poem happens, except that somehow it is associated with the remote inhumanness of the sky and with a human sense of discontinuity from the world that is triggered by it and makes him think of the rooks as being at one with the scene of the moment and of himself as estranged from it. Why this would drive random thoughts away and invoke memories of failed love is not explained or understood. It embodies, in short, the sublime in its unproductive, demystified, postromantic form. But in that space the crucial event of the poem occurs, in which the speaker, suddenly exposed, responds to the spirit of the bleak epiphany and is overpowered by his own suddenly articulated revelation: "I took all the blame out of all sense and reason." If this meant simply, "I blamed myself for the crossed love," as many readings assume that it does, it certainly does not seem like a response that has been prepared for. It surfaces from nowhere. What it seems to mean, instead, is wholly in keeping with the deracinated spirit of the poem: that suddenly, by eliminating blame from thought and reason and with it the associated assumptions of control over human affairs, the poet is confronted with a possibility of human existence that is far more disturbing than mere unresolved guilt could be. As if unhinged by the inhumanness of the sky, he has suddenly confronted the real inhumanness of existence itself and is forced to think about existence as if the cause-and-effect coherence of conjunctive adverbs had been eliminated from it. Ordinarily in human affairs we call upon powers of explanation in order to get at the truth, but we are satisfied with explanations not because they disclose the truth but because they impose the form of human thought upon otherwise inexplicable phenomena. This common and protective strategy has not worked in this moment for the poet, and the intensity of the reaction—rocking to and fro, "[r]iddled with light"—is the measure of the starkness of the revelation. The dream of justice, of being treated justly, is an enduring fantasy, for it is fundamentally a dream of coherence. But in this poem, the universe, or nature, is incapable of justice because it is without the mechanisms of thought that make justice possible. The speaker reflects bitterly that even after death, our very being will be naked before this truth, "punished" oxymoronically and therefore appropriately by "injustice." This is not the Yeats by whom we are accustomed to being addressed. It is the Yeats who made a career of being an existential swashbuckler because he was susceptible to episodes, like this one, of ordinary primordial dread. For this Yeats, the transcendence of such anxieties—of "the lack of life's own values behind my thought"—became a life's work.

The disconcerting logic of "The Cold Heaven" could have been affected by Yeats's extensive reading of Nietzsche, which he seems to have first undertaken in earnest as early as 1902. (Roy Foster has him reading Havelock Ellis on Nietzsche in *Savoy* in 1896.) That logic—or repudiation of logic—is fundamental to Nietzsche's critique, in *The Gay Science*, of both science and metaphysics:

> It will do to consider science as an attempt to humanize things as faithfully as possible; as we describe things and their one-after-another, we learn how to describe ourselves more and more precisely. Cause and effect: such a duality probably never exists; in truth we are confronted by a continuum out of which we isolate a couple of pieces, just as we perceive motion only as isolated points and then infer it without ever actually seeing it. The suddenness with which many effects stand out misleads us; actually, it is sudden only for us. In this moment of suddenness there is an infinite number of processes that elude us. An intellect

that could see cause and effect as a continuum and a flux and not, as we do, in terms of an arbitrary division and dismemberment, would repudiate the concept of cause and effect and deny all conditionality.[5]

If we accept this argument of Nietzsche's about this crucial (and Humean) issue, about the metaphysical agenda implicit in reasoning itself, then we, like the poet in "The Cold Heaven," after experiencing major traumas are left in a very bare place. Not only must we endure the experience itself—"love crossed" being an embarrassingly recurrent example—but in its aftermath we would be obliged to live also with its incomprehensibility. Part of the beauty, Nietzsche argues elsewhere, in the usual sorting out of cause and effect is that it constitutes a narrative that we can then be absorbed into and diverted by—Freud's "master plot," in effect, a way of temporizing with the uncanny. The narrative constituted of cause and effect is in itself a form of order.

Yeats is not often enough given credit for his sophistication in these matters.

> To keep these notes natural and useful to me I must keep one note from leading on to another, that I may not surrender myself to literature. Every note must come as a casual thought, then it will be my life. Neither Christ nor Buddha nor Socrates wrote a book, for to do that is to exchange life for a logical process.

He knew that poetry and even thought are fictions, but he also believed in the power of such fictions to shape and direct human life and in the logic of narrative to give coherence and dignity to the erratic and open-ended human enterprise of becoming. His own life story is the story that makes up the *Collected Poems,* and its obsession was to override the uncertainty that always seems to be at the edge of his thought, to counter with his own formalist lucidity the opaqueness of existence—"the unknown...beyond language," as Hillis Miller expressed it; the "it" that "undermines all thinking, performing, and constructing." He engaged consciously with the corrosive and demoralizing effects of skepticism and set himself against philosophical materialism because of the defeat of the human mind and spirit to which materialism's logic (since he never

5. Friedrich Nietzsche, *"The Gay Science" with "A Prelude in Rhymes" and an Appendix of Songs,* 172–73.

conceded the logic of what Marx meant by dialectical materialism) seemed to him to lead—against, in short, what Sartre called "degradation of consciousness." The path of knowledge having petered out, as he said in a letter to T. Sturge Moore, he intended with Kant's guidance to will existence into being on his own terms.[6] But what was on the other side of such rhetoric—in a sense, *mere* rhetoric—was a darkness.

It is hardly possible to exaggerate the degree to which Yeats's and Nietzsche's thoughts coincide in these respects. The older Yeats becomes in the annals of literary history, the more intelligible this kinship is. It is not possible to know how the kinship was formed. Yeats had read most of Nietzsche's major work by 1905 and had annotated—briefly and selectively—Thomas Common's *Choice Selections.* Richard Ellmann, Denis Donoghue, and David Thatcher have given good, concise accounts of Nietzsche's influence, and Otto Bohlmann and Frances Oppel much longer ones.[7] Still, Nietzsche was not only a man, a writer, and a body of philosophical work but also a whole climate of ideas in the nineteenth century. Neither he nor Yeats would have been dismayed to be told that they were merely voices through which their age spoke.

On the other hand, the credulous, occultist Yeats that we all know and wonder at would have seemed demented to Nietzsche (indeed, many decent and sensible readers find him so). He was poorly equipped for the role of tough-minded, cutting-edge modernist. He claimed to have had an audience once at Rosses Point with the queen of a band of fairies who told him and his uncle about the economy of the fairy kingdom. He told Dorothy Wellesley that the immortality of the individual soul had now been proved beyond doubt and could be so demonstrated in a court of law. He and his Uncle George worked out elaborate astrological charts to explain or forecast any event. He was indignant that George V did not abdicate in protest when Czar Nicholas II was executed. He believed that in the old days the privilege of the nobilities and the courts was to display "the soul of the world" in pageantry for the edification of the poor and to become "to them a type of the glory

6. W. B. Yeats, *Autobiographies,* 461; Hillis Miller, "Yeats: The Linguistic Moment," 204; Yeats and Moore, *Correspondence,* 124.

7. Ellmann, *Identity of Yeats,* 91–98; Denis Donoghue, *William Butler Yeats,* 52–60; David S. Thatcher, *Nietzsche in England, 1890–1914: The Growth of a Reputation,* 139–73; Otto Bohlmann, *Yeats and Nietzsche: An Exploration of Major Nietzschean Echoes in the Writings of William Butler Yeats, passim;* Frances Nesbitt Oppel, *Mask and Tragedy: Yeats and Nietzsche, 1902–10, passim.*

of the world"—proudly walking "clad in cloth of gold" manifesting "their passionate hearts, that the groundlings may feel their souls wax the greater."[8] He thought himself the kind of man who, on the whole, tended to "value all I have seen or heard because of the emotions they call up or because of something they remind me of that exists, as I believe, beyond the world." He read Swedenborg with the solemn credulity of a disciple, especially the parts that sound ghostwritten by Flann O'Brien. He attended séances and was a student of magic for all of his life. He revered the wisdom of ancient philosophers over modern ones. In the writings of neo-Platonists like Henry More he found agreeable arguments for the extendibility of spirits and thus for their compatibility with the material world.

All things considered—or even a few things considered—it seems impossible to bring Yeats under the rule of a single rubric, and it is impossible to imagine what really went on from day to day in his head. It is possible, however, to surmise what our experience would be like if what Yeats imagined to be possible was indeed the case. It would be chaos. Anything that one might choose to be true would be true. Death would impose no limitation and would have no relevance to our thought because it would cease to exist in any meaningful sense. Ghosts would walk the earth at liberty. Spiritual instructors would command our thoughts. Time and space, even as illusions, would cease to be relevant categories. As in the stories of *The Celtic Twilight*, possibility would admit no limit. Such a world, in other words, would be the very opposite of form, and in acquiescing to it (even experimentally) Yeats was allowing himself to be overcome by an inchoate existential environment of his own creation—not unlike the "Eastern way" he describes in the passage from *Memoirs* at the head of this chapter. Yeats does not repudiate the "Eastern way" in that argument. He claims only that it is impractical in "Western life," which has become more focused and concentrated under the rule of the symbol of the Incarnation. Pragmatism—not what is real or unreal—is what is at stake here. It is life's values, not its metaphysical structure, that he speaks of himself in 1910 as doubting, and therefore those are the values that are left to be created by the work of the artist, by the mind, in the formal activity of creation.

8. W. B. Yeats, *The Collected Letters of W. B. Yeats*, 1:325 (hereinafter, the Oxford edition of Yeats's letters will be referred to as *Collected Letters*); Yeats, *Explorations*, 254.

"Hammer your thoughts into unity," one spirit had told him (second-hand through Dante). When he came to do the work of creating value in his poems, the world for him became demystified. The supernatural in the poems became metaphorical rather than real, and in this new metaphysical environment the issues engaged become more accessible to skeptic and believer alike. In short, to restate Dudley Young's point, when magic historically enters the field of rational discourse, it fails, and metaphor—factitious at the source, and self-conscious—takes its place. The poet's task is to remember that and to ensure that metaphorical representation remain value-laden rather than merely descriptive.

The world of Yeats's poems may communicate with the occult world, but ontologically it is different from it as an effect of its having been hammered into a unity. No one who has ever studied the evolution of a Yeats poem through its labored revisions or, for that matter, who has even read "Sailing to Byzantium," would suppose that Yeats as a poet was naively susceptible to automatic writing or to the playful improvisations of surrealism. Whatever attributions Yeats himself might have wished to make, the poems—even the vaguely narrative shape that, collected, they assume from beginning to end—embody and display the activity of consciousness as it projects form and value upon the otherwise formless and valueless (or, at any rate, incomprehensible) world. "Consciousness" in this function refers to a state of mind that is not the unconscious and to the human mind itself, as opposed to what is outside it, whatever we think of the degree to which its content is formed from the outside. "All my life I have tried," Yeats said, "to get rid of modern subjectivity by insisting on construction and contemporary words and syntax."[9] It is possible for the mind to fail at this effort,

9. W. B. Yeats, *The Letters of W. B. Yeats*, 892 (hereinafter cited as *Letters*); cited in Alex Zwerdling, *Yeats and the Heroic Ideal*, 19. Compare Yeats's very shrewd account of what has succeeded Stendahl's nineteenth-century realist ideal: "Certain typical books—*Ulysses*, Mrs. Virginia Woolf's *Waves*, Mr. Ezra Pound's *Draft of XXX Cantos*—suggest a philosophy like that of the *Samkara* school of ancient India, mental and physical objects alike material, a deluge of experience breaking over us and within us, melting limits whether of line or tint; man no hard bright mirror dawdling by the dry sticks of a hedge, but a swimmer, or rather the waves themselves. In this new literature announced with much else by Balzac in *Le Chef-d'Oeuvre inconnu*, as in that which it superseded, man in himself is nothing." Notably, this comes in Yeats's preface to *Fighting the Waves*, where Cuchulain yet again opposes "the invulnerable tide." W. B. Yeats, *Wheels and Butterflies*, 64–65.

to lose the capacity for what Yeats, echoing Coleridge, called "shaping joy." When that occurs, we become pathetic moderns, lost to the old romantic turbulence, and helpless before the mere contents of the mind, overcome, in other words, by desolate reality.

John Holloway has pointed out how Yeats's language creates an independent reality with a nature of its own and how often Yeats openly asserts his claim to do this: "I make," "I declare," "I summon." Dudley Young argues, concerning "Among School Children," that it is the *telling* of the tale of harsh reproof that causes the souls of the two lovers to blend in youthful sympathy—to enter into a world that does not and could not otherwise exist. *Call, declare, make, summon, tell:* such a list begins to sound again like Nietzsche. This Yeats with his head cleared is a Yeats that Nietzsche would understand—the Yeats who (in his Greek mode) rejoiced in battle, as he put it, who found "the sweetest of all music to be the stroke of the sword."[10]

It helps in understanding the kinship between Yeats and Nietzsche to consider that both Yeats's and Nietzsche's view of experience was fundamentally tragic and therefore fundamentally aesthetic (and that each, in his separate era of social crisis, had conservative political grounds for believing this). Nietzsche's assertion that "We possess *art* lest we *perish of the truth*" largely describes his complete agenda, if art can be broadly understood as an expression of the creative will. This was Nietzsche in *The Will to Power,* toward the end of his life. The aphorism only rephrased a more drastic claim (which he later partially repudiated) from *The Birth of Tragedy:* it is "only as an aesthetic phenomenon that existence and the world are eternally justified." If he had been a poet he might have said instead: "I am always feeling a lack of life's own values behind my thought. They should have been there before the stream began, before it became necessary to let the work create [them]." Nietzsche's Zarathustra, addressing those he sardonically calls "wise men" on the errors of their ways, on the gaps in their self-understanding, asserts that what they call the "[w]ill to truth" is in fact a will to render existence thinkable.

> You want to *make* all being thinkable, for you doubt with well-founded suspicion that it is already thinkable. But it shall yield and bend for you. Thus your will wants it. It shall become smooth and serve the spirit as

10. John Holloway, "Style and World in *The Tower*"; Young, *Out of Ireland*, 133; Yeats, *Explorations*, 243.

its mirror and reflection. That is your whole will, you who are wisest: a will to power—when you speak of good and evil too, and of valuations. You still want to create the world before which you can kneel: that is your ultimate hope and intoxication.[11]

Yeats, certainly, could have been so arraigned except that he was not self-deceived as Zarathustra's "wise men" are; he is more conscious, has called into consciousness, of both the creative and the relational aspects of his project.

> As life goes on we discover that certain thoughts sustain us in defeat, or give us victory, whether over ourselves or others, and it is these thoughts, tested by passion, that we call convictions. Among subjective men (in all those, that is, who must spin a web out of their own bowels) the victory is an intellectual daily re-creation of all that exterior fate snatches away, and so that fate's antithesis.... We begin to live when we have conceived life as tragedy.[12]

Zarathustra's ultimate point is that the project must be undertaken but that it also must be understood to be ultimately tragic, and in some sense pointless, because the world is not thinkable except according to the terms—established by the will—under which thinking is conducted.

In an argument in 1928 with T. Sturge Moore over whether philosophy is now wholly dependent upon science, Yeats claimed his own place to be in the particular stream of thought that descends from Kant. Of the two paths to reality, that of knowledge and that of will, Zen Buddhism, he added, "like Blake and Kant, thought the path of knowledge was closed, that of will open." Yeats is on record in many poems as having affirmed this condition of creative intellect; Kant had made unmediated Being itself inaccessible.[13]

The formality of a poem's construction echoes the terms under which thinking in this category is conducted—that is, it reproduces the artificiality of the act of thinking in such a way as to declare the version of the world produced a wholly provisional one. Art "[i]s *but* a vision of reality," Ille claims in "Ego Dominus Tuus." The italics added here

---

11. Friedrich Nietzsche, *The Will to Power*, 435; Friedrich Nietzsche, *"The Birth of Tragedy" and "The Case of Wagner,"* 52; Friedrich Nietzsche, *The Portable Nietzsche*, 225; Yeats, *Autobiographies*, 189.

12. Yeats, *Autobiographies*, 189.

13. Yeats and Moore, *Correspondence*, 124.

are intended to stress the limitation the adverb imposes upon the term it modifies—*vision*. The formal authority of Yeats's poetry must owe in part to the determination that it shows to impose the *imprimatur* of *his* consciousness upon *his* experience, as if at any given moment the world-in-itself could slip again into its opaque, grammarless—that is, formless—state.

In "Lapis Lazuli," the symbolic artifact of the poem's title is significant because it has been reclaimed by the carver and then by the poet from its unmediated origins in mere nature: "Every discoloration of the stone, / Every accidental crack or dent, / Seems a water-course or an avalanche, / Or lofty slope where it still snows." What was geologically random—the cracks and dents—has been not so much reshaped as reenvisioned as representation and made part of a pattern and given meaning, either by the carver (the verb *seems* does not tell us enough) or by the poet, who is in the process of reinventing the reinvention. And the poet then carries himself across into his own kind of virtual reality: "Though *doubtless* plum or cherry-branch / Sweetens the little half-way house / Those Chinamen climb towards" (emphasis added). "I / Delight to imagine them seated there," he says, and there they are, the stone having passed from its state in nature into representation by the carver into an entirely new fiction, now with a story implied, of Yeats's own making:

> There, on the mountain and the sky,
> On all the tragic scene they stare.
> One asks for mournful melodies;
> Accomplished fingers begin to play.
>
> Their eyes mid many wrinkles, their eyes,
> Their ancient, glittering eyes, are gay.

The glittering eyes of those ancient "Chinamen" are gay not only because they are above the tragic scene (though even that is not clear) or because they are ancient and wise but also because they are no longer in life but in art. And this "vision of reality" is an alternative version of reality that Yeats plainly declares to be one of his own imposing.

The philosophy of art for Nietzsche was cognate with a philosophy of life. This could be said to be the rationale of both becoming and overcoming: "[t]o become master of the chaos one is; to compel one's chaos to become form." Walter Kaufmann cites a letter from Nietzsche to Franz Overbeck that puts the issue in conveniently Yeatsian terms: "If I do not discover the alchemists' trick of turning even this—filth into *gold,* I am lost.—Thus I have the *most beautiful* opportunity to prove that for me all experiences are useful, all days holy, and all human beings divine!!!!" Embracing misfortune in this exuberantly defiant way—*amor fati*—would seem implausible except that doing so turns one's existence into an idea and then into a narrative, indeed an adventure. Each new injury is endurable because one believes in the story and because the story is a chosen one, of one's own making. This narrative is what we have instead of a Ptolemaic universe, Nietzsche would go on to say. Art is at war with science not because science has demystified the world but because in doing so "it has dissuaded man from his former respect for himself." "Has the self-belittlement of man, his will to self-belittlement, not progressed irresistibly since Copernicus?" For Nietzsche, in a pre-Lacanian insight, consciousness and language were virtually identical and both designed in the evolutionary scheme for social utility. Language belongs not to individual being but to social being and therefore cannot mediate genuine self-presence. In language we can become "conscious only of what is not individual but 'average.'"[14] And since the means by which we think is metaphorical, what we think must be metaphorical as well. When we appropriate our lives in the way that Nietzsche and Yeats in their separate but overlapping ways claim that we must, we are inhabiting a metaphor, and any achieved self-assurance must always be mitigated by that knowledge. Because of this problem, both Nietzsche and Yeats often seem naively nostalgic for a state prior to language and therefore prior to thought itself. This may be why both writers place so much emphasis upon the body, upon passion and feeling. But even an unwilling sophist knows that language is the only origin, must be made to do, must be bent to the individual will, and that art must engage aggressively in the process of becoming, Being itself and its unintelligible nature having been eternally bracketed by Kant.

"Art ... [is a] ... *means*... of enhancing life," Nietzsche says. "My theme is that the world being illusion, one must be deluded in some

---

14. Nietzsche, *Will to Power,* 444; Walter Kaufmann, *Nietzsche: Philosopher, Psychologist, Antichrist,* 59; Friedrich Nietzsche, *"On the Genealogy of Morals" and "Ecce Homo,"* 155; Nietzsche, *Gay Science,* 299.

way if one is to triumph in it." This second passage sounds like Nietzsche, too, but it is Yeats, neatly sidestepping an aporia. Nietzsche was a pragmatist: what counts is what works. Yeats was even less fastidious about epistemological problems. Kant, he felt, had freed everyone to strive to create his or her own reality even though the raw material of that process would certainly prevail in the end. Alchemy is the right metaphor for this project, but Yeats's story is that of an alchemist who always remains uneasy about the true status of his achievement. He can never be unaware of the baseness of the material with which he works. Even the golden bird in Byzantium, as Sturge Moore politely pointed out to Yeats, is not "out of nature" at all but of nature's very element—of gold to begin with and only then gold enameling.[15]

There are many value problems associated with aesthetic ideology in any form, from both a Kierkegaardian and a cultural-materialistic point of view. (The notion that art that does not enhance life is not art, for instance, was also the policy of the Third Reich, and that policy was only the most innocuous feature of its aesthetic master plan of purifying the race.) But aesthetic pragmatism as a means of appropriating an individual's life has at the very least the merit of being monistic and therefore of avoiding the *ressentiment*, as Zarathustra calls it, and the self-estrangement that dualistic value systems promote. It has the merit as well of grounding value in the experience of life as it is lived and of addressing specifically "*human* problems . . . which . . . being in the world [generates]," as one of Nietzsche's commentators expresses it. Yeats certainly held to some strange dualistic notions during his life, but they were kept apart from the issues of value addressed and set forth in the poems. Yeats had derived from Shelley's *A Defence of Poetry* an idiom for arguing that art should serve the task of enhancing human life:

> Beauty is the end and law of poetry. It exists to find the beauty in all things, philosophy, nature, passion,—in what you will, and in so far as it rejects beauty it destroys its own right to exist. If you want to give ideas for their own sake write prose. In verse they are subordinate to beauty which is their soul.[16]

---

15. Nietzsche, *Will to Power*, 168; Yeats, *Letters*, 534; Yeats and Moore, *Correspondence*, 162.

16. James Sasso, *The Role of Consciousness in the Thought of Nietzsche*, 204; Yeats, *Letters*, 343.

If referred to Nietzsche's irascible obedience to the service of life, this sounds considerably less decadent than if we referred it to the other-worldly ennui of, say, Villiers de L'Isle Adam. Finding what there is of beauty in all things would be understood by Nietzsche as a worthy project, an affirmation of life and a rejection of the counsel of nihilism that he considered to have infected the whole spirit of Europe.

Yeats wrote to his father in 1914:

> I think with you that the poet seeks truth, not abstract truth, but a kind of vision of reality which satisfies the whole being. It will not be true for one thing unless it satisfies his desires, his most profound desires. Henry More, the seventeenth century platonist whom I have been reading all summer, argues from the goodness and omnipotence of God that all our deep desires must be satisfied, and that we should reject a philosophy that does not satisfy them. I think the poet reveals truth by revealing those desires.

He is struggling here to express his version of an attitude toward art that his father himself had tried to express in a letter from America that must have crossed this one. His father, in New York, was explaining the significance of exact portraiture in art. He relates an experience of encountering a young Irish woman in a park. His attention had first been caught by the laughter and play of a crowd of active children. The woman he addressed was, however, shielding from his view a child that he eventually saw to be sickly—"wasted and scrofulous and very sick...; in its wasted neck there were lumps." The young woman supposes, or pretends to suppose, that the child's condition is owed to its teething. John Yeats is struck by her civility, by her Irish prettiness, by the hope-fulness that she perhaps affects for his sake, and by the contrast between her child and the other children—and because of all this he cannot, he says, help looking at her or asking questions about the child. And after he has left he is grieved for days and yet meanwhile tries to recall every detail to keep alive the painful feeling—"in other words, I would have given worlds to have painted a careful study of her and her sick infant and carried it away with me to keep my sorrow alive." "At any rate" he says finally, "have I not made it obvious that all art begins in portraiture? That is, a *realistic* thing identified with *realistic* feeling, after which and because of which comes the Edifice of Beauty." Both father and son in this exchange unconsciously echo Keats: "[T]he excellence of every Art is its intensity, capable of making all disagreeables evaporate, from their being in close relationship with Beauty & Truth.... [W]ith a great poet the sense of Beauty overcomes every other consideration, or rather obliterates all consideration." In doing so, they show not only their own debt to romanticism but early modernism's debt as well, as exemplified in Stephen Dedalus's eventually aborted desire to "transmut[e] the daily bread of experience into the radiant body of everliving life"—in order, in turn, "to forge in the smithy of [his] soul the uncreated conscience of [his—as well as Yeats's and Yeats's father's] race."[17]

It is hard to imagine how far apart Yeats and his father would be on this issue—pretty far one would expect—but Yeats extrapolates gracefully from his father's position to indicate a continuity between his father's and his own that less-subtle minds than his might have missed: that is, that John Yeats's interest in the woman and the child, an unwillingness to be squeamish, was a form of compassion, and that his interest in painting them, out of his sorrow, was an expression of his profound desire that there be some other way for the woman and child to be, that they might exist in "a vision of reality which satisfies the whole being." A reality, in other words, that is other than the one that is. Desire in this usage, one that Yeats derived from his father, is intransitive. It answers to what is absent from the world rather than to what is present in it. It is the expression of the "soul's" being in the world but being discontinuous with it. As Yeats says in a letter of 1895 (to Olivia Shakespear):

> The face of the monkey, with its whimsical, mour[n]ful withered, mocking pretence of wisdom has always seemed to me the symbol of the end of the glory & the triumph of the world, of all the life of desire & hope—and the dead monkey of all these things done with forever, of the time when even desire, the shadow of the quest of the ideal, has passed away & the merely human soul dies.[18]

This is distinctly a vision of hell in life, in which the death of hope from the perishing of desire *is* the hell rather than merely an aspect of

17. Yeats, *Letters*, 588; John Butler Yeats, *Letters to His Son W. B. Yeats and Others, 1869–1922*, 192; John Keats, *The Letters of John Keats, 1814–1821*, 1:192–94; James Joyce, *A Portrait of the Artist as a Young Man*, 221, 253.
18. Yeats, *Collected Letters*, 1:468.

it. It is a condition, notably, when even the soul achieves equilibrium with its environment and no longer stands forth against it in creative overcoming. Desire is the energy of this creative will.

Yeats's father wrote to him years later, in 1914, as if extrapolating now from his son's own point:

> The chief thing to know and never forget is that art is dreamland and that the moment a poet meddles with ethics and the moral uplift or thinking scientifically, he leaves dreamland, loses all his music and ceases to be a poet.... We all live when at our best, that is when we are most ourselves, in dreamland....
>
> The poet is a magician—his vocation to incessantly evoke dreams and do his work so well, because of natural gifts and acquired skill, that his dreams shall have a potency to defeat the actual at every point. Yet here is a curious thing, the poet and we his dupes know that they are only dreams—otherwise we lose them. With our eyes open, using our will and powers of selection, we, together in friendship and brotherly love, create this dreamland. Pronounce it to be actual life and you summon logic and mechanical sense and reason and all the other powers of prose to find yourself hailed back to the prison house, and dreamland vanishes—a shrieking ghost.

The next day, in a continuing letter, he summarizes his argument:

> Art exists that man cutting himself away from nature may build in his free consciousness buildings vaster and more sumptuous than these, furnished too with all manner of winding passages and closets and boudoirs and encircled with gardens well shaded and with everything that he can desire—and we build all out of our spiritual pain—for if the bricks be not cemented and mortised by actual suffering, they will not hold together. Those others live on another plane where if there is less joy there is much less pain.

Then on yet a third day the position is once more reformulated:

> I spoke [yesterday] of art as a means by which a man searches for and finds himself, and afterwards I said that artists were engaged in building habitations in which the spirit might live and enjoy its life in full activity. Yet there was no confusion. When a man builds a house on a site chosen for its beauty making the house also as charming as he can, then he has found himself and also built for his spirit a habitation where it can live at ease. But if a man builds a house, say close to his factory and with all

the utilities and lives in it merely because it possesses all the utilities—but outside his appreciation of these conveniences has no other feeling and no affection for his house, then he is of the type scientific or philistine. He is a man untrained in the art of finding himself and his poor spirit if he has one wanders without a house or habitation.[19]

J. B. Yeats's touchstone in all such theoretical excursions is always Shakespeare; so it seems apparent that he is not speaking of a life-alien, *symboliste* fantasy.

It is an odd feature over the years of Yeats's correspondence with his father that each not infrequently seems to be taking the other's position. In this meditation on the poet's "dreamland" the father—normally, as in the later letter, on the side of philosophical realism and steady seeing—has assumed the son's. Their positions are so nearly interchangeable because they are fundamentally the same; they seem different partly because the nature of the discourse forces the other into an independent argumentative stance. Each is therefore arguing the same case in a different idiom. In effect, they share reflections upon the proper relation of "vision" and "reality" and upon the function in the world of such a creative synthesis. The Irish woman in the park and her suffering have become examples of the "ugliness" we must not keep from our poems, and yet the very evasion that the passage speaks against becomes oddly accomplished in the style in which it is spoken. In his theoretical writing, Yeats invariably manages to weight the aesthetic encounter with reality on the side of keeping the sorrow pure. Yeats's father plainly saw the young woman as both a real person and a compositional subject. When Yeats recycles the father's story two years later for a point in "Anima Hominis," she has become a subject only.

An old artist wrote to me of his wanderings by the quays of New York, and how he found there a woman nursing a sick child, and drew her story from her. She spoke, too, of other children who had died: a long tragic story. "I wanted to paint her," he wrote; "if I denied myself any of the pain I could not believe in my own ecstasy." We must not make a false faith by hiding from our thoughts the causes of doubt, for faith is the highest achievement of the human intellect, the only gift man can make to God. . . . Neither must we create, by hiding ugliness, a false beauty as our offering to the world. He only can create the greatest

19. John Butler Yeats, *Letters to His Son*, 198–200.

imaginable beauty who has endured all imaginable pangs, for only when we have seen and foreseen what we dread shall we be rewarded by that dazzling, unforeseen, wing-footed wanderer. . . . I shall find the dark grow luminous, the void fruitful when I understand I have nothing.[20]

Yeats identifies the artist's vision with religious faith and identifies both as an achievement of the intellect. This faith would appear to be a faith in creation rather than in a creator, or, in other terms, a form of overcoming.

Believers, in the presence of their deity (in worship, for instance) achieve a dignity by association with that presence that is otherwise elusive in day-to-day life. Both Yeats and his father stress this aspect of their own "faith." A world completed by the artist's vision exalts identity, which is otherwise nugatory. This is what Yeats refers to when he speaks of being "rewarded," and he emphasizes more than seems prudent a self-involved exhilaration associated with completed art that seems to relegate the public utility of art to an ambiguous status. On the other hand, this seems to be J. B. Yeats's point as well: "We all live when at our best, that is when we are most ourselves, in dreamland," and artists are "engaged in building habitations in which the spirit might live and enjoy its life in full activity." When desire "has passed away," the "merely human soul dies." "All our art," Yeats himself wrote, "is but the putting our faith and the evidence of our faith into words or forms and our faith is in ecstasy."[21]

"Ecstasy" will seem a little strong to a cooler generation of readers, but it tends to refer in Yeats's critical writings not to a Dionysian rapture but to a vision that the "soul" has—a standing forth from the merely material—in which life is seen completed. It is a faith in the soul's vision that he speaks of, not the empirical experience of the vision itself: "our faith" is that the soul's vision is true, that transcendence is not a fantasy. Yeats is notorious for the artful recklessness with which he uses the term *God*, and he hardly ever means anything more theologically specific in using it than he means when he uses the term *soul*. For the idealist, both terms are, of course, transcendental signifiers of the first order. Here, though, by association with the Cambridge Platonists, he seems to intend to invoke God as a form of inner light identified with vision and imagination—and again, he has echoed Keats:

20. W. B. Yeats, *Mythologies*, 332.
21. Yeats, *Letters*, 583.

> I am certain of nothing but of the holiness of the Heart's affections and
> the truth of Imagination—What the imagination seizes as Beauty must
> be truth—whether it existed before or not—for I have the same Idea of
> all our Passions as of Love they are all in their sublime, creative of essen-
> tial Beauty. . . . The Imagination may be compared to Adam's dream—
> he awoke and found it truth. . . . Adam's dream will do here [in this life]
> and seems to be a conviction that Imagination and its empyreal reflec-
> tion is the same as human Life and its Spiritual repetition.[22]

In his believing moments, Yeats was inclined to affirm a kind of Emer-
sonian theology that both historicized and sanctified what Keats was
content to call "the truth of imagination."

Another version of this idea in "A General Introduction for My
Work" took the form of a testament. The "mechanical theory" will soon
be proved, Yeats says, to have no reality—"the natural and supernatural are knit together."

> I was born into this faith, have lived in it, and shall die in it; my Christ,
> a legitimate deduction from the Creed of St. Patrick as I think, is that
> Unity of Being Dante compared to a perfectly proportioned human body,
> Blake's "Imagination," what the Upanishads have named "Self": nor is
> this unity distant and therefore intellectually understandable, but immi-
> nent, differing from man to man and age to age, taking upon itself pain
> and ugliness, "eye of newt, and toe of frog."

This is more arcane than it needs to be. What is clear is that Yeats is
trying again to claim authority for the inner vision of reality as being
more real than what it sees. Deity and unity are not transcendent and
therefore objectifiable; they are instead of the mind itself and "immi-
nent." It is this immanence that sanctions the "vision of reality which
satisfies the [poet's] whole being"; otherwise it might seem only self-
indulgent. This difference between the immanent reality and the transcendent is described more succinctly in Yeats's last letter to Lady Elizabeth Pelham: "I am happy, and I think full of an energy, of an energy I
had despaired of. It seems to me that I have found what I wanted.
When I try to put all into a phrase I say 'Man can embody truth but he
cannot know it.'" Still, this cautious affirmation, though a corollary of
the earlier one, makes less extravagant claims and is more representative
of the anxiety on such issues that often surfaces in Yeats's poems. It

22. Keats, *Letters*, 1:184–85.

also sets both a Sophist and a Kantian limit. Value must be generated from within human consciousness, and it can be relevant only to specific "human problems," which, in turn, are generated by being in the world. Poetry "exists to find the beauty in all things, philosophy, nature, passion,—in what you will, and in so far as it rejects beauty it destroys its own right to exist." And if man embodies truth without also being privileged to know it, that truth takes the form of the unity of being that he speaks of as being immanent always, though presumably in what D. H. Lawrence would call allotropic forms.[23]

If unity of being is the truth that man embodies, then it is the duty of the artist to seek "a kind of vision of reality that satisfies the whole being." Mere imitation therefore betrays the artist's mission; subjective transfiguration of the outer world fulfills it. "Art delights . . . in the soul expressing itself according to its own laws and arranging the world about it in its own pattern."

> In the last letter but one, you spoke of all art as imitation, meaning, I conclude, imitation of something in the outer world. To me it seems that it often uses the outer world as a symbolism to express subjective moods. . . . The element of pattern in every art is, I think, the part that is not imitative, for in the last analysis there will always be somewhere an intensity of pattern that we have never seen with our eyes.

If we understand "intensity of pattern" to include the vision of the woman with the sickly child as John Butler Yeats "saw" it, with both his eyes and his heart, then we are closer to an understanding of what Yeats meant by saying that he sometimes doubted the existence of life's value behind his own thought. Without John Butler Yeats on that scene in New York with his particular compassionate interest in people, that occasion is without value. Without Yeats's systematic meditation on the events of the Easter Rising, the occasion loses forever that peculiar intensity of pattern that it takes on in "Easter 1916." The two occasions do not derive their meaning from their continuity with a transcendental source; they derive their meaning from the intensity of pattern, a thematic organization, projected onto them by attentive and reflective acts of the mind.[24]

John Butler Yeats liked to bring such matters down to earth:

23. Yeats, *Essays and Introductions,* 518; Yeats, *Letters,* 922.
24. Yeats, *Explorations,* 168; Yeats, *Letters,* 607.

My theory is that we are always dreaming—chairs, tables, women and children, our wives and sweethearts, the people in the streets, all in various ways and with various powers are the starting points of dreams.... Sleep is dreaming away from the facts and wakefulness is dreaming in close contact with the facts, and *since facts excite our dreams and feed them we get as close as possible to the facts if we have the cunning and the genius of poignant feeling,* and since it is true that certain facts, or facts seen in a particular way, may injure our dreams so that they pain us, we acquire a knowledge how to handle them so as to deprive them of their power to do mischief.... All men are artists from morning to night and all night also, creating phantasy, and we who are artists do deliberately and with science and conscious purpose and a great ambition what the others are doing without knowing it. In wakefulness and in sleep when we act, when we think, we are each of us shrouded in dreams—when the soul departs dreams leave us, and not till then.

What ordinary people do and what poets do is different only in degree, not in kind. Poets and artists who enlist in this cause, especially Irish ones, may well think of themselves as priests of the imagination as well as alchemists, as generators of, not commentators upon, value where otherwise no value is. Yeats, in the immodest spirit of the nineties, had willingly allowed this role to be thrust upon him: "The arts are . . . about to take upon their shoulders the burdens that have fallen from the shoulders of priests."[25]

Ezra Pound called Yeats to task in the *Canto* 83 for the imperiousness of his imagination.

> Le Paradis n'est pas artificiel
> and Uncle William dawdling around Notre Dame
> in search of whatever
>   paused to admire the symbol
> with Notre Dame standing inside it.

Donald Davie has elaborated upon Pound's critique and in so doing raises another issue:

> It may be said that W. B. Yeats shares with the symbolist poets, and with a poet squarely in their tradition, such as T. S. Eliot, an imperious,

25. John Butler Yeats, *Letters to His Son*, 216–17; Yeats, *Essays and Introductions*, 193.

appropriating attitude toward the perceived world. When swans get into Yeats's verse, the swan loses all its swanliness except what it needs to symbolize something in the person who observes it: "Another emblem there!" And the poet at the end of "Coole Park and Ballylee" says explicitly that this is also what has happened to Lady Gregory. Similarly, Frank Kermode has demonstrated how far "In Memory of Major Robert Gregory" is concerned with Major Gregory, much less for what he is or was in himself than for what the poet chooses to make him stand for in his (the poet's) private pantheon. It is for this reason, to give an example, that Gregory's activities as a landscape painter are made so salient—so that Yeats may applaud this imperious attitude to the natural world at just the point where it would seem least likely, in landscape painting:

> We dreamed that a great painter had been born
> To cold Clare rock and Galway rock and thorn,
> To that stern colour and that delicate line
> That are our secret discipline
> Wherein the gazing heart doubles her might.

We attend to natural landscape, not for the sake of delighting in it, nor for what it may tell us of supernatural purpose or design, but so that the imperious personality, seeing itself there reflected, may become the more conscious of its own power—"the gazing heart doubles her might."[26]

Yeats would certainly see the point of this, and he would just as certainly not be embarrassed by it. Professor Davie goes on to contrast Yeats's imperiousness with Pound's humility in his characterization of the wasp, *la vespa*, in *Canto* 83, a section he quotes in full. The problem with this line of argument is related to the one that Yeats identified in the letter to his father about intensity of pattern: "In fact, imitation seems to me to create a language in which we say things which are not imitation." Post-Darwinian nature cannot tell us very much that we want to hear about "supernatural purpose or design." Amazing as nature may be, it is not meaningful in itself in human terms, unless one is a social Darwinist, which Yeats decidedly was not. A Hopkins lyric tells us less about what really proceeds in the natural world than about the human desire to reconceptualize that world on its own terms. What we call "nature" is an amoral process in which, at any level, the strong prey

26. Donald Davie, *Ezra Pound: Poet as Sculptor*, 173–74.

upon the weak in order to survive. The amorality of that process is what makes nature work. It cannot work in any other way and certainly not in a moral way. When we think of it in any other terms we are contracting to deceive ourselves, poetically, so to speak. As Oscar Wilde said, even Wordsworth only found in nature "the sermons he had already hidden there." "If . . . we regard Nature as the collection of phenomena external to man, people only discover in her what they bring to her." This epistemological common sense was the cornerstone of Wilde's famous argument that Life—which is otherwise formless and purposeless—imitates Art. Yeats, when he was "four and twenty," had taken Wilde's provocative iconoclasm to heart. "Invited to dine with Oscar Wilde on Christmas day, 1888, [Yeats] consumed not only his portion of the turkey but all Wilde's esthetic system, which Wilde read to him from the proofs of 'The Decay of Lying.' Once expropriated, this was developed and re-unified in Yeats's mind."[27]

The argument here is that we are all dreaming all of the time, and transposing a "dream" into language only removes it one stage further from "the facts," especially the facts of nature. As Professor Davie himself points out, the difference between Pound and Yeats in this respect is "a matter not of mutually exclusive categories but only of where the emphasis characteristically falls"—not a difference in kind, but a difference in degree. Even that difference in degree may be attributed more to what one is professing to be doing—no small matter, admittedly—than what one has achieved. It would be very hard to make an argument that Pound's wasp—a sermon, so to speak, already hidden there—is any less subjectified than Yeats's swans, say, in "The Wild Swans at Coole" except that in one case the mind is swinging by a grass blade and knows it and is needing the consolation of small and simple things, and in the other case it is not (though *imperious* is certainly not the word for the mood of "The Wild Swans at Coole"). And Yeats tells us point-blank that the swan in "Coole Park and Ballylee, 1931," is an emblem, thus calling attention to the difference between the swan of the mind and the swan as itself in the perceived world, establishing his mode as allegory, as Paul de Man would say, rather than symbol. Moreover, once one admits into such an epistemological context the issue of

---

27. Oscar Wilde, "The Decay of Lying," in *Complete Works of Oscar Wilde*, 977–78; Richard Ellmann, *Eminent Domain: Yeats among Wilde, Joyce, Pound, Eliot, and Auden*, 3

what "supernatural purpose or design" nature may reveal to us, one has certainly moved back very close to the issue of the "vision of reality that satisfies the whole being." Imperiousness of one kind or another, as Yeats implies, seems to be built into the very language with which we speak.

It does matter that rather than writing tendentiously about wasps and ants and house cats, Yeats writes tendentiously about eagles, hawks, and swans—after all, he really is one of the last romantics, lashed to the mast of a heroic ideal. But this distinction is not between an unmediated reality on the one hand and a version of it on the other but between two versions—as all such distinctions must be; and Yeats would have argued that the versions we choose are the versions we stake our lives upon. We must choose, if we can, to not become "helpless before the contents of [our] own mind."[28] Paradoxically, the reality of merely perceptual objects is inexhaustible to our awareness; the reality of imaginal objects is not.

Writing in *Twilight of the Idols* about the peculiar metaphysic that language itself is, Nietzsche observes, "we are not rid of God because we still have faith in grammar." Baudelaire had argued earlier (1859) that "systems of rhetoric and prosody are not arbitrarily invented forms of tyranny, but collections of rules demanded by the very structure of a man's spiritual being."[29] If either had meant to refer forward to Yeats here he would have been right. Grammar or syntax for Yeats was not only an affirmation of "the conscious mind's intelligible activity," as Professor Davie describes it, but also the creation of a world that stands in opposition to and transcends the world-in-itself. Grammar itself is an intensity of pattern. Grammar is also a sign of thinking going on in a poem, of a hypotactic organizing, a coordination and subordination of things and ideas; where it is both vigorous and complex, it conveys the illusion of authority, as it subjugates the "things" of perception and thought to the activity of thinking that is taking place. Authoritative syntax is an instance of form itself becoming the subject, an aspect of the declaration of the poem. Grammar is a uniquely human, and therefore existential, construct. Grammar both allows and requires the poet

---

28. Quoted in Zwerdling, *Yeats and the Heroic Ideal*, 19.

29. Nietzsche, *Portable Nietzsche*, 332; Charles Baudelaire, *Baudelaire: Selected Writings on Art and Literature*, 306.

to be discontinuous from nature in the mind. Being made from rules and tensions, it also allows the poet to make artifacts from even the most demoralizing thought, enables a display of overcoming—of managing, of working things out, of subjecting the mere unrationalized fact of the world to the authority of thinking. So Nietzsche was right in this sense; what there is left of God in the world is there in our grammar—but for Nietzsche to have despaired of it, even facetiously, contradicted his own agenda.

Yeats's father had argued that we are all dreamers in our waking life and that, if we are lucky, we continue to be. Yeats's anxiety on this issue is most deeply inscribed in "The Wild Swans at Coole," where it is hidden from consciousness in a subtext. Nineteen years later it is not possible that the swans he speaks of at Coole Parke are the same swans he first saw. Insofar as the swans from nineteen autumns before and the swans he now muses upon are identified, therefore, they are not autonomous entities at all even in the real time of the poem but dream children, so to speak, and real only in the mind or in the mind's creative negotiation with the perceived world. What the poet thinks of the swans—that their hearts have not grown old and that passion and conquest attend upon them still—is no more true of them than it is of himself. What has happened is that the desire that these qualities be embodied somehow in the world has been so intense that it has wholly overridden empirical awareness. The truth of the factual has given way to the truth "that satisfies our profoundest desires," the truth that poetry and art make a place for. It is not possible, either, that Yeats could not know, at some level, that these could not be the same, identical swans. Once we have absorbed that difficulty of the text, it seems clearer that the poem is not about the swans at all but about a way of seeing the swans, and a way of seeing that causes both the natural world and human life—even in an elegiac context (perhaps especially in an elegiac context)—to be enhanced. Such is the power of desire that it generates language, as George Steiner has said, in order "to conceive of, to articulate possibilities beyond the treadmill of organic decay and death."

We secrete from within ourselves the grammar, the mythologies of hope, of fantasy, of self-deception without which we would have been arrested at some rung of primate behaviour or would, long since, have destroyed ourselves. It is our syntax, not the physiology of the body or the thermodynamics of the planetary system, which is full of tomorrows. Indeed, this may be the only area of "free will," of assertation outside direct neurochemical causation or programming. We speak, we dream ourselves free of the organic trap.[30]

If we read "The Wild Swans at Coole" in this way, the question that concludes it no longer seems so oddly redundant. That is, it no longer refers to the swans literally flying off somewhere else and to the poet's waking up one morning to find them gone—to which a reader might well reply, So what? It refers rather to that power that human beings have to dream the world into an intensity of pattern (that poems like this one are only exceptional instances of) and to the fear that that power and the created world with it might suddenly dissipate (or the soul depart, as his father had put it). The poet would then be a modern Coleridge, in dejection, seeing but not feeling, his genial spirits failed, hopeless to win from outward forms, like swans, and lakes, and woodland scenes, "The passion and the life, whose fountains are within." He would have awakened from a dream of the world to be starkly in the presence of only the unmediated world-in-itself—to what is left over after passion, thought, syntax, rhythm, verbal music, and rhyme. That the question is raised at all undercuts the epistemological position from which the poem's prior claims have been made, for it arises from the space behind thought. Insofar as Yeats's poem echoes the ending of "Ode to a Nightingale" ("Fled is that music:...Do I wake or sleep?"), it also raises the same question: not the banal question of whether I am awake or asleep but the question of which self—the awakened one or the dreaming one—is the true "I." "The Wild Swans at Coole" remains doubly elegiac. Bad enough that the poet must age in time; it is far worse that the process threatens also to diminish the power of desire from which he derives his power to transfigure the world. When Yeats says at the end of "The Circus Animals' Desertion" that he now "must lie down where all the ladders start" he intends to refer us once again to this unimaginable prospect—to the condition of mind in which we no longer have the power to appropriate the world, to find a "theme"— the ghost driven out "naked on the roads" "stricken / [by] the injustice of the skies." But in "The Circus Animals' Desertion," he is so far from this actually happening that when, in the first stanza, the subject comes

30. George Steiner, *After Babel: Aspects of Language and Translation*, 227.

threateningly to mind, he repels it—as in "The Cold Heaven" and "The Wild Swans at Coole"—by calling forth and naming it in a formal rhetoric that displaces the world and death, or rather stands in for that displacement.

Dorothy Wellesley reported that even as Yeats lay dying, he was striving to remain most himself, murmuring poetry:

> On Tuesday he did not come to spend the evening with us as arranged, as he was tired. On Wednesday the Turners left for England and we were busy with arrangements. On Thursday morning I went to see him. He was very ill, in fact I saw he was dying, and I saw he knew it. I stayed only five minutes, fearing to tire him. In the afternoon we went again. Mrs. Yeats had said: "Come back and light the flame." I sat on the floor by his bed holding his hand; he struggled to speak: "Are you writ... are you writing?" "Yes, yes." "Good, good." He kissed my hand, I his. Soon after he wandered a little in his speech, murmuring poetry. Later that same evening he was able to give Mrs. Yeats corrections for "The Death of Cuchulain" and for the poem "His Convictions" which he changed to "Under Ben Bulben." On Friday he was worse, and soon passed into what proved to be his last coma. He had much pain from the heart, but morphia helped him. Next day, January 28th, he was dead.[31]

This seems at once too good to be true and easy to believe. Poetry was a mantra for Yeats, an instrument of thought. Perhaps he was believing in the end that it could fend off even death itself. He really did fear "The world outside himself... insofar as it existed in its own right" and thought of himself and poetry as bodied against it because it was "bodied against him."

31. Quoted in W. B. Yeats, *Letters on Poetry from W. B. Yeats to Dorothy Welles-ley*, 214–15.

2

Style

————— ❧ —————

THE RECURRING issue for the W. B. Yeats inscribed in *Collected Poems* was how to live authentically in the world and concede its final authority without therefore also being overcome by it and its problematical indifference to human value. This issue was complicated by the fact that even with his credulous and indiscriminate mysticism in real life, the Yeats of the poems could never be wholly reconciled to, let alone embrace, an alternative metaphysical refuge. A characteristically ingenuous letter to Katherine Tynan about mesmerism from 1890 depicts the problem as explicitly as any of his poems. He speaks of preparing an article describing

> experiments lately made by me, Ellis, Mrs Besant Etc in clairvoyance I being the mesmerist; and experiments in which a needle suspended from a silk thread under a glass case has moved to & fro and round in answer to my will, and the will of one or two others who have tried, no one touching the glass. . . . Probably if I decide to publish these things I shall get called all sorts of names—imposter liar and the rest for in this way does official science carry on its trade. . . . To prove the action of man's will, man's soul, outside his body would bring down the who[le] thing—crash.

This simple experiment of mind over matter also could stand as a model of Yeats's intellectual life. The contest itself is as much the point as any predicted outcome would be, but such a contest would not be possible, obviously, in the aforementioned separate metaphysical space where material, with its inert autonomy, would not exist. A less innocent aspect of the same conviction is apparent in his attraction, at the end of his life, to the ideas of the Eugenics Society. As antidemocratic and pragmatically foolish as such ideas seem now—though both left-wing and right-wing intellectuals endorsed them at the time—and as totalitarian and cruel as they would necessarily have to have become if put into practice (and were when put into practice in Germany in the thirties), they were also consistent with Yeats's interest in outwitting indiscriminate nature, with which he otherwise wished to appear to remain continuous, if only on preferred terms.

> Irish poets, learn your trade,
> Sing whatever is well made,
> Scorn the sort now growing up
> All out of shape from toe to top,
> Their unremembering hearts and heads
> Base-born products of base beds.

The "base-born products of base beds" he refers to in "Under Ben Bulben" must be understood in this respect as extensions of what he thought of as unregulated natural process. The expression of this conflict in the formal aspect of his poems is his presenting the poem as an encounter between the subject's human consciousness and the unconscious world, and showing the poem therefore as the model of an act of being in the world—as a model of *how* to be in the world. "On this point he remained adamant, holding that 'passive suffering was not a subject for poetry,' even as a passive attitude towards nature did not make fine poetry. The creative man must impose himself upon suffering, as he must also upon Nature."[1] This form of the will to power is implicit everywhere in Yeats's poems from *In the Seven Woods* forward. Eventually, even Keats—the proponent of negative capability—can be recruited for and made to illustrate the logic of this mission:

> For certainly he sank into his grave
> His senses and his heart unsatisfied,
> And made—being poor, ailing and ignorant,
> Shut out from all the luxury of the world,
> The coarse-bred son of a livery-stable keeper—
> Luxuriant song. ("Ego Dominus Tuus")

The sophisticated achievement of making poetry as an act of the mind a subject of the poems (illustrated by the elegant verbal architecture of the lines just quoted) required that Yeats develop a style and a

---

1. Yeats, *Collected Letters*, 1:211–12; Yeats, *Letters on Poetry*, 21.

manner of presentation that let the world in his poems remain nearly enough itself for us to recognize it as having been transformed. For such a purpose, for example, the phrase "hollow lands and hilly lands" from "Song of Wandering Aengus" is not effective. As George Bornstein has pointed out, the phrase started out as "barren hills and marshy land,"[2] but in its final form, the image has become more musical than representational, and the landscape has been internalized to a degree that causes the action of internalizing and transforming to be suppressed. It is appropriate for its own context, but in "The Song of Wandering Aengus," the poet has not yet—as himself, as the maker making what we read—entered the world of his own poems.

In "Coole Park and Ballylee, 1931" by contrast, he not only has entered the world of his poems as himself but also speaks explicitly of the poet's act of transforming the phenomenal world in order to bring it under the rule of thought:

> Under my window-ledge the waters race,
> Otters below and moor-hens on the top,
> Run for a mile undimmed in Heaven's face
> Then darkening through "dark" Raftery's "cellar" drop,
> Run underground, rise in a rocky place
> In Coole demesne, and there to finish up
> Spread to a lake and drop into a hole.
> What's water but the generated soul?

Water, obviously, is a great many things besides "the generated soul"; Yeats has taken his usage from a source in Porphyry,[3] and he has therefore switched abruptly from a naturalistic idiom (the otters, the moorhens) to a mythic and allegorical one. For the poet to have bracketed water's other, more conventional properties in order to say that it is nothing else *but* the generated soul is to call attention in a rhetorically conspicuous way to his appropriating act and to establish his claim to an environment in which *only* meaning prevails. When the swan is introduced and then suddenly breaks free of the earth, the poet exclaims, "Another emblem there!" as if to say another emblem in addition to the water identified ten lines before as the soul.

---

2. George Bornstein, *Transformations of Romanticism in Yeats, Eliot, and Stevens*, 78.

3. Jeffares, *New Commentary*, 288.

Upon the border of that lake's a wood
Now all dry sticks under a wintry sun,
And in a copse of beeches there I stood,
For Nature's pulled her tragic buskin on
And all the rant's a mirror of my mood:
At sudden thunder of the mounting swan
I turned about and looked where branches break
The glittering reaches of the flooded lake.

Another emblem there!

By calling attention to these symbol-making acts (especially by linking them with the adjective *another*) he shows us the process by which, and the conditions under which, his symbols are being made. By this means, the symbol-making itself becomes a subtext of the poem, and the symbols achieve the status of what Roland Barthes (in *Writing Degree Zero*) called "healthy" as opposed to "unhealthy" signs. The will to make symbols is shown to confirm the finite condition that generates the need in the first place. It is another example in the poem of confronting the phenomenal world directly in order to reconstruct it. But the irony here is that the poem itself is about being overcome *by* the world—as the setting itself is overcome by wintry desolation, Lady Gregory by age, her beloved estate by economic and political change, and the dream it had been made to symbolize by the indifferent unfolding of material, historical processes. The broken-off sticks on the forest floor then became associated with Lady Gregory's walking stick and thus with Lady Gregory herself. So the swan, the other emblem, is the counterfactual thought of the moment, and the counterfactuality of that thought—fending off desolation and material decay—is as much the point as the ad hoc symbol produced by it. For Yeats, from the beginning, the entire Gregory and Coole Park enterprise has been conceived as, in itself, a cultural symbol-making event that the world was now undoing; and the now-apparent relationality of that enterprise, its fictiveness, is repeated and confirmed in present time by the poet's own fiction-making in the poem on its behalf. This is a poet—a lapsed Platonist, so to speak—who would like to subscribe to the logic of unhealthy signs but who cannot fail to see the opposing case. The world in this poem is certainly not a stable one. In its subtle way, the poem is more modernist than even the modern world itself. The idea of "traditional sanctity" governs the poem but is also undermined by the openly declared provisional quality of the poet's symbol-making protocols. The closer one moves to the creative epistemology of Wallace Stevens, the farther one moves away from "traditional sanctity" insofar as it can be considered to have independent ontological status to begin with.

Once Yeats has put himself in the poems in this way as the poet, W. B. Yeats, many of the strategies of the poems become implicit declarations, means by which all experience is shown to be transformed into poetry, so that in any particular case the poetry itself matters as much as the content of any given poem. Whatever the secondary content of the poem is, the act of making poetry of the world is always potentially the primary content. This is formalism working from the inside out. The poem "as cold and as passionate as the dawn" that the poet aspires to write for his imagined solitary fisherman, which becomes the poem we are reading, is not only a poem that transcends the anti-intellectual rhetoric and the vulgar populism of modern Ireland as he sees it in "The Fisherman" in 1918—the ascendancy of the lowest common denominator—but also a poem whose formal reserve is an expression of its content and whose resolution is intelligible only in the privileged idiom of poetic discourse. The act of writing the poem is named itself as the gesture of transcendence: "Before I am old / I shall have written him one / Poem maybe as cold / And passionate as the dawn." In this respect a poem is a model of how, in life outside the text, the poet may imagine himself to achieve a similar renegotiation with the real world, whose content he does not control. The poem's stern artifice is a representation of its being a wholly willed and human achievement—not just an event of consciousness like observing the time of day, but an appropriating act. Traditional stanza forms and prosody serve this same purpose, conferring a kind of architectural dignity. "The Two Trees," with its obsessive artificiality, could be said to epitomize this function, since its very stylization expresses its own point and, again, makes an explicit connection between the act of writing and the act of being in the world—"Gaze into thine own heart," in other words.

Paradoxically, artifice in its most visible form on the page—a stanza form, a rhyme scheme—also constitutes and represents a barrier and a sign of where the self is compelled to stop. It is therefore like the world, too, at the same time that it expresses the poet's appropriating act of consciousness. In the choice to declare the artificiality of his act—endorsing the healthy sign—the poet concedes a distinction between himself and his reader, on the one hand, and the world he works in creative opposition to, on the other. Yeats said that stanza form and meter enabled him to subdue mere subjectivity. Mere subjectivity would be a subjectivity that was not conscious of itself. Obviously Yeats is not one to denounce or pretend to have overcome subjective expression. So what seems to be meant here is that subjectivity is being contained by the obedience to form, which is to say, performing in yet another way the representative act of the poet living both within the limits of the world and in opposition to those limits. At the same time, Yeats knows that there is a kind of futility built into this process. He is on record as saying that when he has tidied his thoughts, they end by seeming less profound, as if the authority of tidiness ensured the momentary—as well as eventual—suppression of desire. Yeats's version of this experience replays Nietzsche's argument that language, indeed consciousness itself, is a kind of ordering into which awareness enters only to surrender some indefinable quality of its own primordial, autonomous life.[4]

The Yeats who takes it as a challenge to shoehorn a very complicated, complete thought into the untransgressible limits of a conventional stanza form—a "complete coincidence between period and stanza," as he put it—is demonstrating what is possible within the given, not the heart's cry but the mind's assertion against necessity. The aged man in "Sailing to Byzantium" as a *poet* is anything but a "paltry thing," and Yeats, we know, must know that, for he is plainly and self-consciously demonstrating it. He may, in other words, be disempowered by age in one category of his being, but he is empowered by it in another and is required by the energy of that power to override the content of what he says by the very composed authority with which he says it. The dread of aging is subdued by its counterfactual rendition in the rhetoric in the same way that the confinement or restraint of the *ottava rima* stanza is all but overpowered by the assertiveness of the speaker's syntax. It is partly because of this display that we are unable fully to concede the surface logic of the poem, for here in the writing itself is an agent of desire so fully self-enabled as not to be driven to any refuge, let alone that of a neurasthenic disincarnation. The pathos at each stage seems unconvincing because it is an occasion for counterreaction in the energy of the poem's vocabulary and syntax. It is certainly true, as Richard Ellmann has said, that Yeats's way "did not lie in the suspension of the active faculties," as he had thought Joyce's and Pound's had;

4. See Yeats, *Letters*, 892, 629; and Nietzsche, *Gay Science*, 297–300.

"to the end he remained stubbornly loyal in his art to the conscious mind's intelligible structure."[5] Yeats's syntax is more than simply orthodox; it is also an elaborate, symbolic repudiation of existential inertia.

In the final stanza of "In Memory of Major Robert Gregory," there is no forward momentum like that of "Sailing to Byzantium" for that *would* be beside the point.

> I had thought, seeing how bitter is that wind
> That shakes the shutter, to have brought to mind
> All those that manhood tried, or childhood loved
> Or boyish intellect approved,
> With some appropriate commentary on each;
> Until imagination brought
> A fitter welcome; but a thought
> Of that late death took all my heart for speech.

What *is* in evidence in this structure alone is a complicated activity of fabrication in the process of contemplating, adjusting, and establishing grammatical priorities (of subordination and coordination) and subtle cause-and-effect relationships. What one would expect here, from a simple-mindedly expressive style of one whose heart for speech has been taken, would be some form of parataxis, certainly not hypotaxis of this baroque and self-consciously achieved order. The style itself is silent assertion in the presence of the silencing thought of death.

In a related way the convention of rhyme for Yeats is a mastery of limitation by virtue of its being a perceptible effect of the use of limitation. Rhymes, though they are in one respect impediments, are made to seem not to be:

> Beyond the ridge lived Mrs. French, and once
> When every silver candlestick or sconce
> Lit up the dark mahogany and the wine,
> A serving-man, that could divine
> That most respected lady's every wish,
> Ran and with the garden shears
> Clipped an insolent farmer's ears
> And brought them in a little covered dish.

---

5. Yeats, *Letters*, 522; Richard Ellmann, "Joyce and Yeats," 636.

A fully self-contained narrative is fitted here into this single eight-line stanza. Its being a narrative means that a forward movement is desirable, and the single-sentence structure obviously ensures this movement. Somewhat less obviously, the rhymes are effortlessly overrun in this progression until the point comes where the narrative ends, and where rhymes, having opened out in the second quatrain, then draw the story neatly to a close. On the one hand, the barrier that rhyme symbolizes by stopping the line at the end has been transcended; on the other hand, the potential for closure that rhymes, particularly in this stanza form, symbolize has been manipulated by the poet (identified in the poem as a poet) for his own purposes before our eyes. Barrier, limit, and closure are all apparent to us at least subliminally in the convention of syntactical practice, in the stanza form, and in the rhymes. But rather than subjugating the poet, they are subjugated by the poet and appropriated for his rhetorical self-representation. The compositional strategies become in themselves a subtle existential drama, and this rhetorical experience is reinforced by, and reinforces, the poet's identification with the subjects in the story—with the aristocratic *hauteur* of Mrs. French and with its extension into the servant's unhesitating transgression on her behalf.

Obviously there is nothing unusual about a poet's manipulating and overcoming rhyme. What makes Yeats's a special case is that he speaks in the voice not just of a man but of a poet "thinking and feeling" his way through the poem. This poet's recurring theme is the effort of human consciousness to command the otherwise random and unmediated material of history and the world and to supplant them or reconstitute them in the privileged estate of the poem. The authority of this effect can be demonstrated by comparing the stanzas in "The Tower," or almost any stanza from a mature Yeats poem, with the mannered syntax and consequent awkward rhyming in the first four lines of "The Sad Shepherd":

> There was a man whom Sorrow named his friend,
> And he, of his high comrade Sorrow dreaming,
> Went walking with slow steps along the gleaming
> And humming sand, where windy surges wend.

Sorrow's friend is more hapless in these lines than he needs to be. The inversion of the phrase that would normally be "dreaming of his high comrade Sorrow" so as to move "dreaming" to the end of the line is not only an ungainly effect in itself but causes the rhyme to sound even more contrived than it otherwise would have. The normal grammar is naively garbled in order to produce the rhyme. In the next line the rhyme interrupts the normal grammatical unit and becomes itself undercut by the awkward enjambment that results. This could be argued to be deliberate, an aspect of the poem's artificially antique style; but it does not convey poetic authority nor strength of purpose. Not that it has to of course: "The Sad Shepherd," in these formal respects, as in its theme, is about defeat rather than conquest, and the defeat of the power of what is here metaphorically called "singing" at that.

> And then the man whom Sorrow named his friend
> Sought once again the shore, and found a shell,
> And thought, *I will my heavy story tell*
> *Till my own words, re-echoing, shall send*
> *Their sadness through a hollow, pearly heart;*
> *And my own tale again for me shall sing,*
> *And my own whispering words be comforting,*
> *And lo! my ancient burden may depart.*
> Then he sang softly nigh the pearly rim;
> But the sad dweller by the sea-ways lone
> Changed all he sang to inarticulate moan
> Among her wildering whirls, forgetting him.

Here, in short, is an early exception that proves the rule, a poem in which the poet has occluded himself and that not only reports but also enacts his failure to achieve an appropriate rhetorical form of self-presence.

Once this poet does enter the poems as himself—at about the point of "Adam's Curse" as it is commonly said—his formal command of poetic device, of the material of the poet's world (rhyme, meter, syntax, and their interaction) becomes in itself an aspect of his self-presentation. How complex and therefore, in a sense, self-validating the effects of this mastery can be may be illustrated by the familiar example of "No Second Troy":

> Why should I blame her that she filled my days
> With misery, or that she would of late
> Have taught to ignorant men most violent ways,

Or hurled the little streets upon the great,
Had they but courage equal to desire?
What could have made her peaceful with a mind
That nobleness made simple as a fire,
With beauty like a tightened bow, a kind
That is not natural in an age like this,
Being high and solitary and most stern?
Why, what could she have done, being what she is?
Was there another Troy for her to burn?

"No Second Troy," like "The Cold Heaven," is a sonnet without the final couplet, displaying the art of resonant sonnet closure without recourse to the most obvious conventional means for doing so, the two extra lines. The intensity is an effect of the relentless movement through the barely resisting rhymes of the first two single sentences, each of which constitutes in itself a five-line shadow stanza arrested in the middle of the rhyme so as to push forward subtly at the same moment that it has come to rest. This is especially evident in the four-stress phrasing of "Being hígh and sólitary and móst stérn." The conclusiveness of this line's tone causes us, in turn, to anticipate a closing rhyme that is yet to appear; so when "stern" is answered in the last line with "burn" the effect of closure is that much more emphatic and complete. The contrast of rhetorical authority between the poet here and in "The Sad Shepherd" is plain enough. What is less obvious is that, in empowering himself, the poet empowers his female subject as well, and by this means he becomes identified with her. (It was a dream of Yeats's and Maud Gonne's when they were younger lovers that spiritually they should become one.) This new power that the woman can embody is noumenal more than political in that it is in excess of history, in excess of ordinary temporal grounding. In this regard she is one with the poem as well as being its spoken subject.

This poet's role, when it becomes identified with this rhetoric of self-assertion, is thus always in itself potentially a transgression, however enthralled by traditional sanctities the poet might otherwise appear to be. His role as a poet is to defy gravity, so to speak, with whatever means he has at his command and to keep this project before the reader continually, to "impose himself upon suffering." This will be the case even when he and his reader are aware that the defiance is only finally a rhetorical illusion, a formalist achievement posing as an existential one and doomed in the real world by the very restraints that his conceded formal limits are meant to signify. The ironies of this position are openly conceded in part 3 of "Vacillation," where the rhetoric therefore becomes willfully overdetermined:

> No longer in Lethean foliage caught
> Begin the preparation for your death
> And from the fortieth winter by that thought
> Test every work of intellect or faith,
> And everything that your own hands have wrought,
> And call those works extravagance of breath
> That are not suited for such men as come
> Proud, open-eyed and laughing to the tomb.

The word *tomb* flares up surprisingly here not only because of its position at the end of the stanza's and the sentence's martial progression, but also because, being an image, it is the dominant sound in the last rhyme. So the pride and the open-eyedness (which flare, too, because of the spondaic accent) are brought up short and overcome; but the complete effect of the stanza remains one of a stalemate, illogical and paradoxical as that is. We can give assent to this illogic only to the degree that the rhetoric itself compels us to, because of its own resistance to the fact of death and to the silent but nevertheless restraining pattern of the meter and the prescribed stanza form. Yeats's situating the key concepts—*begin, test, proud*—at the initial position in three lines reinforces this effect; but the decisive influence, again, is the momentum that is generated in the unrolling of the single sentence and its progressive elevation of pitch. Harold Bloom, a last romantic of our own era, says of these same lines: "That way of writing is simply beyond admiration, that high and extraordinary style in which nevertheless everything is beautifully articulated, beautifully subordinated to a kind of overwhelming aesthetic event. It goes from height to height, and you feel it can't really be sustained at that pitch, and then he takes it even higher."[6]

One of the ways Yeats has of reinforcing this level of rhetoric and therefore of evading the tidiness that leaves the experience of the poem

6. John Taylor, "Bloom's Day: Hanging Out with the Reigning Genius of Lit Crit.," 55.

"less profound" is to press his language slightly over the threshold of conventional meaning. By this means, he both keeps the entrenched semantic conventions of the authority over limits in place and also overrides them. This is a version, in his choice of diction, that is also enacted in his rhyming and syntax. As a performative rhetorical gesture—as opposed to a cleaner communicative one—the language's suddenly not quite making sense becomes in itself a part of the point. A world is momentarily generated in the purely verbal space that is free of conventional referential restraints, just as consciousness in the poem is free of necessity.

> It is time that I wrote my will;
> I choose upstanding men
> That climb the streams until
> The fountain leap, and at dawn
> Drop their cast at the side
> Of dripping stone; I declare
> They shall inherit my pride,
> The pride of people that were
> Bound neither to Cause nor to State,
> Neither to slaves that were spat on,
> Nor to the tyrants that spat,
> The people of Burke and of Grattan
> That gave, though free to refuse—
> Pride, like that of the morn,
> When the headlong light is loose,
> Or that of the fabulous horn,
> Or that of the sudden shower
> When all streams are dry,
> Or that of the hour
> When the swan must fix his eye
> Upon a fading gleam,
> Float out upon a long
> Last reach of glittering stream
> And there sing his last song.

So long as pride in this sequence is identified as a human attribute, it is wholly comprehensible. When it leaps from Burke and Grattan to "the morn / When the headlong light is loose," it becomes problematical. The transition creates a new and unfamiliar conceptual forum and therefore, by implication, a new region of possibility for it to inhabit. It does not matter to this objective that "pride" like "that of the sudden shower" in a conventional semantic world does not make sense. What does matter is that it almost seems to make sense and that it comes forward from a usage that would make sense in the simplest prose discourse. It is that transition that makes the difference. The reader must see the poet in the poem pressing to achieve this range of possibility. The transition must be perceived as an *action* of consciousness as well as the *result* of such an action; and the norm of conventional intelligible diction is as critical to this effect as the release of that diction into wider parabolas of implication. The sense of the entire transaction is of a world (guaranteed in the poet's language) in which words may be freed of ordinary referential restraint and yet possess the authority of reference as well. Conventional referentiality has taken on the role of conventional syntax, which is to anchor and to connect symbolically to the real world so as both to underwrite and to enable the dialectical event of transcending it—a performative gesture, in other words, which exemplifies the effort to live authentically in the world while also pressing the discursive limits of accommodation. It does not hurt that the word in this case is *pride* and that the very concept it symbolizes is being represented in the way in which usage has been augmented and extended. Also, it should not pass without notice that the indeterminate usage here emerges not just from a human context but from a political one as well, and that it therefore unobtrusively advances the project of "naturalizing" the conservative agenda. Floating signifiers that claim immunity from rational scrutiny are useful, obviously, in political as well as in poetic strategies.

In "The Wild Swans at Coole," the assertion "Passion or conquest, wander where they will, / Attend upon them still" has the same indeterminate resonance. Outside the ambiance of the reverie of this poem—that is, in ordinary discourse—it is very difficult to say what this statement means, though it is certainly a compelling utterance in its own setting. The sound qualities alone that arise from the configuration of diminishing vowels *("wander where they will"),* from the alliteration, and from the texture and weight of the words *passion* and *conquest* move the poem's language away from reference into a function that is just outside the reach of ordinary cognitive understanding. The terms applied to the swans seem chosen as much for their musical attributes as for the conceptual attributes they confer. So Yeats's swans have transcended simple nature and his language has transcended simple representation, yet this event is motivated by desire rather than by observation, though proceeding from observation and then away from it.

A natural outcome of Yeats's symbolist apprenticeship is always in evidence in these transactions. His symbolist inclinations are domesticated by experience and choice but remain in evidence nevertheless, and they are pointedly put into evidence in the high rhetorical drama of this poem. Even the oxymoronic phrase in "Easter 1916"—"a terrible beauty is born"—points to a condition of being that seems just beyond the reach of empirical thinking, especially when that terrible beauty is extravagantly claimed to have been born in a context in which "*all*" has been "changed *utterly*." Or, in "A Prayer for My Daughter," not only the compelling phrase "radical innocence" but also the entire last two stanzas would be material enough for a new chapter of *Seven Types of Ambiguity*. Yeats's language in such enterprises would not hold up much better under Empson's scrutiny than Wordsworth's lines from "Tintern Abbey" have, though the ambiguity in both cases is at some level deliberate, of course. It is a symbolist extension of language's reach so as to show, in the formation of the poet's position in the world— and in the reader's, by association—the effect of the limitations under which we think. ("Only... when we have put ourselves in all the possible positions of life, from the most miserable to those that are so lofty that we can only speak of them in symbols and in mysteries, will entire wisdom be possible.")[7] Wordsworth hedges his own case by saying "*sometimes* I have *felt*." But Yeats never wavers:

> Considering that, all hatred driven hence,
> The soul recovers radical innocence
> And learns at last that it is self-delighting,
> Self-appeasing, self-affrighting,
> And that its own sweet will is Heaven's will;
> She can, though every face should scowl
> And every windy quarter howl
> Or every bellows burst, be happy still.
> And may her bridegroom bring her to a house
> Where all's accustomed, ceremonious;

7. "W. B. Yeats' Speech at the Matinee of the British Association Friday, September 4th, 1908," in W. B. Yeats, *Uncollected Prose*, 2:370.

> For arrogance and hatred are the wares
> Peddled in the thoroughfares.
> How but in custom and in ceremony
> Are innocence and beauty born?
> Ceremony's a name for the rich horn,
> And custom for the spreading laurel tree.

Not wavering is an aspect of the stance. This wholly optative assertion is framed in the idiom of logical dispute ("considering that," etc.) as if nothing could be more self-evident than what follows; and though the authority of the truth-proposition statement gives way in the last stanza, it nevertheless carries its support forward subliminally, shoring up the more problematical return to the mode of what passes here for prayer. Meanwhile the symbolist tropes float free and assemble into different combinations—innocence, beauty, custom, ceremony, rich horn, laurel tree, soul, Heaven. This is not to say that Yeats's language cannot be wrestled to the ground of discursive meaning. The point is that the otherwise familiar terms are made to seem strange by the new combinations they are made to form and that their role in the story of the rhetoric is to extend the limits of possibility—or rather, by their very indefinite nature, to symbolize the desire for that extension. The poet's concluding the poem with a rhetorical question, especially this not-very-persuasive one, leaves the issue suspended but also ensures that suspension remains the issue.[8] At the end of "Among School Children," the question "How can we know the dancer from the dance?" is sufficiently ambiguous to produce the same vague effect of extended horizon.

The pattern that is shown here repeats itself in the most canonical of Yeats's poems and therefore becomes a form of signature. As a signature, it is a territorial marker of the poet's fictional regeneration

---

8. Charles Altieri presents "A Prayer for My Daughter" as a model of "Yeats's sense of the significance of the poetic act itself—the act of naming or apprehending the world through the imaginative capacities of poetic language" and a model, too, therefore, of the kinship between the poet in this role and the traditional tragic heroes who "share one basic quest: the desire to impose their own emotional and imaginative forms on their world." The poem's rhetoric, he concludes, particularly the elaborate double chiasmus at the end, "supports the poem's affirmation of poetic imagination because its elaborate artificiality insists that the poet's language is the product of a forming mind and not merely an imitation of the processes of nature." Altieri, "From a Comic to a Tragic Sense of Language in Yeats's Mature Poetry," 156, 162.

through poetry, which is to say, on his own terms. He is most likely to call upon indeterminate grammatical forms or indeterminate language at the end of poems so as to produce an effect of closure and of release at the same time:

> Now I shall make my soul,
> Compelling it to study
> In a learned school
> Till the wreck of body,
> Slow decay of blood,
> Testy delirium
> Or dull decrepitude,
> Or what worse evil come—
> The death of friends, or death
> Of every brilliant eye
> That made a catch in the breath—
> Seem but the clouds of the sky
> When the horizon fades,
> Or a bird's sleepy cry
> Among the deepening shades.
>
> ("The Tower")

> I am content to follow to its source
> Every event in action or in thought;
> Measure the lot; forgive myself the lot!
> When such as I cast out remorse
> So great a sweetness flows into the breast
> We must laugh and we must sing,
> We are blest by everything,
> Everything we look upon is blest.
>
> ("A Dialogue of Self and Soul")

> No matter what I said,
> For wisdom is the property of the dead,
> A something incompatible with life; and power,
> Like everything that has the stain of blood,
> A property of the living; but no stain
> Can come upon the visage of the moon
> When it has looked in glory from a cloud.
>
> ("Blood and the Moon")

To isolate only one of these instances is to see how compelling the mere rhythms of Yeats' poetic speech can be. "Everything I look upon is blessed" would give no reader difficulty; but "I am blessed by everything" is a different matter, which the rhetorical and metrical momentum of the lines discourages us from scrutinizing. The meaning of the word *bless* itself becomes problematical and seems to have been deliberately made problematical so as to accomplish the indicated release from the otherwise threatening impingement of the outer world. So vivid is this exertion of the ego toward momentary transcendence that when the poet forgives himself, the world is felt to forgive him as well, as if it could in the first place, and as if, in the second place, there were now no real difference between the self and the world. It is not only remorse that is overcome in this passage but also a naive dichotomy between subject and object and, with the erasure of that distinction, time itself. The closure of the poem has set the poet free.

Ezra Pound's argument that Yeats could not see the cathedral of Notre Dame inside the symbol and Donald Davie's extension of it (in *Poet as Sculptor*) reminds us that the strategies of Yeats's rhetoric are repeated in his appropriation of the natural world, that nature, when it enters Yeats's poems, becomes pointedly denatured—except, that is, in its manifestations where it is forbidding because finally it is only itself. This redefining process is seldom so overt as in "Coole Park and Ballylee, 1931," but it is never fully concealed, either. The logic of the poet's own position would require him less to conceal it than to put it on display. Pound is perfectly right about his not seeing Notre Dame inside the symbol, but what is right about Yeats in this case, if the logic holds, is right about almost everyone else, too, Pound included. As an artifact, Notre Dame *is* a symbol; its design incorporates symbolic character. Otherwise an army barrack would serve as well for religious ceremony, except then that would be symbolic, too. What Pound and Davie seem to be speaking of is not Yeats's confusion of the world and his own perception of it, but Yeats's unembarrassed openness about what he is doing. It plainly cannot be the case that some people see the world objectively and some do not (though some presumably try harder than others). Not even to claim to be perceiving the world objectively would seem—again, in Barthes's commonsensical terms—to be more of a healthy sign than an unhealthy one, suggesting at the very least legitimate dialectical conflict. As Hugh Kenner expresses it: "Against the poet as force of nature he placed of course the poet as deliberate personality."[9]

Yeats's appropriation of mechanical or vegetative nature takes the form of radically humanizing it and of detemporalizing it. The cumulative, subliminal impression from reading the *Collected Poems* is of a nature wholly instrumental to human awareness of itself and to human desire. This is the case even though in empty tropes, so to speak—as mere wind, or as rock and thorn, or as hawk and hare, or as aging and death—it not only represents but *is* what is outside of consciousness and subject to manipulation only in thought, only in formalist enterprise. The knowledge of this immutable reality—of nature's otherness—is what requires the counteroffensive of aesthetic transformation. Yeats's wandering Aengus is a good example here. Although he has grown old with wandering, he still yearns for the "silver apples of the moon, / the golden apples of the sun" and still supports a desire to dwell in a condition in which the normal processes of nature have been miraculously suspended. He is pointedly not wandering in a direction; he is in a narrative without end. And—again—the lapis in "Lapis Lazuli" is of no interest in itself, as a geological formation, until its "accidental" features are incorporated into an imposed human design. "Art is art," Yeats says with Goethe, "because it is not nature."[10] What Davie sees as Yeats's rejection of the natural world as an emblem of divine creation, Yeats clearly regards as an effort to envision human freedom, and this of course evades the problem of the condition of finiteness that Davie's term *creation* implies. Wilhelm Worringer's argument that cultures that are threatened by nature produce stylized art, and Joseph Frank's modernization of his theory, certainly apply to Yeats, but they do not produce in Yeats's work the spatial form that Frank seems to argue to be a necessary consequence.

> The heart of [*Abstraction and Empathy*] consists in [the] discussion of the spiritual conditions which impel the will-to-art to move in the direction of either naturalism or its opposite. Naturalism, Worringer points out, always has been created by cultures that have achieved an equilibrium between man and the cosmos. Like the Greeks of the classical period, man feels himself at one with organic nature; or, like modern

9. Hugh Kenner, "The Sacred Book of the Arts," 16.
10. Yeats, *Letters*, 440.

man from the Renaissance to the close of the nineteenth century, he is convinced of his ability to dominate and control natural forces. In both these periods man has a relationship of confidence and intimacy with a world in which he feels at home; and he creates a naturalistic art that delights in reproducing the forms and appearances of the organic world. Worringer warns us, however, not to confuse this delight in the organic with a mere impulse toward imitation. Such imitation is a by-product of naturalism, not its cause. What we enjoy is not the imitation per se but our heightened sense of active harmony with the organic crystallized in the creation or apprehension of a naturalistic work of art.

On the other hand, when the relationship between man and the cosmos is one of disharmony and disequilibrium, we find that nonorganic, linear-geometric styles are always produced. To primitive peoples, for example, the external world is an incomprehensible chaos, a meaningless or terrifying confusion of occurrences and sensations; hence they would hardly take pleasure in depicting this world in their art. . . . Accordingly, their will-to-art goes in the opposite direction: it reduces the appearances of the natural world to linear-geometric forms. Such forms have the stability, the harmony, and the sense of order that primitive man cannot find in the flux of phenomena as—to use a phrase of Hart Crane's—"they plunge in silence by."[11]

In experimental modernism, the transcendent ego is effaced, or distributed, along with the linear time that it otherwise inhabits, whereas with Yeats the ego is foregrounded because its engagement with nature and temporality is always the subtext of the poem at hand. In effect, Yeats has remodernized the will-to-art of Greek and Renaissance naturalism by stressing the heightened "sense [illusion] of active harmony" that can be "crystallized" in what only appears to be a "naturalistic" work of art. This is a continuing story from the beginning to the end of *Collected Poems*. The point is not so much a matter of what nature is made to symbolize as that it is made into symbols and therefore brought into the arena where human self-creation can be believed to take place. With Coleridge, Yeats has reversed the emphasis that Wordsworth argued for in the Preface to *Lyrical Ballads*. Rather than the passions of men being incorporated in the beautiful forms of nature, the beautiful forms of nature are incorporated in the passions of men. Nor is nature called upon merely to sanctify human desires. What is important is

11. Joseph Frank, *The Widening Gyre: Crisis and Mastery in Modern Literature*, 53–54.

that the exchange take place, regardless of whether it is, in the mind, for good or ill.

> Once more the storm is howling, and half-hid
> Under this cradle-hood and coverlid
> My child sleeps on. There is no obstacle
> But Gregory's wood and one bare hill
> Whereby the haystack- and roof-levelling wind,
> Bred on the Atlantic, can be stayed;
> And for an hour I have walked and prayed
> Because of the great gloom that is in my mind.
>
> I have walked and prayed for this young child an hour
> And heard the sea-wind scream upon the tower,
> And under the arches of the bridge, and scream
> In the elms above the flooded stream;
> Imagining in excited reverie
> That the future years had come,
> Dancing to a frenzied drum,
> Out of the murderous innocence of the sea.

It is the mood of excited reverie that transforms mere wind in the first stanza into a symbol of future years in human time. Before the remaining meditation of this poem can proceed, the abstract neutrality of nature must be brought into the mind and framed by human reference, even if that reference is as threatening as nature itself. This is the first necessary act of "A Prayer for My Daughter": that what is otherwise merely wind become a metaphor, the future years dancing to a frenzied drum. If we observe that not much is said in what follows in the poem about these future years, it seems more apparent that the change from wind to future years has been merely an enabling device, a mirror that we step through. Any humanized context is more comprehensible than none at all, and his daughter's achieving the idealized aristocratic composure that the poet goes on to describe seems somewhat less pointless when it is challenged by destructive human qualities such as hatred and bitterness than when faced with the circumambient inhuman reality—"murderous innocence"—of nature and the sea, which is the poem's first subject. Once an even vaguely human dispensation is established by the metaphor, nature is no longer threatening in itself and becomes an obliging enabler of the remainder of the meditation.

> May she become a flourishing hidden tree
> That all her thoughts may like the linnet be,
> And have no business but dispensing round
> Their magnanimities of sound.

Metaphor has many functions in poetic discourse, obviously, but its first effect is always domestication, bringing the uncanny under the human rule of rhetorical intention. This effect is especially obvious when the comparison is slightly surreal (or what Paul de Man would call allegorical), as it is here, with the tree as the daughter and the thoughts as birds, and the effect therefore calls attention to the exchange taking place in the metaphorical language. If Anne Yeats were to be associated instead with, say, a gazelle, as Eva Gore-Booth is in a later poem, the work of domestication would not be so striking. But even when he does describe Eva Gore-Booth as a gazelle, conferring grace and exotic beauty upon her, both the gazelle and the veldt it would normally inhabit are made to seem acquiescently available. Yeats is consistent in this process. In metaphors, the traffic is always running from nature to the human, whether the image is an adapted common idiom or special to Yeats:

> Was it for this the wild geese spread
> The grey wing upon every tide?
>
> > ("September 1913")

> For even daughters of the swan can share
> Something of every paddler's heritage.
>
> > ("Among School Children")

> How should the world be luckier if this house,
> Where passion and precision have been one
> Time out of mind, became too ruinous
> To breed the lidless eye that loves the sun?
> > ("Upon a House Shaken by the Land Agitation")

In this last segment, rather than the reverse, eagles, in bits and pieces, become honorary members of the Gregory family. Nature, when it cannot be so adapted, threatens the very ideal of human freedom that it is called upon to symbolize. Metaphor, then, is a stabilizing agent and works on behalf of a deeper purpose than the merely rhetorical ones.

When human beings become animals, trees, flowers, or clouds in these poems it is not, any more than it is in Ovid, a tribute to nature but a blocking out of nature's autonomy.

Yeats's celebrated frankness on the subject of sexuality should be understood as at least a part of the psychological and rhetorical enterprise in which the world, in its form (in this case) of human biology (as opposed to the idealized erotic subject of the mind) can be given representational prominence so as to be visibly recharacterized and adapted to the system of his own thought. Frankness may be the right word for Yeats's attitude toward sexual matters, compared to the stances of some of his more demure contemporaries, but it is not precisely right for the language in which sexuality is represented:

> Though pedantry denies,
> It's plain the Bible means
> That Solomon grew wise
> While talking with his queens,
> Yet never could, although
> They say he counted grass,
> Count all the praises due
> When Sheba was his lass,
> When she the iron wrought, or
> When from the smithy fire
> It shuddered in the water:
> Harshness of their desire
> That made them stretch and yawn,
> Pleasure that comes with sleep,
> Shudder that made them one.
>   ("On Woman")

This passage could be argued to be an eloquent case for the power of circumlocution in writing of the sexual act. But to think of the sexual act being presented here one must think through at least one layer of myth and one layer of metaphor only to find that the mediating activity of both the myth and the metaphor are as much an aspect of the subject as what they eventually lead us to. Rather than being merely presented, sexuality is being rhetorically augmented and transformed in that rhetorical process to accommodate itself to the heroic scale of life that the poet has reconstituted for his poet's world. Associating himself with Solomon and his partner with Sheba even detemporalizes this most poignantly temporal of all human phenomena, though, of course, that in itself is part of the point—as it usually is in representation.

> What else He give or keep
> God grant me—no, not here,
> For I am not so bold
> To hope a thing so dear
> Now I am growing old,
> But when, if the tale's true,
> The Pestle of the moon
> That pounds up all anew
> Brings me to birth again—
> To find what once I had
> And know what once I have known,
> Until I am driven mad.

Even the forces of eternal regeneration become sexualized, and sexuality itself has become metaphysical.

A similar strategy in "Solomon and the Witch" has Sheba's "crying out" in sexual pleasure—an otherwise hermeneutically innocent act, one would think—translated by Solomon into more occult terms:

> Who understood
> Whatever has been said, sighed, sung,
> Howled, miau-d, barked, brayed, belled,
>   yelled, cried, crowed,
> Thereon replied: "A cockerel
> Crew from a blossoming apple bough
> Three hundred years before the Fall,
> And never crew again till now,
> And would not now but that he thought,
> Chance being at one with Choice at last,
> All that the brigand apple brought
> And this foul world were dead at last."

Sheba's crying out is made analogous mainly to animal sounds before it is, so to speak, apotheosized as the utterance of a mythical bird from before fallen time and nature. The wit of this passage, and of the poem, is in the mock-serious hyperbole, and it suggests a wholesome capacity for self-parody on Yeats's part, since here he appears (in the role of

Solomon) as a butt of his own joke, ponderously unwilling, as usual, even in sex, to leave well enough alone. In this respect, "Solomon and the Witch" is a modest course correction as well, a more mature version of the rhetorical male swagger of "On Woman" to the degree that it is critically self-referential. Nevertheless, it is on account of such metaphorical transactions as these that it remains difficult to think of sexuality in Yeats's poetry as natural, that is, of nature. Even the all-but-pathological lecherousness of the speaker of "The Wild Old Wicked Man" is only part sex and part existential posturing.

Sexuality is its most natural, its unmediated, biological self in Yeats's poems when it has failed:

> How came this ranger
> Now sunk in rest,
> Stranger with stranger
> On my cold breast?
> What's left to sigh for?
> Strange night has come;
> God's love has hidden him
> Out of all harm,
> Pleasure has made him
> Weak as a worm.
> ("The Chambermaid's First Song")

> From pleasure of the bed,
> Dull as a worm,
> His rod and butting head
> Limp as a worm,
> His spirit that has fled
> Blind as a worm.
> ("The Chambermaid's Second Song")

Sexuality is most like nature, in other words, when it is indisputably no longer subject to the control of the will or the imagination, and in this form, for the poet, it is a disconcerting paradigm. The lessons for Yeats are quite grave, and they underlie all of his thought and motivate his work. It is not as far as we might think from the inarticulate moan of the shell into which the Sad Shepherd sings to the "fled spirit" of the chambermaid's songs. This is why, when after 1930 Yeats emerges in the personae of libidinous old men and old women (as an androgynous and abstract sexual energy), the story of this life, and the degree to which its being written *is* the life, seem to have reached the irreducible core of its subject matter. It is only when he lacks a "theme"—any theme—that the poet must lie down in the wholly material rag-and-bone shop of the heart. When what he himself names as "counter-truth" that he has made up ("And then a counter-truth filled out its play") ceases to be credible, the unthematized truth-in-itself must be confronted with a new one:

> I sought a theme and sought for it in vain,
> I sought it daily for six weeks or so.
> Maybe at last, being but a broken man,
> I must be satisfied with my heart.

And, of course, in "The Circus Animals' Desertion" he goes on to achieve a holding action, which he calls attention to achieving by making a theme out of not having one. Even the indignities of old age, impotence, and impending death may be thematized and therefore deflected if they can be made to become a part of the larger narrative of the poet's regeneration through the power of imagined life. This, of course, is what art does, but it may also be all that it does. Yeats could have been hearing Nietzsche on this as on other points:

> The deeper one looks, the more our valuations disappear—meaninglessness approaches! We have *created* the world that possesses values! Knowing this, we know, too, that reverence for truth is already the consequence of an illusion—and that one should value more than truth the force that forms, simplifies, shapes, invents.[12]

In two related essays on Yeats, John Holloway and George Bornstein have given subtle accounts of how Yeats generated a coherent world in his poems by endowing the otherwise disparate objects in it with related meanings, or, as Holloway characterizes it, "the creation, by a series of as if vatic acts, of a whole world of objects ordered as their creator desires."

> Logic, reality and fiat make a unity: no mere mirror of the physical cosmos, but a newly made one. Yeats's "world" in the later poems comprises not simply the objects he promulgates, but also and along with them the

12. Nietzsche, *Will to Power*, 326.

acts of thought by which these are promulgated and manipulated. This is what follows from—or creates, depending on how one looks at it— the passionate subjectivity of the poem: an ever-present continuity in them of their vehemently feeling, thinking, willing creator.[13]

This is different from Blake's claim to have created his own system so as not to be enslaved by another man's, and the distinction must be acknowledged, since it goes to the heart of the issue of how poetry for Yeats was an opportunistic appropriation of the material world. *A Vision* was Yeats's attempt to create a system so as not to be enslaved by another man's, though the more he tinkered with it, the more it became a process rather than a system. It has not been many years since it was common to describe the recurring symbols in Yeats's poems as representing unchanging emblems that had the same value or meaning regardless of the context in which they appeared, as if the structure of the poems merely reflected the higher metaphysical order of *A Vision*. But even the ordinary truth of the matter identified in Holloway's and Bornstein's arguments is more complicated than it at first seems. The symbolic interlockings that make Yeats's world coherent and meaningful also change. The so-called symbolic system of any given poem is always only emblematic and provisional in that tower, stream, swan, moon, tree, hawk, and so on, are always in effect movable signifiers. They are elements of a phenomenal world that has been reduced to a condition of ready-to-hand potentiality. And since such potential phenomena recur in the poems, they have a special status by virtue of their recurring and therefore circumscribing the world—robbing the universe of its vastness, as the narrator of *A Passage to India* says of another such adaptation. When the poet uses the word *emblem* in a poem—as in, "In mockery I have set / a powerful emblem up"—he is declaring an ad hoc transaction, the creation of a symbol for a specific rhetorical context. It is the same as saying, "I declare this tower is my symbol," and then going on to explain what in "Blood and the Moon" specifically— as opposed to other poems—his multipurpose tower is going to be a symbol of. In Coleridge's terms, this usage is closer to allegory than it is to symbol. It is modernist rather than romantic, a sign of what romanticism has become.

13. George Bornstein, "Yeats and the Greater Romantic Lyric" in *Romantic and Modern: Revaluations of Literary Tradition*, 91–110; Holloway, "Style and World."

The point is not so much that the tower always signifies one thing or the swan another, but that each always has a strong signifying identity in context when it recurs, and often in relation to the other images in its small family of tropes. (Swans are not starlings; Norman towers are not mobile homes.) When we interpret these configurations and learn to anticipate them, we are experiencing a kind of value that we recognize as being imposed upon the world that is otherwise wholly absent from it—an imperialism of the reflecting subject that is calling attention to the nature of its own act. The activity of the mind, and therefore the mind's presence, is evident in the shifting about of the interpretations of the images that are stable mainly to the degree that they become familiar because they recur. "[C]urious shifts in value take place in [Yeats's] symbols," Richard Ellmann points out, citing, for example, the "dance" as it symbolizes differing things in "The Double Vision of Michael Robartes," "Among School Children," and "Crazy Jane Grown Old Looks at the Dancers":

> The tree can be the "great-rooted blossomer" of "Among School Children" or the "broken tree" of the old pensioner. The bone may suggest the meaninglessness of physical life, as in the "slender needles of bone" of "The Crazed Moon," or its strong roots, as in the tenacious memory of the "bone upon the shore" in "Three Things." The sea-shell stands for the miracle of divine creation in "Crazy Jane Reproved," but for the lovely emptiness of wealth in "Meditations in Time of Civil War." The moon is immutable perfection in "Blood and the Moon" but mutable illusion in "The Crazed Moon" and perhaps "The Cat and the Moon." Yeats allows nothing to petrify, and keeps his symbols in movement from poem to poem. Yet in each poem the symbol is integral in its meaning and effect.[14]

This unsystematic system is different from Blake's also in that it has reference, to a large extent, to objects in the material world that one can visit in real time and see and smell and touch, or to historical events that can be examined and verified through access to other representations and sources, so that one who is not the poet is able to reflect upon the exchange between phenomenal and symbolic, and upon the heightened sense of difference between the two, which is always the point of such transactions in Yeats's poems.

14. Ellmann, *Identity of Yeats*, 169–70.

The reaches of this strategy cannot very well be circumscribed. John R. Harrison complains that Yeats tended to exploit "images taken from Christian rituals, without including Christian teaching or dogma."[15] One could see how, to some believers, this would be offensive and, to others, a hopeful, appropriatable sign; yet the same could be said of Jews or Buddhists or Hindus, since Yeats is never so blithely autocratic as when he is pillaging sacred texts or doctrines of established religions. This may be seen as a solemn theosophical deference to the universality of religious truth. But in practice, it calls attention to the self-sufficient authority of the poet's own intellect and its capacity to adapt all phenomena to the superior ecology of its own system. For western readers, the adaptation of Christian symbols makes this action all the more conspicuous and, therefore, from the poet's point of view, all the more effective in terms of his own directly or indirectly declared rhetorical project.

In the end, this project turns out to be fundamental to all the poems: to engender work that was a model of the labor of being in the world, and this meant showing forth the creative act. It meant always giving the appearance of being in the middle rather than at the beginning or end of something. It meant never lapsing into commonplace or stereotyped or institutionalized views, even when they might seem more reassuring than their idiosyncratic alternatives (as in the last section of "Vacillation," when Yeats rejects the "relief" his "heart might find" in Christian faith). And it meant, for Yeats, running not only against nature but even against his own nature, as well, so that what stays in view in the poems is the mind in action, perpetually readjusting its relationships with new circumstances and with itself: "The self-conquest of the writer who is not a man of action is style."[16] Indeterminacy in this project—Yeats's politics otherwise notwithstanding—becomes addictive for its own sake and, because of the occasions it presents for the modernist, it becomes a paratactic drama of self-overcoming. Nietzsche had addressed this issue, too:

> Alas, what are you, after all, my written and painted thoughts! It was not long ago that you were still so colorful, young, and malicious, full of thorns and secret spices—you made me sneeze and laugh—and now? You have already taken off your novelty, and some of you are ready, I

15. John R. Harrison, *The Reactionaries: A Study of the Anti-Democratic Intelligentsia*, 56.
16. Yeats, *Autobiographies*, 516.

fear, to become truths: they already look so immortal, so pathetically decent, so dull![17]

The issue of whether Yeats was or was not a Platonist, which in the past seemed to move just beneath the surface of all of the critical discussion of his work, lends itself to being constructively redefined. It is true that he seemed to wish to constitute in his poems—in "words alone"—a model of a Platonic world in which the raw material of human experience could be radically idealized, so that at least the possibility of eternal verities could be implied. In poems, ideas about how the real world might be could remain undisturbed by the complicated demographics of actual historical and social processes. It was always clear that the ideas of Yeats's poems could not become a basis for a realistic social policy. It did not take European fascism to show that. So in this respect, writing itself could be considered to be a temporal version of a Platonic safe house, an environment in which ideas could theoretically be venerated without being contaminated by the real world or, in turn, without jeopardizing the real world by a dangerous disapotheosis from theory into practice. This was the entire basis of the quarrel between Yeats and Maud Gonne, though Maud, contradicting herself, and not on the whole minding the way she had been represented, tended to agree with Yeats as far as his own work was concerned—and it was, after all, Maud Gonne's principled obedience to action, to praxis, rather than to reflection, that drew her into the arena of both anti-Semitic and Nazi causes. On the other hand, Yeats never even approached the Christianized Schopenhauerism of the late Eliot: "For it is ultimately the function of art, in imposing a credible order upon ordinary reality, and thereby eliciting some perception of an order in reality, to bring us to a condition of serenity, stillness, and reconciliation; and then leave us, as Virgil left Dante, to proceed toward a region where that guide can avail us no further."[18] In Yeats's poems, the idealizing act of consciousness takes place not in anticipation of the fullness of revelation but in its absence. He called this void by different names, but the protagonist of his poems is always in conflict with it. Even the wheel of *A Vision* turns ineluctably in this direction, toward a pure darkness. For

17. Friedrich Nietzsche, *Beyond Good and Evil: Prelude to a Philosophy of the Future*, 236.
18. T. S. Eliot, "Poetry and Drama," in *On Poetry and Poets*, 94.

the poet, naturally, the analogue of absence is silence, a condition of nonbeing, the fear of which is the motive of his thought and action. As Yeats says, in "The Long Legged Fly": the mind "moves upon silence." What is worse is that the modern mind must be aware that this must always be the case.

3

History and Politics

—————— ❧ ——————

Y EATS'S MEDITATION about doubting life's own values behind his thought (quoted in Chapter 1) was published as a note to "Upon a House Shaken by the Land Agitation" (1910), and on the whole, the note gives a more coherent view of the issue that the poem addresses than the poem itself does. Here is the poem, followed by the explanatory note (from Jeffares's *New Commentary*) in its entirety.

> How should the world be luckier if this house,
> Where passion and precision have been one
> Time out of mind, became too ruinous
> To breed the lidless eye that loves the sun?
> And the sweet laughing eagle thoughts that grow
> Where wings have memory of wings, and all
> That comes of the best knit to the best? Although
> Mean roof-trees were the sturdier for its fall,
> How should their luck run high enough to reach
> The gifts that govern men, and after these
> To gradual Time's last gift, a written speech
> Wrought of high laughter, loveliness and ease?

I wrote this poem on hearing the result of reduction of rent made by the courts. One feels that when all must make their living they will live not for life's sake but the work's and all be the poorer. My work is very near to life itself and my father's very near to life itself but I am always feeling a lack of life's own values behind my thought. They should have been there before the stream began, before it became necessary to let the work create its values. This house has enriched my soul out of measure because here life moves within restraint through gracious forms. Here there has been no compelled labour, no poverty-thwarted impulse.

70

The note enables us to understand the degree to which the value Yeats speaks of in the poem is generated ex nihilo as a human construction— as a "house," as written speech—and how that then determines his aesthetic understanding of political values and how for him the political, the existential, and the symbolic were intertwined.

> Art delights in the exception, for it delights in the soul expressing itself according to its own laws and arranging the world about it in its own pattern.... But the average man is average because he has not attained to freedom. Habit, routine, fear of public opinion, fear of punishment here or hereafter, a myriad of things that are "something other than human life," something less than flame, work their will upon his soul and trundle his body here and there.[1]

Here Yeats states as clearly and succinctly as seems possible what he would understand the goal and therefore the ideology of formalism to be—or, in the political sphere, what Phillip Marcus calls "artistic power," the potential art has for shaping life. Art is "exceptional" in that it answers only to the "soul" and reconfigures life in obedience to the soul's pattern rather than in obedience to some other prevailing discourse or to public opinion—implying that all of human life is "arrangement," by one set of competing discursive forces or the other, and that nothing is given. The argument in the poem and in both prose commentaries is unselfconsciously classist on the surface, but it is individualistic and antithetical at its core. Its political dimension is an extension of the logic of formalism generally. If poets and artists are the creators and custodians of the highest values in human life (as Nietzsche had argued that they must be, in the absence of any external source), and if art, by example, is to inspire the "average man" to "attain to freedom" (in part, as Shelley expressed it, by defeating "the curse which binds us to be subjected to the accident of surrounding impressions"),[2] then for the sake of all others who are borne down by their labor, physically and psychologically, poets and artists should be free to do their work. Institutions that support them in this enterprise should be enabled to flourish—otherwise, only politics and market forces and the

---

1. Yeats, *Explorations*, 168.
2. Phillip L. Marcus, *Yeats and Artistic Power;* Percy Bysshe Shelley, "A Defence of Poetry," 295.

"accident of surrounding impressions" prevail. If the work of poets and artists does not generate and distribute capital, it does generate and distribute cultural value—the symbols of the kind of freedom that can be attained to—and should be insulated from the reductive logic of the marketplace. Yeats's argument, without of course his saying so, is as much anticapitalist as it is antidemocratic, though in practice the two tend to come to the same thing, since capitalism with its indiscriminate distribution mechanisms—creative destruction, as it is called—is what makes possible the kind of social reorganization Yeats has in mind. His is a repetition of the classical English view descended to him from Samuel Johnson and Shelley through John Ruskin, Matthew Arnold, and Oscar Wilde: that poets are, or at least should be, the true legislators of the world, whether they be acknowledged or not—especially to the degree that "legislation" otherwise tends to be nudged along by Adam Smith's "Invisible Hand."

At this time of crisis in Coole Park's fortunes (by 1910 the estate was deeply in debt), Yeats was thinking of the Gregory estate not so much as a source of patronage, on the one hand, or as part of a larger, political hegemony, on the other, but as an irreplaceable symbol-making enterprise, which, as an ironic effect of the Irish decolonization, he was now seeing not as dominant but as subversive and antithetical. This was a way also to think of the issue in at least vaguely political terms—that is, as not altogether hopeless—since the only alternative on the horizon seemed to him to be the aforementioned market forces, the reductive commercial agenda of the urban middle classes, and the leveling conformity promoted by the Irish Roman Catholic Church. "[T]o be traditionalist in the modern world," Seamus Deane says of this view of Yeats's, "was to be revolutionary."[3]

The inhabitants of the tenant classes concealed in the poem in the phrase "mean roof-trees" could not be expected to show much interest in this debate except to the extent that they might secure a station in life that would permit them the luxury of becoming interested in it. Indeed, the appeal to history in "Upon a House Shaken by the Land Agitation" exclusively from the Protestant Ascendancy perspective could be taken as a form of coded discourse that the tenant classes—materially, at least—might well be better off without. These classes are the

3. Deane, *Celtic Revivals*, 49.

same as those whose ancestors' rootedness Yeats and John Synge and Lady Gregory had extolled, and their folklore was central to the project of re-Celticizing Irish culture. They were by this point emerging into a political and social ascendancy of their own. It seems uncharacteristically ungenerous here for Yeats to have set the story of their historically straitened circumstances outside the frame.[4]

When at the end of his life Yeats became an advocate of eugenic solutions to what was widely thought of as the democracy problem (a ludicrous notion in itself, scientifically, considering what we know now about the vagaries of genetic outcomes), his logic was inattentive to the actual results that dynastic marriages and selective breeding among the ruling classes have to present for the historical record. He had only to review his own century to turn up such examples as, say, Czar Nicholas II, whose demise Yeats deeply lamented in public—a despot whose regime was complacently decadent by even the most generous standards and whose skills in the arts of statecraft could have been outmatched by the average Dublin wine merchant. Yeats was also not willing to accommodate the statistically demonstrable fact that social and environmental conditions as well as either selective or fortuitous breeding produce human specimens. Even Nietzsche thought that Prussian families ought to intermarry with Jews in order to invigorate their declining bloodlines. Yeats did not seem to give credit to the fact that his own education, which had enabled him to make such arguments, was an effect of the same historical processes that alarmed him so in his own lifetime.

---

4. In relation to such political and economic crises, Lady Gregory herself could exhibit a blend of sympathy and hauteur that converted them into something oddly literary. During the famine of 1898, she had said to Yeats, according to her diary, "'that we who are above the people in means & education, ought were it a real famine, to be ready to share all we have with them, but that even supposing starvation was before them it wd be for us to teach them to die with courage [rather] than to live by robbery'" (Roy F. Foster, *W. B. Yeats: A Life,* 1:194). Even this measured generosity seems a little disingenuous in light of the fact that during the indisputably real famine, in 1847, her husband had been the author of the infamous "Gregory Clause" in the new Poor Law Legislation, which stipulated that "any family holding more than a quarter of an acre could not be granted relief, either in or out of the workhouse, until they gave up their land." This meant that the most desperate tenant families were forced either to starve or to give up their land. If they gave up their land, the landlords could, of course, then avail themselves of it. See Colm Tóibín, "Erasures," 17.

He also seemed unable to recognize that, owing to the glacial pace of those processes, members of his own family would have been unable to vote until as late as two years after he was born.

Yeats's father's counsel that he not introduce political or ethical argumentation into his poems, lest someone respond in the same terms, was prudent. One could answer the question of how to improve the tenants' situation at great length. (They had appealed to the Land Court, established by the Land Act of 1881, for a reduction of rents.) Such a debate could only be conducted, however, in the terms that the rule of existential formalism implicitly excludes. The semantic oddity of the phrase "laughing eagle thoughts" is a signal that Yeats is not intending for us to think here in material or representational terms at all—and, indeed, given its logic, the poem is a masterpiece of rhetorical supervision. It also demonstrates the degree to which the ideology of formalism and this assured command of the resources of poetic language are interdependent—in this project, that is, of arranging life according to its own pattern. Everything about the poem's rhetoric—the oxymoronic phrasing, the elaborate web of synecdoche and metonymy, the illusion of transcendence achieved by the images of flight—has the effect of setting the reader at a distance from points of reference outside the frame that would compromise the poem's agenda. To the extent that Yeats is thinking here of the Gregory family alone—of his friends and of what he knew—his claim is not wholly implausible. He seems always—even to the end, as James Pethica has suggested—to have been more deeply invested in friendship than in politics. But the rhetoric he deploys here implicitly represents the Gregorys as benevolent exemplars of their class, and a generalization on that scale would have been harder to substantiate in prose.[5]

5. W. B. Yeats, *Last Poems: Manuscript Materials,* xxiv. "The theoretical self-image of the Anglo-Irish was aristocratic and gentlemanly, but in practice, as Edmund Burke sarcastically noted, they were a middle class masquerading as an aristocracy. . . . Two centuries after Goldsmith's strictures . . . Louis MacNeice . . . remarked that (with the exception of Lady Gregory's and one or two others) the Big Houses contained no culture worth speaking of, 'nothing but an obsolete bravado, an insidious bonhomie and a way with horses.' They were brought down less by IRA firebombs than by a combination of fast women and slow horses—in other words, by decay that came mainly from within. This was recognized by Synge when he wrote that they were neither much pitied nor much deserving of pity" (Kiberd, *Inventing Ireland,* 449).

In the various excellent discussions of Yeats's conservative politics and how they might be said to weigh against him on a given day of judgment, the issue that is not often addressed directly is the degree to which the idealist psychologism that he shared with Nietzsche affected their formation. The Yeats of "Upon a House Shaken by the Land Agitation" or of "No Second Troy" is the Yeats also of "The Two Trees," where one is enjoined not only to look upon one or the other of the two trees of life, to dwell in the mind in one world or the other, the inner or the outer—to decide what to permit within the frame—but also to do so knowing that in either case, what one sees is what one gets. However wishful this wishful thinking would turn out to be, "The Two Trees" requires its audience to take it seriously as an epistemological proposition. Without any overt reference to politics, "The Two Trees" might be called a prototypical political poem for Yeats, because of its repudiation of the political *episteme*. Its medium is its message. Symmetry, stylization, pastoral antiquity, and a merely literary passion are marshaled to fend off the "outer world" and its ravens of "unresting thought" who "sniff the wind." The wrought dream of the world transcends the world in itself. And the injunction is carefully, even philosophically, phrased: it is not that the outer world does not exist; it is that it is better not to brood upon its nature because it always threatens to invade or infiltrate the sanctuary of what Yeats later, self-critically, acknowledged to be "pure mind." In a way typical of high modernism, he has set value and history in opposition to one another.

For all his wariness of abstraction, Yeats's view of world history was abstract and literary to the point that it ruled his understanding of what ontological history in fact is and of how the past in it is genealogically related to the present. At one level, this is a frame of mind that he shares with everyone, but it is especially common with visionaries like Gibbon, Hegel, or Marx, who understand and represent history as a narrative and therefore appropriate it epistemologically in order to make a particular narrative or superstory manifest. Yeats's abstractions were simpler, especially when put to the service of mythicizing the Anglo-Irish ascendancy. Seamus Deane calls it "Romantic aesthetics," in the interest of "hermeneutic value." "In Coleridge, in Blake, in Carlyle, in William Morris, history is essentially engaged with the fortunes of the Imagination and, therefore, almost indistinguishable from aesthetics"—from metaphor, that is, which lends "to widely dispersed materials a

provisional coherence." "I daresay," Yeats wrote to a friend in regard to
the Home Rule debates in 1912, "that politics will not in our time
escape from statements that have but temporary value, but I believe
that a man of letters should have no part with them, for his life if it has
meaning at all is the discovery of reality." The reality that he speaks of
is not the reality of the historian. What Yeats had said of his own tem-
perament in relation to science was relevant to his sense of history as
well: "I am philosophical not scientific, which means that observed
facts do not mean much until I can make them a part of my experience."
Thus art is again arranging the world about it in its own pattern. Yeats's
intermittent but lifelong allegiance to the *anima mundi* and the *spiritus
mundi*—perhaps by intention—had the effect of bracketing the historical contingency of human consciousness and took for granted the
possibility of an unmediated contact with the past, as if historical change
altered nothing of how and what people think. This paradigm also had
the appeal of causing one's own consciousness—and one's very being—to seem atemporal as well: "The Tale of Troy is quite near to me,
probably much nearer than anything I read in this morning's paper. . . .
I am not limited by time. I am as old as mankind."[6] This way of reading history immunized him from having to ground his interpretations
in empirical data. His mission as a poet combined with his unwavering
allegiance to the Gregory family made it inevitable that he would seem
to idealize, without scruple, aristocracy, landowners, and Protestant
families, even where there was adequate evidence to contradict his
views in the history of modern Ireland alone. As long as they could
serve as symbols of his values—just as O'Leary and the "wild geese" of
"September 1913" had—it must have seemed irrelevant to him that
propertied classes, however generous otherwise, have an institutional if
largely unconscious bias toward preserving the continuity and therefore
the conditions of their ascendancy and its associated privileges, and that
the word *tradition* therefore readily lends itself to the task of conceal-
ing unglamorous subtexts.

Paul Scott Stanfield points out that Yeats thought of the aristocracy
largely as a model of the forms of individual freedom to which everyone should be privileged to aspire—again, in other words, abstracting
from history an existential paradigm. Edward Said argues that even

6. Deane, *Celtic Revivals*, 30; Foster, *W. B. Yeats: A Life*, 1:460; Yeats, *Explorations*; Yeats quoted in Foster, *W. B. Yeats: A Life*, 1:512.

allowing for his "late reactionary politics," Yeats always wrote poetry of resistance, however cryptically encoded the politics may be in a given poem, and that his themes of freedom and self-realization looked past decolonization to imagine a liberation that is more than just a matter of "seizing power"—or to imagine how, as in Gramsci's model, to achieve afterwards "the marriage of knowledge to power or of understanding with violence." This argument would be credible particularly to the degree that one thinks of the Roman Catholic Church as a colonial power in itself: "Imperialism after all is a cooperative venture," Said says, restating a truism. "Both the master and the slave participate in it."[7]

Yeats found his models where he could. All of the strong women in his poems—when they are not co-opted by other forces—are symbols for him of what has been achieved in human life and might still yet be. Mabel Beardsley, in "Upon a Dying Lady"—with her playful wickedness, her disdain of priests, her consideration of her friends' pain more than of her own, and her unbroken will even as she is dying—is made to seem a reassuring embodiment of freedom in a fundamental, inexpressible form. She is imagined ("I have no speech but symbol," the poet says) to be bound for "the predestined dancing-place" that is for the heroic, where they are free of all cultures and both sexes are united, a place for "all / Who have lived in joy and laughed into the face of Death." The heroic personalities of *A Vision* are all resistors and creators, antithetical rather than submissive subjects, and in their apotheosized status in the system, they fend off colonization by the wills of others— economic, political, intellectual, spiritual—and even the oppression that is life itself.

Yeats had internalized and made into his own dogma all of the arguments of the German romantics, from Schiller through Hegel and then Nietzsche, which presented art not only as a symbol of the freedom from necessity—a liberation of the spirit—but also as an agent of that freedom. Shelley had, too, of course: "for want of the poetical faculty... man, having enslaved the elements, remains himself a slave."[8] To the degree that art is the agent of freedom, democratic processes become freedom's impediment by urging society away from the exceptional

---

7. Paul Scott Stanfield, *Yeats and Politics in the 1930s*, 44; Edward W. Said, *Yeats and Decolonization*, 236–37.

8. Shelley, "Defence of Poetry," 293.

toward the lowest common denominator. Yeats probably never formulated this paradox quite so explicitly in his mind, but its logic underlies the theme of "Upon a House Shaken by the Land Agitation." Art's identification with freedom, and art's being an agent of freedom, is the foundational principle of Yeats's conservative politics—which were not so much antidemocratic, perhaps, as republican in the classical Platonic sense.

In his vocation as a poet, Yeats extrapolated from his readings of history into a stylized present and future, and when, as it turned out, real history unfolded in its crude and misbegotten way and was different in character from metahistory, he was caught off guard intellectually. A more inclusive historiographical principle would have helped him avoid such surprises. Like nature, history offered otherwise appropriatable material to him, except that ontological history—history as raw material (that is, not yet far enough behind to be theorized)—is a good deal more complex for human life and impinges more directly upon the routine of one's daily existence. Relationships to it cannot be successfully ritualized until it becomes the past. Yeats lived through a cruel and turbulent era in the twentieth century, but what must often have seemed to him (in the midst of it) to be impending chaos was in part history in the unmediated form that it takes when it is experienced in real time. Conceivably, the accompanying anxiety that afflicted him would not have been much different for him in any age that he might have been living in. An empirical historian could have consoled him at least on this point. Ontological history and epistemological history can never be the same. Anyone achieves a marginal transcendence of history simply by thinking about it and therefore by imposing upon it the form of his or her own thought, becoming an observer so as not to be a product. Until the end of his life, Yeats has raised this simple psychological principle to the level, literally, of an art form.

Denis Donoghue attributes Yeats's vagueness on such issues to what Thorstein Veblen called "trained incapacity," tactfully without going on to state the obvious, that this was an incapacity that Yeats, as a lyric poet, nurtured in himself because, in a sense, it is the point of lyric poetry.

> It should be remembered . . . that like other writers in his time Yeats derived a politics from an aesthetic. He did not approach politics in its own terms. So the question of "trained incapacity" arises. Veblen used this phrase to refer to a situation in which as man is prevented from seeing certain things by the fact that they are not emphasized in the gram-

mar of his professional skill. Training in one direction makes a disability in another. It may be argued that modern writers, skilled in one way and dedicated to their own idiom, are for that reason disabled in other respects, including respects readily available to less talented men.[9]

T. Sturge Moore had been equally tactful on this issue many years before, when rebuking Yeats for being unwilling to acquiesce in the logic of his brother G. E. Moore's methodical empiricism.

> The dialectics of my brother, like those in some of the dialogues of Plato, seem cumbrous and confusing because he omits no single step as obvious: and obviously he must not do so because he is arguing against those who make the simplest and most fundamental mistakes, and they make them merely because they did not follow all the steps entailed because it seemed fastidious to do so; therefore, they jump and come croppers.
>
> It needs a very considerable effort and some familiarity with thinking at so slow a pace before one can fall into step and appreciate the truth of the minute points made. Literature, especially poetry, works in an opposite way, flies rather than crawls, and so to be good at poetry is itself a handicap in philosophy. Many philosophers and most amateurs are only interested in the imaginative aspects of speculation; the search for truth bores them stiff. They are fertile in hypotheses but build on the sand of many treacherous assumptions. They therefore appeal to fashion not to reason and have their giddy day and then are superseded. But the search for truth goes on bringing more and more of experience within the reach of science. It is like all pioneering a lonely job and makes little show in the world which it nevertheless transforms willy-nilly.[10]

It is shrewd of Sturge Moore to define the issue in this way, since his brother's relentless identification of thinking with method and his separation, like a chemist, of ideas into their constituent substances, would be precisely what Yeats's "Happy Shepherd" would describe as "Grey Truth." In turn, G. E. Moore would no doubt consider the Blakean illogic of "The Two Trees" immature. The appropriate response from Yeats (or Nietzsche or Blake) would be that however rigorous analytical thinking must be, people live metaphorically, and it is in its claim on that sphere of being that poetry rather than analytical philosophy presumes to rule.

---

9. Donoghue, *William Butler Yeats*, 131–32.
10. Yeats and Moore, *Correspondence*, 98.

Yeats's conviction that real data of other discourses can be compelled to shade over in the mind into the realm of art is what makes the argument of "The Two Trees" implicitly political. To secure the argument, he invokes the authority of love and claims it to be exclusively the property of the imagination. By extension, he denies the sanction of love to all who dwell in the fatally compromised materialistic world—where love is argued not to be possible. The inescapable implication is that the world beyond the mind, undreamt and untransformed, is empty of value because empty of form, and that erotic love is a fiction that saves one from that world. We are left to imagine the demographic effect of such a policy, but it is not very difficult to do.

This seems to be one of the points of this line in "Adam's Curse": "[y]et now it seems an idle trade enough"—that the times are unpropitious for love because they are democratic and realistic, not like the earlier historical periods when courtship was literate and ritualized. So the age is to blame for the failure of love, and no sooner does that thought focus in the poet's mind in "Adam's Curse" than the whole idiom of the poem subtly changes and the lovers in his elegiac reverie become separate from time to become blended with lyrically enhanced nature—which is to say, with art. In such disquisitions as these, there is seldom any doubt of the poet's position on the surface. But when we recall Yeats's saying that he doubts life's value behind his own mind, then we may guess that such affirmations of the power of the mind to create the reality in which it dwells are, in fact, dialogues with himself, early versions of the dialogue of self and soul in which the latter is still young enough to be credulous. If this is the case, it is not implausible to argue that the "now" in "Adam's Curse" is not only a *now* of the age but also a *now* of the speaker's mental condition. Now, in this age, or in other words, in the environment of this time, the possibilities of love *seem* limited, even for those who envision more, and therefore *become* limited—a "trade" in fact, like any other. In this reading, one may imagine the time when one could love in the old high way of love, but that is only projection, too, the past as uncontingent in conflict with the untranscendable, contingent present. If one were to enter that past, it would become the untranscendable present, too (and the present, nicely enough, would become the imaginable future). Perhaps, then, the Adam's curse of the title refers not to the labor required to achieve beauty after the Fall of Man, but to the labor required after the Hegelian fall into consciousness in order to believe in beauty as anything more than a figment that we have to think ourselves back into time in order to realize. A political subtext is even less visible in "Adam's Curse" than in "The Two Trees," but we should notice that, in both cases, in order for the highest love to flourish, time must be reified or derealized in its form as the present. What is in the present cannot be transcended in the mind; what is in the past can be, and it is therefore endowed with value. By virtue of their having been marginalized by history, women could be imagined to stand closer than men to the freedom symbolized by art—hence, the poet's ultimate wish for his own child, in "A Prayer for My Daughter," that she should find her way outside the currents of history to a place in her life where the innocence of history could be rooted in continuity, ceremony, and custom: art in the ritual form of so-cial practice. This also accounts for his imagining that Mabel Beardsley's soul will fly to "the predestined dancing-place" where the brave of myth and history, impartially and ahistorically, have in common that they "have lived in joy and laughed into the face of death."

By contrast, what seems to have distressed Yeats most about the political women he admired was not the kind of politics they espoused but the demeaning level—the undancelike level—of practice at which they functioned. Both Maud Gonne and Constance Gore-Booth were more avidly republican than Yeats could ever permit himself to be. Anti-British as he was, the treaty that created the Free State compromise not only satisfied him but also is now usually thought of as a metaphor for his own ambiguous relation to both Irish and English cultures. But the practice of politics could not have appealed to him, because ideas in action in the political sector have a way of very quickly losing their sanctity as ideas. Actual politics—the deals and alliances with other-wise unacceptable people, the exhortations and manipulations of crowds, the endless solicitation of money, the crude simplifications of rhetoric, the absolutizing of short-range goals—disrupts the attractive coher-ence of political thought and calls metaphorical thinking altogether into question. He had lived through his own spirit-breaking version of this kind of labor for a cause, and what he saw as happening to his own "colt" could as easily happen to anyone else's:

> The fascination of what's difficult
> Has dried the sap out of my veins, and rent
> Spontaneous joy and natural content
> Out of my heart. There's something ails our colt

> That must, as if it had not holy blood
> Nor on Olympus leaped from cloud to cloud,
> Shiver under the lash, strain, sweat and jolt
> As though it dragged road-metal. My curse on plays
> That have to be set up in fifty ways,
> On the day's war with every knave and dolt,
> Theatre business, management of men.
> I swear before the dawn comes round again
> I'll find the stable and pull out the bolt.

Hence the one consistent pattern of Yeats's life of entering the sphere of political endeavor and then sooner rather than later withdrawing back into the refuge of his own creative vision. Quite aside from the content of her political views, Maud Gonne's commitment to political action meant in Yeats's view that she was unwisely indentured to the randomness, particularity, and contingency of material history. It was from this condition that poems like "Fallen Majesty" aspired to rescue her—even when the mission has begun to seem slightly absurd.

> Although crowds gathered once if she but showed her face,
> And even old men's eyes grew dim, this hand alone,
> Like some last courtier at a gypsy camping-place
> Babbling of fallen majesty, records what's gone.
> The lineaments, a heart that laughter has made sweet,
> These, these remain, but I record what's gone. A crowd
> Will gather, and not know it walks the very street
> Whereon a thing once walked that seemed a burning cloud.

Both the last courtier—not unlike Matthew Arnold's "Scholar Gypsy," evading the "disease of modern life"—and gypsies themselves are willful anachronisms, as are poems, for that matter, in Yeats's world. Memory is by definition *ana-chronos*, against time. Under these conditions it seems possible for the poet to speak of transfigured beauty, but he is chastened while doing so by a self-deprecating irony, spoken from a place where modernity still prevails.

Yeats attempted to rationalize Maud Gonne's defection from the ideal by claiming that her fault was not personal but contextual, the splendidness of her spirit being unmatched by an adequately heroic occasion—the famous theme of "No Second Troy." The problem is that this way of resolving the issue in his mind (or at least pretending to) depended upon the classic fallacy of comparing apples and oranges. The Troy that we think we know is not even remotely of the same order of reality as that of Dublin in the first two decades of the twentieth century. There was no second Troy for her to burn; there was no first Troy, either, in the terms the poet stipulates, or at any rate, none to which we have any significant intellectual access. The Troy that Yeats is thinking of is *only* a city of the mind, and if we could go back to the real city, we would almost certainly not find—in *its* real time—citizens of more heroic or stylized and picturesque attributes than those who inhabit our own century. Certainly we have no evidence to the contrary except the story Homer (whoever indeed he was) and Virgil told. So the tragedy is even greater than Yeats was moved to imagine. Maud Gonne's greatness is such that she should have inhabited literature, not life, and that of course is impossible, an aporia peculiar to any conflation of art and history. Even the ancient Irish bards whom Yeats revered and identified with can only be understood to have sung of imaginary history. And their position in relation to real history in their time could not have been much different from Yeats's position in relation to the real history of his own.

In his presentations of Maud Gonne in his poems, Yeats resisted distinguishing between Maud Gonne as an actor in his plays and Maud Gonne as a *character* in his plays, as existent in literature only, in other words, where he seems to have wanted to keep her contained—where he seems at times to have wished to keep everything contained. A striking exception is "The People," where Maud Gonne not only speaks in her own voice—literally transcribed from a letter to Yeats—but also makes a compelling moral claim for the primacy of real, peopled life over the easy and evasive stylization of it in the refuges of art. The poet in this poem, "whose virtues are the definitions / Of the analytic mind," is "abashed" by his friend's argument and by this confrontation with "the purity of a natural force." Thus at the end of the poem, he is also deprived of his poetic powers. Ironically, this outcome confirms the necessity for the poetic distance from the real for which his poem is meant to be reparation.

In his part of the dialogue in "The People," as in his other poems, Yeats seems to be claiming the superiority of one age over the other, but what he is really claiming, as "The People" seems to acknowledge, is the superiority of art over life. In this one respect Yeats's poems on this theme have an obvious affinity with *The Waste Land,* though Eliot's understanding of the irony and futility of such strategies was considerably more subtle than Yeats's. Yeats's presentation of the subject is complex because of its simplicity. Maud Gonne is already "in" literature by virtue of being in the poems, her identity simplified and iconic. So, therefore, are the times she inhabits and contends with there, and so, for that matter, is the simplified Yeats who is thinking of her. So in order to imagine a past era that would be adequate to her spirit, he is required to make the despised present literary as well, and Maud Gonne ends up being moved around only in different literary territories or regions of the mind. So it is not a matter, after all, of comparing apples and oranges but of comparing artificial apples to real ones. When he was claiming the authority of history to support a particular argument, he was not speaking of history but of literature, and yet he had to be able to claim history for his own side—as a more otherworldly symbolist might not have—because he was genuinely concerned with the outcome of a current political and economic struggle in his own country. He saw that as a struggle to control the consciousness of his race, and so it was both political and literary in his view. Metahistory had to be made to seem like real history and therefore affirmable so as to provide a model that was not hopelessly inaccessible in real life. This political Yeats was in equal measure both a pragmatist and a symbolist, but his faith in progress on even this limited front waned in the end.

When the two impulses—toward the present, and away from it, toward metahistory—came into conflict in his poems, instead of collaborating, they produced, ironically enough, the kind of crisis of understanding that we associate with Yeats's most compelling work. He may not have been capable of reconciling himself to his own century but he did recognize a sense of responsibility to it. When Robert Gregory was killed in Italy—accidentally, as it turned out, thus making his real story inconsistent with the heroic one that Yeats invented on his behalf—Yeats characterized Gregory in the subsequent poems in a way that allowed him to project his own ambivalence onto Gregory. Neither Robert Gregory of the elegy nor Robert Gregory of "An Irish Airman Foresees His Death" is political in any conventional way. Instead, the Irish airman is made to seem ideologically apolitical and is implicitly commended for it. An artist in his own right, he composes his own

death. He has chosen to commit himself to history, but that history becomes in his mind a poet's history, atemporal and beyond chronological
imperative.

> A lonely impulse of delight
> Drove to this tumult in the clouds;
> I balanced all, brought all to mind,
> The years to come seemed waste of breath,
> A waste of breath the years behind
> In balance with this life, this death.

Yeats had some evidence to confirm that such thoughts were in Gregory's mind in the period shortly before his death.

> Though he often seemed led away from his work by some other gift, his
> attitude to life and art never lost intensity—he was never the amateur. I
> have noticed that men whose lives are to be an evergrowing absorption
> in subjective beauty...seek through some lesser gift, or through mere
> excitement, to strengthen that self which unites them to ordinary men.
> It is as though they hesitated before they plunged into the abyss. Major
> Gregory told Mr. Bernard Shaw, who visited him in France, that the
> months since he joined the Army had been the happiest of his life. I
> think they brought him peace of mind, an escape from that shrinking,
> which I sometimes saw upon his face, before the growing absorption of
> his dream, the loneliness of his dream, as from his constant struggle to
> resist those other gifts that brought him ease and friendship. Leading
> his squadron in France or in Italy, mind and hand were at one, will and
> desire.[11]

Yeats thought he knew Gregory well enough to speak of him with
authority. But he was also faced with the problem that Gregory had
died fighting voluntarily for an English cause in the Royal Flying
Corps in a time when conscription of Irish citizens to fight England's
war—while the treaty negotiations were suspended—was, for good
reason, the most inflammatory issue in Irish political life. So the poem
has to make a virtue of necessity and argue that Gregory is not really
fighting for England but from an apolitical commitment to action alone.
In order for that claim not to seem ethically suspect, the poet has to

11. Yeats, *Uncollected Prose*, 2:430–31.

brush aside any imaginable influence that Gregory's otherwise committed life might have on historical outcomes. The lonely male impulse of
sprezzatura is ultimately one of self-completion though self-annihilation.

"The Irish Airman Foresees His Death" is an affecting poem mainly
to the degree that it can appeal in its audience to the same desire for
transcendence—for an uncompromised freedom and a oneness of "will
and desire"—that Gregory is made to exemplify in the poem. In that
respect, it is more effective when it is read following the Gregory elegy,
where it is normally placed, so that Gregory the dreamer seems fairly
to erupt from the morose environment of his own verse memorial and
to escape the community of friends and kindred of which the elegy
speaks—not only Kiltartan's poor, in other words, but also his mother,
Yeats and his bride, and all the claiming retinue of Yeats's dead and
regretted friends. But the political point Yeats ends up.indirectly making is similar to the point made about Maud Gonne in "No Second
Troy"—there is no second Troy to burn. The pure dream of freedom can
be consummated only in isolation. Real history, in process with its clut-
ter, cannot fail to disrupt the identity of time with spirit. In this respect,
Gregory might just as well have been fighting for Prussia as for England.
It would not have been un-Irish for him to have done so. The ultimate
consolation is action and the death itself, because then one does not
have to bear witness to the anarchy and vulgarity of the metastasizing
present.

This gratifying irreality is luxury only of the dead, and Yeats is compelled to concede the point two years later in the poem "Reprisals":

> Some nineteen German planes, they say,
> You had brought down before you died.
> We called it a good death. Today
> Can ghost or man be satisfied?
> Although your last exciting year
> Outweighed all other years, you said,
> Though battle joy may be so dear
> A memory, even to the dead,
> It chases other thought away,
> Yet rise from your Italian tomb,
> Flit to Kiltartan cross and stay
> Till certain second thoughts have come
> Upon the cause you served, that we
> Imagined such a fine affair:

Half-drunk or whole-mad soldiery
Are murdering your tenants there.
Men that revere your father yet
Are shot at on the open plain.
Where may new-married women sit
And suckle children now? Armed men
May murder them in passing by
Nor law nor parliament take heed.
Then close your ears with dust and lie
Among the other cheated dead.

This sequel has been said to be an indictment of Gregory for his failure to be obedient to the responsibilities of his Irish nationality and of his class, for having chosen glamorous death abroad, serving an English cause, over unglamorous service at home (and the phrase "Italian tomb" certainly sounds sardonic). That Yeats himself may have felt this way is evidenced in the fact that he was finally unwilling to publish the poem for fear of giving further offense and pain to Gregory's widow, who was pro-English. But if we think of the two poems as two sections of one poem, it may be understood as another early version of the dialogue of self and soul. The speaker of "Reprisals," who eventually becomes the self in the dialogues, is thus a detached and comprehensive observer who is therefore capable of offering a critique of the soul's transcendental subjectivity. The result is yet another aporia that is redeemed by a recourse in tragic irony. No matter how pure one's allegiance may be to the abstracted heroic virtues of the Irish Airman (Gregory as "our Sidney and our perfect man" and "all life's epitome"), those allegiances must always connect somewhere to someone else's political reality. Actions count in a real world as well as in an idealized one, and the real world—the one behind thought—unlike the idealized literary one (featuring, for instance, "Troy," or, for instance, war as "a fine affair"), is not one that is subject to the individual's manipulation. History itself plows on. Other stories are going on in which one is not only not the protagonist but even a minor, barely relevant character. The collective effect of those stories is what we know in any given moment as ontological history, unpredictable by definition and not resolvable into a formal pattern, except in retrospect and factitiously.

The men who murdered Ellen Quinn and tenants on the Gregory estate had fought in the Great War in the same cause that Gregory had died serving. During the worst atrocities of the Black and Tans, it must have seemed that England not only had failed to keep faith (by reinstating the treaty) but also had simply turned to combat on a different front with a now-seasoned military force. Gregory's ego in Yeats's poem could contain only his own intransitive desire. The theme of "Reprisals," then, seems less that deeds have consequences than that, in some incomprehensible but definitive way, they do not, and that the relentless invasion of the present (the wind upon the tower) will proceed unabated, mocking the solipsist, unrestrained and untouched by the values sealed away in an idealized past. Gregory, as a shade in "Reprisals," having witnessed the most recent and intimately cruel instance of this principle at work, is enjoined to close his ears with dust so that he may rest in peace and so that "common" thoughts can be chased away again; but the "other" that these thoughts are of does not go away in the world in time as easily as all that, as Yeats knew and yet was always, to his credit, relearning. "Wisdom is the property of the dead" he was to write eight years later. The dead, in other words, do not have to live in the present. They have achieved identity with history because, for them, history has stopped. In "Reprisals," it is not only the other Irish dead who fought for England who are cheated, but also anyone who expects the form of the present to be continuous with the formalizing projections of consciousness or of their representations in the past.

One part of Yeats thought of "Reprisals" as a political act. He wrote to Lady Gregory that he had sent it to the *Nation* "less because it would be a good poem than because I thought it might touch some one individual mind of a man in power." Yeats's politics always have to be understood as an aspect of his fluctuating optimism, as an expression of his faith in human nature's capacity to renew by reenvisioning itself. This would be to believe in the power of thought represented by poetry— "artistic power"—to redefine the terms under which political life is conducted, to have his own work impart value to life. The oddly isolated course of Ireland's history was conducive to this frame of mind, as if Ireland itself were a poem always on the verge of being completed, its history distinguished by vivid gestures, recurring patterns, and rhyming episodes that never seem to have had any practical effect. Robert Emmet's death was such a gesture for Yeats, and he spoke of it in such a way as to redefine—to accord with his own eccentric, and Irish, purposes—the whole point of political action: not to achieve specific outcomes, but to form symbols that will enrich cultural memory:

Emmet had hoped to give Ireland the gift of a victorious life, an accomplished purpose. He failed in that, but he gave her what was almost as good—his heroic death.... And out of his grave his ideal has arisen incorruptible. His martyrdom has changed the whole temper of the Irish nation. England celebrates her successes.... In Ireland we sing the men who fell nobly and therefore made an idea mighty. When Ireland is triumphant and free, there will yet be something in the character of her people, something lofty and strange, which shall have been put there by her years of suffering and by the memory of her many martyrs. Her martyrs have married her forever to the ideal.

As Elizabeth Cullingford says, "The poetry of revolution makes the prose of constitutional politics look shabby."[12]

To succeed by this reasoning is to transpose the ideal into the compromised arena of the real. Even when Ireland succeeds, Yeats says, and becomes triumphant and free, that ideal kept incorruptible by death—having receded, upon death, into distilled history—may remain alive as something lofty and strange; but he implies that the ideal is more likely to survive if Ireland remains *un*free. This is not an altogether absurd notion for a poet to advocate, but it cannot prepare him to act effectively at the political level that Maud Gonne or James Connolly or even Parnell, aloof and autocratic as he was, operated, and it compels him to remain ambivalent throughout his life about the execution of even his own political convictions.

The Easter Rising was more pliable material for poetry than Robert Gregory's death because the cause for which the martyrs died was a cause worth dying for, not so much the freedom of Ireland as Yeats saw it, but their *dream* of that freedom. After working his way through his own doubts in two less-distinguished versions of the event, he was able finally to see the martyrs and their deaths as having revived romantic Ireland as Robert Emmet had epitomized it: out of the grave, the ideal rises incorruptible. When thinking empirically about the Rising, we cannot say that the death of the martyrs in any way truly changed their natures. If John McBride was a drunken, vainglorious lout in life, he only ceased being a drunk and a lout because he had become dead, that is, had stopped being real and become literary. The apotheosis that the martyrs experienced was an apotheosis in the mind of the culture, not

---

12. Yeats, quoted in Elizabeth Cullingford, *Yeats, Ireland, and Fascism*, 561–62; Yeats, *Uncollected Prose*, 2:318–19; Cullingford, *Yeats, Ireland, and Fascism*, 6.

an actual event, and it came at the cost of death. Their having died, having ceased to be a part of the ongoing present, entitles them to a transcendent status that the fallible living are denied. They are no longer themselves but poems, and they are with Troy. Perhaps inadvertently but perhaps not, this transformation is symbolized by (some of) their names lending themselves to being set down in a verse: "McDonaugh and McBride / And Connolly and Pearse." The rhetorical subterfuge of this gesture is that although Yeats claims in the course of the poem to have been drawn over by the terrible event to seeing their point of view, he has in fact drawn them over into becoming expressions of his own. They have been moved from the raw material of politics and the contingency of action into the framed coherence and freedom of poetry. The ironies of that integration constitute one aspect of the "terrible beauty" that is born, and correctly named.

Considered in this context, the beauty of the *Vision* system is that it enabled Yeats to equate everyone in real time to characters in history and, by this means, to receive them into history itself without their having to undergo the otherwise conventional prerequisite of being dead. In the most famous case of such apotheosis, Maud Gonne virtually becomes Helen of Troy, and her life in the present—where in practice she is more like Pallas Athena—becomes continuous with Helen's life in a wholly fabulous past. In these respects, *A Vision* is not about the past at all but about the present, in that it provides Yeats with a way of seeing the present as if it had already become the past and had taken on the attractively unrough contours that the historical past invariably has. That Yeats found it necessary to redesign the always-inchoate present in this way in order to be able to assimilate it—to think of historical process as having been, so to speak, thought of already and hence predictable and structured—shows how nearly symbiotic death and life were for the functioning of his imagination, if not for his psychic well-being as a whole. *A Vision* was an act of appropriation and aggression against the present—any present, in effect, not just the one that Yeats happened to have landed in. Its diagrams, wheels, gyres, and cones displace recorded history, and the present with it, even further from the level of particular fact than histories usually do. In effect, it reduces history to geometry, to a metaphysic that seems true but is false because it is abstract. It was Yeats's most Pythagorean venture, and considering the ghastly period of Ireland's history during which it was written, it seems somehow both gloomy and serene.

A Vision shares with "The Second Coming" (or "The Second Coming" shares with it) the mathematical understructure of a formula that progresses by its own logic toward solution. The first part of "The Second Coming" and the terrors of revolution and anarchy that it represents is depressurized by the second part. The vision that is given is of the inevitability of this process of release of modernism into the streets and upon the world. It is represented, like the wind upon the tower, as a nonhuman force—the falcon released from the control of the falconer—and there is nothing to be done. The great beast, imposing and dreadful as it is, enters the poet's consciousness as a stylized condensation of the chaos depicted in the first part, and therefore as a kind of explanatory principle. With its emergence, the poem moves from unintelligible chaos into an eerie but, on the other hand, stately working out of a process—like a formula. "Now I know," he says, and the confusion and terror of unknowing from the first section is abated in a marginal victory for human thought—a victory because of the revelation and the symbol, but marginal because what the symbol signifies remains the unknown.

The stylization of history and the retrojection or historicizing of the present in *A Vision* permitted Yeats to have his romantic politics both ways. The romantic revolutionaries like Emmet and O'Leary whom he revered—who succeeded in the imagination by failing in reality—and even the Irish airman who foresees his death—can be made to seem to have acted in exactly the kind of history that was compatible with their aristocratic and transcendent natures. Their failure to have stayed at the helm of public leadership and therefore leaving the tending of it—as Parnell in effect did—to meaner-spirited politicians, can be seen perhaps not to matter, since the inevitable, objective cycle will run its course anyway. Much as Yeats complained in his bleak moments of revolution in Europe and of what he called the mob and of the Catholic middle class in Ireland, *A Vision* presents him implicitly as reconciled—"As though God's death were but a play." It is a remarkable case of how events of the ordinary phenomenal world can be psychoanalytically accommodated by being referred to the logic of an explanatory, that is, metaphysical system. The activity of the mind reconstitutes reality.

Yeats seems never to have attempted an analytical understanding of the cause-and-effect relation between history as unmediated fact and history as myth or fiction. Not many people do. However, when the

Troubles came in 1919 and then the Civil War, his own secluded neighborhood in County Clare was literally and metaphorically invaded, and he was forced to consider that his own thinking about the nature of history and the world had little to do with the form that events took. This unwelcome revelation required him, as a visionary custodian of values, to feel extraneous and isolated, but he then shrewdly cut his losses by claiming a compensatory authority for analytical thought, a kind of existential virility. It was also the beginning of the end of what little faith Yeats had left in art's power by "presenting models to shape life" (notwithstanding his optimistic exhortations at the end in "Under Ben Bulben").[13] The two monuments of this crisis, "Nineteen Hundred and Nineteen" and "Meditations in Time of Civil War," both analyze and disparage his own idealism and show a new grim maturity in his thinking about the reality of social processes. Prior to these two crises for his nationalist hopes, there was the more global cataclysm of the Great War, which, though unnamed, is invisibly present in both poems in the rupturing ferocity of its effects. (Roy Foster points out that "Nineteen Hundred and Nineteen" was actually published in 1921, making "seven years ago" become 1914—though the poem is dated 1919 in *The Tower* volume itself.) However rational history might eventually be made to seem from the distant perspective of *A Vision*, on the ground it could be known for once as the very embodiment of the irrational.

"Meditations in Time of Civil War" is the later of the two poems (though it precedes the other in *The Tower*). It is, perhaps, *therefore*, a series of meditations upon failed expectations rather than upon war; it barely touches upon the war itself, though the war figures in the background throughout as an embodiment of the reality principle that contradicts the life of the mind. That presence accounts for the poet-speaker's labored self-contempt in this poem, which is also excruciatingly complex. "Ancestral Houses" sets this tone by thinking the unthinkable out loud: that life itself—behind thought, undreamed—is not the glittering jet of a fountain and richness of being in its own shape and motion, as Yeats appears to have wanted Homer to be able to believe, but an emptiness that all the forms of our imagining surround and enclose in order to conceal—a "marvelous empty sea-shell flung / Out of the obscure dark of the rich streams." The inherited glory of the rich is there-

13. Marcus, *Yeats and Artistic Power*, 150.

fore only such an empty signifier, a yearning toward a dignity in life that is not there—and, at worst, a sweetness reared in stone by otherwise unsweet, "bitter and violent" men, a sweetness, in short, that "none there had ever known" or would ever know. For the credulous apologist of "Upon a House Shaken by the Land Agitation," this is a quite radical thought:

> What if those things the greatest of mankind
> Consider most to magnify, or to bless,
> But take our greatness with our bitterness?

In other words, what if art and the irrationality of violence are indivisibly linked by cause and effect, and art is made possible by the violence of appropriation but also then generated by violence as the necessary dream of its antithesis? The tone is derisive here, not as a Marxist's critique might be but as an apostate believer's might be, holding himself and his own contribution to the issue in contempt.

> O what if gardens where the peacock strays
> With delicate feet upon old terraces,
> Or else all Juno from an urn displays
> Before the indifferent garden deities;
> O what if levelled lawns and gravelled ways
> Where slippered Contemplation finds his ease
> And Childhood a delight for every sense,
> But take our greatness with our violence?

Though it seems to be the main theme recurring in each of the meditations, the subject of inheritance, what can be passed down "changeless" through the ages, is really a subset of the theme of failed expectations, and the next logical move for the poem is toward a reconciliation with the facts. His own "house," unlike the stately ascendancy home, has been chosen to be founded upon for its austerity and isolation. This is so that his heirs, rather than declining into decadence from excess of privilege, may rather develop inwardly—exalt the lonely mind—finding in this place "Befitting emblems of adversity," reminders of what is always there to be overcome. This may or may not work out, the poem goes on to say. The sword of Sato, emblem of a now perhaps wholly imagined time when the gift of honoring the soul was passed down as a craft, encourages hope and purpose (the sword "may moralise /

My days out of their aimlessness"). The time now, however, is one of disintoxication:

> Life scarce can cast a fragrance on the wind,
> Scarce spread a glory to the morning beams,
> But the torn petals strew the garden plot;
> And there's but common greenness after that.

Here in this lovely metaphor is another unusual reconciliation. The lines say that this, as life is, which is not all bad, may be the way things are—whatever we wish for or long toward, and regardless of the emblems of art and power and adversity, like the sword. If that is the case, then it is enough to have founded here from the right motives—to pass on to heirs the vigorous mind that he inherited, whether it decline in them or not—and to express and embody love and friendship, which are enough. The lines that commemorate this acceptance are among the most affecting in all of Yeats's work, for they cut through to the core of the issues of mortality and time and exhibit vigorous intellection rather than symbolist evasion:

> May this laborious stair and this stark tower
> Become a roofless ruin that the owl
> May build in the cracked masonry and cry
> Her desolation to the desolate sky.

> The Primum Mobile that fashioned us
> Has made the very owls in circles move;
> And I, that count myself most prosperous,
> Seeing that love and friendship are enough,
> For an old neighbour's friendship chose the house
> And decked and altered it for a girl's love,
> And know whatever flourish and decline
> These stones remain their monument and mine.

The complexity of the thought of "Meditations in Time of Civil War" derives from a principle of parataxis at work in it, disestablishing any single mood or attitude or any verifiable schema of cause and effect. When the robust soldiers of both sides come to his door, he is envious of their vigor, and his envy forces him into an abstraction so complete that the moorhen chicks he watches on the stream are barely real to him as what they are, as if he had never seen them before—"I count these feathered balls of soot"—and he withdraws, as poets will, into his "chamber" and into the cold snows of a dream.

Then, in the next section, envy gives way to uncertainty and fear. The war is the same, but its features are different: a man killed, a house burned, a soldier's body trundled by, no clear facts. Yeats's characterization of the war is eerily reticent but at the same time compelling. He is drawn toward the excitement and vitality it generates and even toward its violence; but he is withdrawn before its incomprehensibility. In war, as Dudley Young points out, parataxis is the rule, not the sweet dream of life or learned reasoning or epic narrative.

> We had fed the heart on fantasies,
> The heart's grown brutal from the fare;
> More substance in our enmities,
> Than in our love.

Civil war, it goes without saying, is the most incomprehensible and unpredictable of all outcomes. Both in its real and symbolic natures, it disrupts the mind's dream of a continuous national past and future and of justice and reality held together. Man has become "simply the victim of a process of events" and "consciousness...only a sort of epiphenomenon."[14] And Yeats should not have been able to miss the point that this period of reciprocal terrorism—only a modest beginning, as it has turned out—was the direct outcome of the events of the Easter Rising and the terrible beauty not only born but now unwilling to lie poetically still.

The Civil War is the unmediatable present incarnate. So the refrain in section 6 invoking the honeybees who will build in the empty nest of the stare—in "the crevices / Of loosening masonry"—has its primary psychological meaning from its referring hope to some space that is essentially meaningless in human terms. The bees themselves are wholly oblivious to human purpose or failed designs or to the metaphorical status that we cannot fail to impose upon them. They are a benevolent version of the wind in "A Prayer for My Daughter," productively rather than murderously innocent. They are as close as Yeats ever gets to the wasps and ants of *The Pisan Cantos*, for this is also as close as Yeats's mind gets to hanging by a grass blade.

---

14. Young, *Out of Ireland*, 21; Robert Snukal, *High Talk: The Philosophical Poetry of W. B. Yeats*, 179.

O honey-bees
Come build in the empty house of the stare.

Ironically, however, a human version of this creaturely innocence can
only be imagined as a wholly solipsistic removal, a disconnection from the
morally unintelligible world outside: my house, he says, my children, my
wife and friends, my sword, my pear tree, my wall, my stares, my bees.

When the poet salvages this experience with his poet's visions at the
poem's end, they, too, are paratactically associated. First, there are two
opposed human states, both nevertheless representing aspects of the
same poet's state of mind: the Dionysian seductiveness of "senseless
tumult" on the one hand, and a dream of a pure aphasia on the other,
where memory and thought and even desire cease to exist. Second, and
more distressing than the other two because it is without human form
(no "self-delighting reverie, / Nor hate of what's to come, nor pity for
what's gone / Nothing but grip of claw, and the eye's complacency"),
there is a desolate reality—unmediated by thought, without sentience
or purpose, though brought vividly to mind by the irrationality of human
action and the rupturing of the continuity between idea and fact. Yeats
has thought, in this time of upheaval and conflict, that to be a dreaming poet is to be irrelevant and epicene. But now he reflects bitterly
that, given the way things are and where the road leads, he should
count his blessings. So he does:

> I turn away and shut the door, and on the stair
> Wonder how many times I could have proved my worth
> In something that all others understand or share;
> But O! ambitious heart, had such a proof drawn forth
> A company of friends, a conscience set at ease,
> It had but made us pine the more. The abstract joy,
> The half-read wisdom of daemonic images,
> Suffice the ageing man as one the growing boy.

Still, this is corrosive self-criticism not only because of the Wordsworth-
ian quaintness of the idiom at the end but also because it implies no
progress gained, no growth with history, as if his own moral and psychological makeup had become a distorted reflection of "the soul's unchanging look."

This point will be driven home in "Nineteen Hundred and Nineteen":

> We pieced our thoughts into philosophy,
> And planned to bring the world under a rule,
> Who are but weasels fighting in a hole.

And, again, "Nineteen Hundred and Nineteen" is clearheadedly not about "the way things used to be then, and the way they are now" but about the way things used to be *perceived to be* and the way, in fact, they *have always been*. To read simplistically from *A Vision* back to "Nineteen Hundred and Nineteen" is to obscure the profound ambiguity of the poem. The nightmare riding upon sleep—the poem's ruling figure—is the anarchy of reality breaking through the sweet reassuringness of the dreams of polity and civil order and washing over the irrelevantly "ingenious lovely things" of art, from which, it seems, the political dreams of poet-intellectuals have been extrapolated. All have become "toys" and all are subtly derided by the poet—art especially: "Phidias' famous ivories / And all the golden grasshoppers and bees." The sacred statue of Pallas Athene becomes merely an "ancient image made of olive wood," as if even rudimentary aesthetic sensibility were no longer in operation. It is as if the creative power of the mind had failed at its most ordinary level and the sculpture had gone back into its origins in raw material. We had imagined, he says, that such things are outside the influence of the moon's gravitational influence pitching common things about. But, he adds in section 2, although all men are dancers when under the spell of art, their tread upon the earth "Goes to the barbarous clangor of a gong." The force of this thought is that of some previously omitted, essential data, and of a new configuration of the other data into a timeless but grotesque verity. That the real world has not changed in these respects is clearly implied in the sixth stanza of section 1. Greece in Phidias's own time could have been no exception, though we imagine, from the imperfect evidence that we have, that it was.

> That country round
> None dared admit, if such a thought were his,
> Incendiary or bigot could be found
> To burn that stump on the Acropolis,
> Or break in bits the famous ivories
> Or traffic in the grasshoppers or bees.

At the poem's end, when the ghost of Robert Artisson revives, he comes forward from the fourteenth century rather than from what, for

Yeats, would be some darker, more analogous time. He and his inhuman mindlessness, this implies, are always here, as are the Dame Kytelers with the extravagant irrationality of their desire. Herodias's daughters, epitomized by Salome, emerge naturally in the context of this nightmare, for it is their collective role to violently separate mind and body, to destroy the culture's capacity for dreaming counterworlds into being or even of piecing "thoughts" into coherent philosophy. Their purpose is unknown, and they themselves are blind. Contrary to what we might expect in a Yeatsian vision, they do not have even an apocalyptic role. They are simply purposelessness embodied, which is, for the poet, the most threatening chthonic power of all.

In this context, the poet's self-doubt and compunction from "Meditations in Time of Civil War" are revived in bitterness:

> A man in his own secret meditation
> Is lost amid the labyrinth that he has made
> In art or politics.

When in the next stanza the swan, an ad hoc image of the soul, leaps into the desolate heaven, the poet's reaction is rage, for the desolate heaven has become an abyss, to be leaped into where otherwise one would expect soaring. Forms of the word *desolate* recur in these two companion poems. The word's most famous incarnation elsewhere in Yeats's work will come in "Meru":

> but man's life is thought
> And he, despite his terror, cannot cease
> Ravening through century after century,
> Ravening, raging, and uprooting that he may come
> Into the desolation of reality.

The word is used precisely. It means alone, uninhabited, cut off, and so, by extension, unmediated by human thought or speech, the tabula rasa of subjective idealism. It is the fear of that profoundest mockery, the soul in desolation, that provokes the poet's rage to decreate,

> To end all things, to end
> What my laborious life imagined, even
> The half-imagined, the half-written page;
> O but we dreamed to mend
> Whatever mischief seemed

> To afflict mankind, but now
> That winds of winter blow
> Learn that we were crack-pated when we dreamed

A main issue of "Nineteen Hundred and Nineteen" is that the violence in the outer world has introjected. So it is not simply "they," or "we Irish," but "they and I"—"we"—who are but "weasels fighting in a hole"; and this revelation is all the more unsettling, for it is now appearing to have always been the case.

> We, who seven years ago,
> Talked of honor and of truth,
> Shriek with pleasure if we show
> The weasel's twist, the weasel's tooth.

Yeats's identifying with those for whom the image might be more appropriate is a sign of what, on the occasion of this poem and this historical moment, he most fears: a failure of nerve, as Donald Davie expresses it, and an isolation from the power of the "conscious mind's intelligible structure." A related point is that "Meditations in Time of Civil War," in being placed before "Nineteen Hundred and Nineteen" in *The Tower*, even though it was written later, resolves the issues introduced in the two poems on the side of anger rather than self-pity and withdrawal. We are moved forward by the momentum rather than drawn inward and back. Later, in "The Circus Animals' Desertion," this poet will say to himself, trying again to face the truth,

> and yet when all is said
> It was the dream itself enchanted me:
> Character isolated by a deed
> To engross the present and dominate memory.
> Players and painted stage took all my love,
> And not those things that they were emblems of.

Here, the context is not political, but the point is the same, or close to it. His dream of the world has wavered between a desire to change it and a desire to be removed from it, and there is no knowing which is better or worse.

In December 1921, anxious about civil war as it might impinge upon his family, Yeats wrote to Olivia Shakespear from Oxford:

In the last week I have been planning to live in Dublin—George very urgent for this—but I feel now that all may be blood and misery. If that comes we may abandon Ballylee to the owls and the rats, and England too (where passions will rise and I shall find myself with no answer), and live in some far land. Should England and Ireland be divided beyond all hope of remedy, what else could one do for the children's sake, or one's own work? I could not bring them to Ireland where they would inherit bitterness, nor leave them in England where, being Irish by tradition, and by family and fame, they would be in an unnatural condition of mind and grow, as so many Irishmen who live here do, sour and argumentative.[15]

Apart from his natural concern for his children and for the future of Ireland, we should also notice here an implied intellectual issue. The children are to be relocated so as to escape this bitterness that proximity to the conflict has provoked. It is not a question of physical danger. In 1930, Yeats inscribed in his diary a curriculum for Michael in school that, for all practical purposes, would achieve the same effect:

A LETTER TO MICHAEL'S SCHOOLMASTER

Dear Sir,

My son is now between nine and ten and should begin Greek at once and be taught by the Berlitz method that he may read as soon as possible that most exciting of all stories, the *Odyssey*, from that landing in Ithaca to the end.... As he grows older he will read to me the great lyric poets and I will talk to him about Plato. Do not teach him one word of Latin. The Roman people were the classic decadence, their literature form without matter. They destroyed Milton, the French seventeenth and our own eighteenth century, and our schoolmasters even to-day read Greek with Latin eyes. Greece, could we but approach it with eyes as young as its own, might renew our youth. Teach him mathematics as thoroughly as his capacity permits. I know that Bertrand Russell must, seeing that he is such a featherhead, be wrong about everything, but as I have no mathematics I cannot prove it. I do not want my son to be as helpless. Do not teach him one word of geography. He has lived on the Alps, crossed a number of rivers and when he is fifteen I shall urge him to climb the Sugar Loaf. Do not teach him a word of history. I shall take him to Shakespeare's history plays, if a commercialised theatre permit, and give him all the historical novels of Dumas, and if

15. Yeats, *Letters*, 675.

he cannot pick up the rest he is a fool. Don't teach him one word of science, he can get all he wants in the newspapers and in any case it is no job for a gentleman. If you teach him Greek and mathematics and do not let him forget the French and German that he already knows you will do for him all that one man can do for another. If he wants to learn Irish after he is well founded in Greek, let him—it will clear his eyes of the Latin miasma. If you will not do what I say, whether the curriculum or your own will restrain, and my son comes from school a smatterer like his father, may your soul lie chained on the Red Sea bottom.

Then, many years later, he grandly represented his role as editor to be the purifier of cultural memory:

If war is necessary, or necessary in our time and place, it is best to forget its suffering as we do the discomfort of a fever, remembering our comfort at midnight when our temperature fell, or as we forget the worst moments of more painful disease.

Thus he excluded the war poets, who described only "passive suffering," which was not, Yeats said, a "theme for poetry."[16] In these arguments, only partly facetious, Yeats prescribed a mode of encountering the realities of past and present history: The conflicts in themselves do not go away by moving away from them. They may be held at bay in thought and feeling, however, by putting distance between them and the mind. It is what happens to the inner life and its capacity for creating its own world that matters most—even when the irrationality of the forces set loose in recent history make that effort more dubious and therefore more difficult. How and why this effort is problematical is easy to express in Yeats's own terms: Would the eyes of the old men staring down upon "all the tragic scene" in "Lapis Lazuli" be glittering and gay if in fact it were Ellen Quinn's and her children's bodies they were staring down upon? Presumably not, unless they were far enough away. Kant, Nietzsche, Pound, and Yeats all believed war to embody a certain "sublimity," as indeed it does in one terrible sense. But of course, in another sense, that sublimity is war's most literary and therefore least important aspect. When the aesthetic distance is abridged and war's carnage is foregrounded, the epistemological data change radically.

16. Yeats, *Explorations*, 320–21; W. B. Yeats, ed., *The Oxford Book of Modern Verse: 1892–1935*, xxxiv–xxxv.

As Douglas Archibald has pointed out, Yeats's political attitude during the period of *The Tower* had once more become one of ambiguous detachment. The "pride of people that were / Bound neither to Cause nor to State" becomes mystically one with the pride of the morn "[w]hen the headlong light is loosed," or with the pride of the "fabulous horn" or of the sudden shower—whatever all of this means. Finally, this pride merges with the pride of the *hour*—not the swan—but the hour when the swan floats out upon the "Last reach of glittering stream / And there [sings] his last song."[17] His politics, in being diffused in this vague way, become dehistoricized and are made to seem both natural and transcendentally impervious.

Of course, it is not unusual for conservative intellectuals to justify their ideologies with metaphorical appeals to origins in nature. Yeats had Burke as his model, with his representation of the state as an organic entity like a tree, and he had Burke's general argument that the metaphorical resources of language—*because* they are imprecise—are the most rhetorically useful ones: "not clear, but strong expressions are effective."[18] Yeats's strategy in this case, however, seems intended not so much to advance a specific historic cause as to depoliticize his own relation to history by going behind it into a preemptive, theoretically wordless, and hence pre-ideational, oddly Rousseauistic condition. His models and his points of reference are most frequently from a historical period, but such periods now being (in his view) irretrievably gone, they also have the special sanctity of being no longer, in the worst sense, historical—as, for instance, in "The Curse of Cromwell," where Cromwell's curse is a ruthless, leveling force in history itself. What is literally gone cannot be recovered, but at least in poetry and memory—in formalized time within real time—"things both can and cannot be," in poetry and memory, and in dreams:

17. "[T]hat pride is instantly generalized, made less personal and removed from class consciousness...by its association with a cluster of natural symbols." Douglas Archibald, *Yeats,* 142.

18. "Berkeley proved that the world was a vision, and Burke that the state was a tree, no mechanism to be pulled in pieces and put up again, but an oak tree that had grown through centuries." Yeats, *Uncollected Prose* 2:459. See also Alasdair MacIntyre, "Poetry as Political Philosophy: Notes on Burke and Yeats," in Vereen Bell and Laurence Lerner, eds., *On Modern Poetry: Essays Presented to Donald Davie,* 145–57.

But there's another knowledge that my heart destroys
As the fox in the old fable destroyed the Spartan boy's,
Because it proves that things both can and cannot be,
That the swordsmen and the ladies can still keep company,
Can pay the poet for a verse and hear the fiddle sound,
That I am still their servant though all are underground.
　　　　O what of that, O what of that,
　　　　What is there left to say?

I came on a great house in the middle of the night,
Its open lighted doorway and its windows all alight,
And all my friends were there and made me welcome too;
And when I pay attention I must out and walk
Among the dogs and horses that understand my talk.
　　　　O what of that, O what of that,
　　　　What is there left to say?

That only this peasant speaker, dogs, and horses "understand" implies
that what is there to be retrieved has always already been there. In
"Hound Voice," such knowledge is declared an awakening from existential slumber for those few who "were the last to choose the settled
ground," those for whom to be civilized and normalized as history
requires is to be discontent.

We picked each other from afar and knew
What hour of terror comes to test the soul,
And in that terror's name obeyed the call,
And understood, what none have understood,
Those images that waken in the blood.

Some day we shall get up before the dawn
And find our ancient hounds before the door,
And wide awake know that the hunt is on;
Stumbling upon the blood-dark track once more,
Then stumbling to the kill beside the shore;
Then cleaning out and bandaging of wounds,
And chants of victory amid the encircling hounds.

The hound voice is not the voice of unreason but of unattenuated
being—fearful as that is. It expresses affirmation of some still-accessible,
primal core of being where history is irrelevant and cannot reach.

Paul Scott Stanfield makes the point that in his works dealing with the Easter Rising—"The O'Rahilly," "Three Songs to the One Burden," "Easter 1916," "The Statues," and *The Death of Cuchulain*—Yeats was "trying to ensure that in future that ambiguous event would have not a deValeran [i.e., Republican] but a Yeatsian meaning." He felt that he had learned from Balzac that "[i]f poetry is conscious of its own power, it can outstare history and even become accepted as history." This would be to make history and historical figures—and the very nature of history—responsive only to the values that Yeats sanctioned. But of course underlying both the self-confidence and implicit optimism of this strategy is a profound pessimism and a distrust of the unmanaged historical process in itself—of life's own value behind his particular thought. In both of these respects, Yeats's attitude toward history is entirely in accord with the oddly nihilist arguments that Nietzsche puts forth in *The Use and Abuse of History*. Yeats continued intermittently to be able to believe that art could shape human nature by raising its aspirations and even intervene in the process of natural selection by what Stanfield calls "educating desire"—that is, by modifying human mating choices and thus improving the genetic outcomes of procreation.[19] This role for art is implied in his last, more or less official, utterances in "Under Ben Bulben," where it is poets and sculptors—not priests or eugenicists—who are enjoined to "Bring the soul of man to God" and "Make him fill the cradles right."

Yeats's commitment to the necessity of Kant's three postulates—freedom, God, and the immortality of the soul[20]—implicate God, as his poems do when the name is used, as the highest authority and criterion for moral identity, an authority that, associated with the entailed immortality of the soul, is above the authority of (and more demanding than) any merely secular state apparatus. In the three convictions he speaks of, "freedom" is therefore a consequence of belief in the second two and a privilege available to any individual, regardless of nationality or class (who is not presumably preoccupied with prior claims of economic dispossession). This is Yeats's metaphysical pragmatism at work. For him, freedom is not only the real issue but the point of this triumvirate, and for that objective it is the *belief* in God and in the immortality (and therefore antimaterialist sanctity) of the soul that matters, not

19. Stanfield, *Yeats and Politics,* 139, 154–55.
20. Yeats, *Explorations,* 333.

their indisputable, autonomous reality. But to talk seriously about a state founded on Kant's three "convictions" entails quite directly the issue of the degree to which God's otherwise merely stipulated existence can be verified, and not only the extent to which but also the way in which God could be said to intervene in human affairs. Before endorsing such an enterprise, one would wish to know a great deal more about God's agenda than Yeats (or Kant, for that matter) was ever willing to supply. The state founded on Kant's three "convictions," in other words, is a characteristically vague and wholly metaphorical concept of Yeats's that seems, by its very nature, to resist grounding in actual political practice. Yeats's political theories, such as they are, often seem cogent for him to the degree that they are impractical, viable within the economy of their own making and only in the terms permitted by their conceiver.

To predicate and then impose an actually functioning political state founded on Kant as Yeats was reading him is virtually a contradiction. Such a state by definition could not be imposed. Yeats must have been aware of this problem at some level, for in the end, he turned away from history and into his poetry's version of history where the soul, as he put it, arranges according to its own laws. His poems create Kant's ideal state, and—notwithstanding the surprisingly liberal record he achieved as a Free State senator—this ideal state, in its way, was even more elitist than Pound's and therefore, oddly, not fascist. Yeats could not have been happy for long with any real state, Mussolini's included. The phrase *aesthetic ideology* was not current when Yeats was alive, but his work was there waiting to exemplify its logic when it became so. Just as Nietzsche had argued that existence was justifiable only in aesthetic terms, Yeats's politics gradually withdrew into the shelter of aesthetic humanism. His idea of freedom was the freedom of art on the Kantian model of aesthetic experience, and ultimately this meant being free of attachment to any political world and all of its associated institutions. Art and freedom, in this respect, were cognates. This great dream predisposed him not only toward leaders like Parnell, who seemed to him to rise above the masses both literally and symbolically, but also toward those whose concerted ambition was to advance the arts. His brief envisionment of "the despotic rule of the educated classes" as a solution to Ireland's troubles was based on this naive principle, and it made him also unwilling or unable to consider the significant differences between the Gregorys on the one hand and, say, the Medici on the other. Indeed that difference did not matter in one sense, given the degree to which his ideology had evolved independently of the data of legitimate historical evidence. "Yeats's audience belongs to no immediate times," Seamus Deane has said. "It lives in the future or in a past that will be the future. Between these two modes of time, past and future which is the more past, intervenes the cataclysm or crisis."[21]

So Yeats created in his poems the political and historical world that could not be reproduced in real life. Marx would have known exactly what to say about it, that it presumed the absence of material causes. By taking a transcendentally long view, Yeats had turned on its head Marx's foundational dictum that it is not consciousness that creates society but the reverse. Given Yeats's own internal battle between his anxiety over the course of human life and his dream of its perfection, taking that long view—long enough not to be complicated unnecessarily by facts or to entail thick description, but still historically linear in some sense—must have seemed to him a worthy if only strategic compromise.

Indeed, as Stanfield carefully shows, it was the belief in what he called "Italian philosophy" (from Vico, Croce, and Gentile) that "the individual creates his external, material circumstances"—ironic as this seems for Italy's history in retrospect—which caused him to be sympathetic with fascism as a creative and antithetical political force, particularly as it valued rather than rejected the past and as it allowed that "various past periods are the realisations of possibilities that still exist within us."[22] On the other hand, Yeats was essentially trapped by his own artistic philosophy, dependent as it was—like Nietzsche's—upon a belief in the ultimately tragic condition of human life. This predication compelled him to deny not only the possibility of Hegelian or socialist progress but of all human progress whatsoever. This belief kept art at the center of human life rather than politics, since the point of all great art was to affirm "tragic joy." If life were not fundamentally tragic, and if some, say, Marxian version of dialectical evolution were to come to fruition, then art's role would cease to be fundamental and become merely ancillary. So melioristic change and art in its highest sense for Yeats could not coexist. Fascism, until it turned out to be just another

---

21. Yeats, *Letters,* 811–12; Deane quoted in Terence Brown, *Ireland's Literature: Selected Essays,* 88.
22. Stanfield, *Yeats and Politics,* 72–73.

version of mob rule, must have seemed to Yeats at some point a kind of tertium quid, a way in which art and change could be reconciled.

When such dialectical enterprises miscarry, one political model left is the Platonist one that Socrates proposes at the end of book 9 of *The Republic*. He is describing to Glaucon the measures that the intelligent man must practice in order to achieve inner peace:

> "He will follow the same principles over honours, private or public. If he thinks they will make him a better man he will take and enjoy them, if he thinks they will destroy the order within him, he will avoid them."
>
> "If that is his object, he won't enter politics," he said.
>
> "Oh yes, he will," I replied, "very much so, in the society where he really belongs; but not, I think, in the society where he's born, unless something very extraordinary happens."
>
> "I see what you mean," he said. "You mean that he will do so in the society which we have been describing and which we have theoretically founded; but I doubt if it will ever exist on earth."
>
> "Perhaps," I said, "it is laid up as a pattern in heaven, where those who wish can see it and found it in their own hearts. But it doesn't matter whether it exists or ever will exist; it's the only state in whose politics he can take part."
>
> "I expect you are right."[23]

More than twenty-five centuries of human history later, in 1951, Theodor Adorno put forward a gloomier model of this construct. In the process—having lived, as a Jew, through the period of European and Russian history that Yeats died just soon enough to miss—he was able to represent in the form of philosophy precisely the problem that, for Yeats, would always confront the discourses of art and that even Yeats would never be able to transcend:

> The only philosophy which can be responsibly practised in face of despair is the attempt to contemplate all things as they would present themselves from the standpoint of redemption. Knowledge has no light but that shed on the world by redemption: all else is reconstruction, mere technique. Perspectives must be fashioned that displace and estrange the world, reveal it to be, with its rifts and crevices, as indigent and distorted as it will appear one day in the messianic light. To gain such perspectives without velleity or violence, entirely from felt contact with its objects—

23. Plato, *The Republic*, 420.

this alone is the task of thought. It is the simplest of all things, because the situation calls imperatively for such knowledge, indeed because consummate negativity, once squarely faced, delineates the mirror-image of its opposite. But it is also the utterly impossible thing, because it presupposes a standpoint removed, even though by a hair's breadth, from the scope of existence, whereas we well know that any possible knowledge must not only be first wrested from what is, if it shall hold good, but is also marked, for this very reason, by the same distortion and indigence which it seeks to escape. The more passionately thought denies its conditionality for the sake of the unconditional, the more unconsciously, and so calamitously, it is delivered up to the world. Even its own impossibility it must at last comprehend for the sake of the possible. But beside the demand thus placed on thought, the questions of the reality or unreality of redemption itself hardly matters.[24]

It seems worth repeating here that the glittering eyes of the ancients in "Lapis Lazuli" are gay not just because they are ancient and up high and staring upon only a distant, rarefied version of the tragic scene in "the mountain and the sky" but also because they are in art—literally—rather than in life. The women in the first stanza of the poem are "hysterical" because (as the poem concedes, to its credit) they are in life, where real history is on the verge of working out, in Yeats's absence, one of its most horrific manifestations.

24. Theodor W. Adorno, *Minima Moralia: Reflections from a Damaged Life*, 247.

4

Identity

———— 🖋 ————

P OETRY, OR MORE specifically, writing itself, was Yeats's ready-to-hand immortality, an atemporal dimension within which one could be reborn again and again: "[A poet] is never the bundle of accident and incoherence that sits down to breakfast; he has been reborn as an idea, something intended, complete. . . . He is part of his own phantasmagoria and we adore him because nature has grown intelligible, and by so doing a part of our creative power." "I think all happiness depends on the energy to assume the mask of some other life, a re-birth as something not one's self, something created in a moment and perpetually renewed." One reason that it makes sense that we take Yeats's occult practices and beliefs seriously is not just that they refer us to symbols and metaphors that are recycled in the poems, but that they refer us to an ontological model that the poems simply reconstitute in another, more coherent form. In the Yeats arcana, spirits visit the material world, the dead address and can be addressed by mortals, souls are real entities rather than merely metaphors, and the immortality of souls is assured—it is never even doubted. In this setting, death is a mere fiction; death has been denied. In the poems, the poet is reborn each time as a different self, as an idea even, not just a self, and nature becomes intelligible. In becoming intelligible, nature is no longer where being human stops and something else begins—"the obscure limit of our spiritual being," as Gentile expressed it[1]—our temporality, so to speak, spatialized. Instead, it has become an extension of the self, an extension of thought.

Yeats is not wrong about this. We do, in some sense, adore the poet for reassuring us on these issues, for making the world in language become the real world and the world outside it stand back, however briefly.

1. Yeats, *Essays and Introductions,* 509; Yeats, *Mythologies,* 334; Giovanni Gentile, *The Theory of Mind as Pure Act,* 251.

He himself is a case in point. It is extremely difficult for even otherwise tough-minded people to think of Yeats as a socially constructed subject, a specific and predictable concentration of temporal and material events: parents, social class, historical moment, prevailing or competing power discourses, modes of production. We tend to think of him in the way he represents himself in the poems, and no biographer, no matter how sedulous, will ever be able to contain the poet we speak of when we say "Yeats" within the idea of the man who was—so to speak, behind his own thought—the bundle of accident. Until the past decade, biographers have gone wrong again and again by taking Yeats to have been in fact what he presents himself as being in the poems and reading from the poems back into the life. In John Kelly's minutely annotated collections of Yeats's letters and in Roy Foster's recently completed biography, the cumulative new biographical evidence only affirms that his poems were an alternative life for him and therefore permitted an alternative identity.

Foster's biography is scrupulous and exhaustive, a historian's biography confined to the hard evidence of the public record. The most accessible public record for the 1865–1914 period, which volume one covers, concerns the organization and evolution of the Irish National Theatre, from 1896 through 1914, and this is naturally, therefore, the material that Foster concentrates upon. Yeats the poet—the one we think of as "Yeats"—seems buried under this record, as indeed he seemed to himself to have been. In life, Yeats was the day-by-day micromanager of endless internal disputes, public relations officer, political advocate, traveling fund-raiser, and solicitor of patronage for virtually twenty years. This was what rent "Spontaneous joy and natural content / Out of my heart," as he put it. In art, meanwhile, he was the dreamy "Yeats" of *The Wind among the Reeds, In the Seven Woods,* and *The Green Helmet and Other Poems*—of "The Secret Rose," "He Wishes for the Cloths of Heaven," "The Withering of the Boughs," "The Ragged Wood"—which were produced in this same period. Between these two Yeatses, there is an astonishingly great gulf fixed. Reading Foster's harrowing account of the fourth and fifth decades of Yeats's life, one does not wonder that Yeats began to feel that something was ailing his colt and that he must "find the stable and pull out the bolt" and release him again, kicking up his heels, into phantasmagoria. The quantity of detail that Foster supplies for this period was the quantity of the weight of detail that Yeats lived through. This record on the page makes it all the more clear how shrewd and perceptive Yeats has been in "The Fascination of What's Difficult" on the psychology of becoming overextended in public life at the cost of the inner life—not just for the poet but for anyone for whom existential poeisis remains a challenge.

Conversely, it is all but impossible to hold in focus and achieve depth of field both the credulous "WBY" of Foster's second volume, who was transfixed by resourceful George and her "controls" from the other world, and the Yeats who, only a year before, had achieved the severe clearheadedness of "Easter 1916" or who, during his submission to George's ministrations, could rise to the apocalyptic authority of "A Prayer for My Daughter" and "The Second Coming." The Yeats that lived in the world both as the bundle of accident and as the poet is necessarily lost to us forever, but that lost Yeats fashioned another one who lives in his place and has therefore left behind in his poems the illusion of having overcome contingency and circumstance—of having overcome biography itself. Ordinarily, one would think of there being a man and then poems made by him—as in *The Man and the Masks* or *Man and Poet*—but in Yeats's case, the process seems to have worked the other way around. Instead of the "real" self being projected into the poems, the invented self in the poems began at some point to project itself back into biographical reality. Marjorie Perloff has concisely summarized the situation we are left with: "Surely no other poet of our century has been at once so present and so absent in his poems."[2]

Even the "Yeats" of the poems that we feel entitled to speak of is a noumenal presence who is perceptible mainly as a voice and as a style. To achieve a style in this sense, Nietzsche had said in *The Will to Power*, is "[t]o become master of the chaos one is; to compel one's chaos to become form." Seamus Deane cites Valéry as regarding this transformation as a kind of heroic *symbolist* achievement: "A man who measures himself against himself, and remakes himself according to his lights, seems to me a superior achievement that moves me more than any other. The first effort of humanity is that of changing their disorder into order, and chance into power. That is the true marvel."[3] In Yeats's poems, the

2. Marjorie Perloff, "'The Tradition of Myself': The Autobiographical Mode of Yeats," 573. Denis Donoghue also elegantly summarizes these issues in his review of volume 2 of Foster's *W. B. Yeats: A Life* in *Harper's Magazine*, December 2003.

3. Nietzsche, *Will to Power*, 444; Deane, *Celtic Revivals*, 43.

voice and style are the form that unifies and, like the invisible logic of architecture, strengthens the relationship of many identities. This consistent, recognizable, but merely formal being enables us to know that each new self emerges from the same source. We know this formal Yeats by his absence, in the sense that the more the identities change, the more perceptible and recognizable the style that binds them together becomes. "Hammer your thoughts into a unity" seems finally to have meant no more than this, given that there is certainly nothing unified about the content of his thought.

We know this "Yeats" by his absence in another way as well.

> Civilisation is hooped together, brought
> Under a rule, under the semblance of peace
> By manifold illusion; but man's life is thought,
> And he, despite his terror, cannot cease
> Ravening through century after century,
> Ravening, raging, and uprooting that he may come
> Into the desolation of reality.

Thinking is becoming. Thinking creates and decreates, and what happens in cultures is recapitulated in the creation and decreation of one's own being. Existence precedes essence, and it also evades essentialization. We know the Yeats who comes down to us in the poems as this impersonal energy that drove him incessantly to revise his own poems, to make and unmake selves: "The friends that have it I do wrong / When ever I remake a song / Should know what issue is at stake / It is myself that I remake"—and this was in 1908. Such a strategy gives voice to the unappeasable and insatiable life that thinking is, and it depicts a way of being in touch with life by adaptation as life changes rather than gliding serenely above it. This all but anonymous energy itself is the irreducible Yeatsian quality. Autobiography, in this sense, William Howarth says, "is not just a 'calling' or public duty, but the creative act that autobiography itself demands. Writing a book assures . . . that the controlling force in life is neither God nor man alone but the imagination, where both of those powers are constantly potential. . . . Only the process of *becoming* is essential." ("Whatever flames upon the night / Man's own resinous heart has fed.") In *On the Genealogy of Morals*, Nietzsche argues that "All great things bring about their own destruction through an act of self-overcoming: thus the law of life will have it, the law of the necessity of 'self over-coming' in the nature of life."[4] Nietzsche is speaking specifically of Christianity and of how the intellectual rigor informing its pursuit of the ascetic ideal, the concept of truthfulness as a morality, eventually set into motion the demystification of its own dogma. This is a point in intellectual history, before Husserl and Heidegger and then Derrida, where the logic of deconstruction is first identified, as such, as a metaphysical principle, as a "law of life." Yeats's continuous presence in the poems is a manifesting of this noumenous, deconstructive force that generates renewal through self-decreation. The "true" identity—that conforms to "the law of life"—is a dynamic absence of one.

It will follow, ironically, that the representations of time in Yeats's poems must be dialectical. The dialectical Yeats of the poems could not inhabit the world that the conservative political Yeats envisioned, since the one was anarchic, fluid, and pluralistic, and the other was hierarchical, stable, and sequestered. This dialectic is most obvious in the way the wish to become artifice as the golden bird in "Sailing to Byzantium" is subverted by the opposing, primordial energy generated in the poem, so to speak, from underneath. Despite the severe clarity of the poem's rhetoric, the poem is not a linear intellectual progression. The "idea" that the poet is born into in "Sailing to Byzantium" is not a fanciful inhuman eternity but a stabilization in language of a destabilizing ambivalence, neither aspect of which can exist authentically apart from the other, in life or in poems.

In "Among School Children" public, quotidian time is silently annulled and appropriated. Idealized time restores the poet first to his young manhood and then to a point in space and time that he never even inhabited ("and it seemed that our two natures blent / Into a sphere from youthful sympathy"; "She stands before me as a living child"). The point of this subtext is that the reassemblage of linear time enables several selves to thrive within the same mental environment and that memory in this Bergsonian function, as a recourse from the otherwise irreversible forward motion of time, is what poetry itself is for Yeats.

---

4. See George Bornstein's account of the Yeats of this question in "Remaking Himself: Yeats's Revisions of His Early Canon"; William Howarth, "Some Principles of Autobiography," in James Olney, ed., *Autobiography: Essays Theoretical and Critical,* 113; Nietzsche, *Genealogy of Morals,* 161.

The inner logic of his view of this issue was paraphrased by Yeats's counter-Futurist, Italian contemporary Giuseppe Ungaretti: "Internal duration is composed of time and space beyond chronological time; the internal universe is a world where reversibility is the rule. This time never flows in a single direction, never orientates itself in the selfsame manner; one can trace back its course to one knows not what inaccessible source, yet it is at the same time immediately present within us."[5] The seeds of any present's decreation are always sown from the beginning.

In the poem "In Memory of Eva Gore-Booth and Con Marcievicz," the Gore-Booth sisters are temporarily recovered and rediscovered in a simpler but similar way by having history reconstructed for them:

> The light of evening, Lissadell,
> Great windows open to the south,
> Two girls in silk kimonos, both
> Beautiful, one a gazelle.
> But a raving autumn shears
> Blossom from the summer's wreath;
> The older is condemned to death,
> Pardoned, drags out lonely years
> Conspiring among the ignorant.
> I know not what the younger dreams—
> Some vague Utopia—and she seems,
> When withered old and skeleton-gaunt,
> An image of such politics.
> Many a time I think to seek
> One or the other out and speak
> Of that old Georgian mansion, mix
> Pictures of the mind, recall
> That table and the talk of youth,
> Two girls in silk kimonos, both
> Beautiful, one a gazelle.

> II

> Dear shadows, now you know it all,
> All the folly of a fight
> With a common wrong or right.

5. Quoted in Peter Nicholls, *Modernisms: A Literary Guide*, 109.

> The innocent and the beautiful
> Have no enemy but time;
> Arise and bid me strike a match
> And strike another till time catch;
> Should the conflagration climb,
> Run till all the sages know.
> We the great gazebo built,
> They convicted us of guilt;
> Bid me strike a match and blow.

The two sisters are passed back and forth at the poet's discretion from one historical context to another, their becoming, so to speak, reversed so that they may continue to be both as they were ("two girls in silk kimonos") and as they are represented as being at the end of their lives ("lonely," "withered," and "skeleton-gaunt"). The poet's stated wish to abolish time, as poets may, on their behalf—to seek them out and "mix / pictures of the mind, recall / that table and the talk of youth"— is enacted by the poem, and this achievement is as much in the poet's own interest as in theirs. But of course in the kind of conservative palatial, historic time with which Yeats identifies their glamorous past ("Of that old Georgian mansion") and honors through them, this kind of configuration would not be possible in the first place.

In Yeats's poems, the fluid, subversive, and hidden version of temporality tends to be in conflict with or incompatible with the arguments or the affirmations represented on the poem's rhetorical surface, where heraldic time is more apparent. The "Yeats" that inhabits, indeed flourishes, in that hidden and subversive dimension, is an invisible agent, while another recognizable "Yeats" is simultaneously present to us as persona in the rhetoric. Whichever "Yeats" is under scrutiny in a given moment of critical discussion is therefore always—to refer back to his own idiom—"incomplete" to the degree that the other is not called forth and acknowledged. In these two poems, as in others where time is an issue, Yeats makes a point of having enabled such a transformation so that his own identity in the poem becomes implicitly shamanistic. The poet becomes the agent who can achieve such miraculous feats, who commands time and disorder rather than being commanded by them. Once this role is established in the poems, many themes related to identity are given freedom to unfold as effects of it.

The analogy that Yeats implies when he speaks of being transformed from a "bundle of accident" into an "idea" is equivalent to the
relationship of the dancer to the dance. He speaks of rebirth in the poem
not simply as another person but as an idea. This is the transformation,
as it turns out, that "Among School Children" reports: as an "idea"
there, having cast off the temporal sixty-year-old body and the socially
constructed "public" man in the second stanza, he is beyond the reach
of the very processes that he has just been arguing to be inescapable.
After all, as he says, how can we experience the full mystery of becoming apart from the enacting of it, know the dancer apart from the dancing, the bundle of accident as also an idea? But the identity of the dancer
with the dance—like Wordsworth's "something far more deeply inter-
fused"—is probably wholly coherent and intelligible to us only in the
presence of the poem itself, into whose privileged environment we are
permitted to enter, where we are the music only while the music lasts.

But that, of course, is why it is necessary to be *re*born: because the
music doesn't last. If the music did last, the phenomenal world and all
of its rich opposition to the becoming self, to the human, would have
slipped away, and since we may know ourselves only in meeting the
challenge of that opposition and otherness, we ourselves would have
slipped away with it. That necessary phenomenal world is not only just
material things but also real, unmediatable time, so not only the things
of the world but also the real, ongoing, temporal character of the world
must be reproduced by the poet, as well—and deferred to. Being *episodi-
cally* transcendent—being *repeatedly* reborn—is the only really plausible option. Being reborn in that larger, enveloping context is the way
both to show time's authority as a law of the phenomenal world and to
show its susceptibility to being serially transcended in consciousness
and memory. This problem is a particularly tough one for Yeats to the
degree that he radically affirms the particular over the type and is thereby
indentured, by his own preference, not to a stylized Byzantium but
also to what is begotten, born, and dies. What causes his "medieval
knees" to bend in "The Municipal Gallery Re-visited," gazing upon
the portraits of Lady Gregory and Synge, is the despairing realization
"that time may bring / Approved patterns of women or of men / But
not that selfsame excellence again"—that is, the patterns may recur, as
they do in portraiture, but the real flesh-and-blood people whom we
love do not: they simply die.

The recurrent dilemma is that he has to contend psychologically both with time as it is and as he prefers it to be. Yeats's Magi are not *dis*satisfied with the calvary's turbulence but *un*satisfied—unsatiated—and they continue to seek through the process of real history for a reengagement with the opposite of what they, in their distant sculpturedness, have become. They hope to experience again, in whatever form, the paradoxical union of mystery and beast, of dance and dancer, of idea and fact. For this paradox even to make sense as a paradox, it must be embedded in authentic time in its most incomprehensible autonomy. For the same reason, the swans in "The Wild Swans at Coole" may be symbols, but they must remain swans as well. They remain swans because they are not contained or delineated by a specific allegorical schema—as they would be, for instance, if they were Blake's or Shelley's—and they are therefore notably still creatures of ordinary phenomenal time. They have significance fixed upon them, but only such significance as is provisional and vague enough not to have turned them into something else. This striving to have things be naturalistic and symbolic simultaneously is an overriding motive with Yeats so that both the worlds of idea and of unmediated fact—like both the forms of time they are identified with—have equal claims or presence, when the one does not subvert or dominate the value of the other. It is because of this interaction that the sense of real time—which his creatures inhabit—remains persuasive. "The world of the spirit," as Paul de Man expresses it, and "the world of sentient substance" have managed to coexist without cancelling each other out.[6]

What is tragic in Yeats is not being able to be forever at one with the poem. But that disappointment is mitigated by the fact that, in some way, the poet wills his own falling away or falling back just as in some sense he wills into existence that which he falls back from. If nature becomes too intelligible, it becomes more intelligible than we ourselves have any hope of being without ceasing to be any longer recognizable to ourselves. This is the continuing crisis of making a life, of becoming, of being both dancer and dance. The wild swans at Coole

6. Paul de Man, *Blindness and Insight*, 32: "Understanding can be called complete only when it becomes aware of its own temporal predicament and realizes that the horizon within which the totalization can take place is time itself. The act of understanding is a temporal act that has its own history, but this history forever eludes totalization."

certainly seem like real swans in Yeats's representation of them in the poem, but since they cannot be the same swans that the poem's speaker counted nineteen years before, for him to imagine that they are the same swans is to measure his own deterioration in time against a wholly imaginary—and therefore impossible—standard. So if and when he "awakes" one day from this dream of the world, the question will remain whether he is better or worse off for having passed through this experience. His experience is enriched by the vision that becomes the poem, but he himself is diminished by it. Nature becomes intelligible as an effect of his desire. It becomes part of his creative power; but grown intelligible it reminds him of what he cannot be and must always fail to become.

This is a secondary but visible theme of "Adam's Curse": that humans, being the contingent, unintelligible configurations that they are of language, irrational drives, historical circumstances, and social class, cannot become their dreamed of, stylized selves—ideas of themselves— *except* in poems. Yeats is sensible and unmodern enough to think of human dignity as a virtue and at least to wish to subjugate the embarrassing vagaries of raw sexual passion to the rituals of courtship. The idea of a true self and of love as an ennobling influence described in the third stanza of "Adam's Curse" is not a wholly frivolous one, faintly absurd as it is nevertheless made to seem.

> I said: "It's certain there is no fine thing
> Since Adam's fall but needs much labouring.
> There have been lovers who thought love should be
> So much compounded of high courtesy
> That they would sigh and quote with learned looks
> Precedents out of beautiful old books;
> Yet now it seems an idle trade enough."

But the poet's models are literary (other bundles of accident reborn as ideas), who in turn cite models from other literary texts, and the poet must know this ultimately. The "now" he refers to is as much a condition of personal disillusionment in his own life span as it is a cultural paradigm shift. It is no longer possible for even the poet himself to think in such terms, he concedes, and human life has been diminished simply in being seen from this ground-level, quotidian perspective. Picturesque nature is brought in poignantly at the end of the poem both to stand for the dream of love and its failure and also to set the dream further at a distance from real human possibility:

> We sat grown quiet at the name of love;
> We saw the last embers of daylight die,
> And in the trembling blue-green of the sky
> A moon, worn as if it had been a shell
> Washed by time's waters as they rose and fell
>
> About the stars and broke in days and years.
> I had a thought for no one's but your ears:
> That you were beautiful, and that I strove
> To love you in the old high way of love;
> That it had all seemed happy, and yet we'd grown
> As weary-hearted as that hollow moon.

Unsimple irony rules in the real world. The very laboredness of the poet's courtship, in the name of an ideal, has caused it to fail. Human lives may be *metaphorically* represented by the sky and the moon—tenor and vehicle can be identified here and their relationship plotted—but, bundles of accident that real lives are, they fall hopelessly short, even in their tragic occasions, of the impersonal, barely expressible beauty of the natural world. To imagine a kinship between the lovers and the twilight scene in "Adam's Curse" is only to cause the awkwardness and embarrassment of failure in the real world to seem more acute. When nature becomes a part of our creative power, it creates the ironic effect, at the same time, that it causes us to see that power's limitations. The stubborn poet-dreamer of *Collected Poems* never learns his lesson about this, but to do so would be to resign himself, as Auden expressed it, to "walking dully along," instead of dancing, and without the dance, as we know, there is no dancer.

In Yeats's universe, walking dully along is simply another way of submitting to the impersonal gravity of being mortal. Poems, which we may be said to be born into as ideas, are not just singing schools— "monuments of unageing intellect"—they are also dancing schools. If we generalize this conceit to refer to something like "the wisdom of the ages" (what in "The Tower" Yeats calls "a learned school"), then, collectively, "learned Italian things," "the proud stones of Greece," "poet's imaginings and memories of love" become formed into an idea that one may be reborn into, as well. These are measures or models for our becoming that are idealized abstractions from our having been. His protest to the contrary notwithstanding—"I mock Plotinus' thought / And cry in Plato's teeth"—the poet has not given up on "abstract things" altogether. His point about the "learned school" is Platonic thinking, at least in the sense that it presupposes models: "Now I shall make my soul," he says, and the "soul" that he says he will now "make" is an abstraction, also. In Anglo-Irish usage, the phrase means to prepare the soul to meet death, and this usage assumes that the soul is always already there as an idea—another trope for the formed *pattern* of experience within us that repeats itself in time, as opposed to the mere bundles of accident as which we die. To prepare this "soul" is also to call upon it in the meditation upon time as impending death. The effect of this invocation is to be able to envision, in metaphor, the form that an ultimate reconciliation might take:

> Now I shall make my soul,
> Compelling it to study
> In a learned school
> Till the wreck of body,
> Slow decay of blood,
> Testy delirium
> Or dull decrepitude,
> Or what worse evil come—
> The death of friends, or death
> Of every brilliant eye
> That made a catch in the breath—
> Seem but the clouds of the sky
> When the horizon fades,
> Or a bird's sleepy cry
> Among the deepening shades.

Nature here has been made intelligible and benign as the result of the poet's reflecting upon the role of pattern in human experience and in the larger scheme of things into which individual lives eventually recede. The extraordinary image of the distant clouds receding into darkness on the horizon's edge is a painterly representation of this event. That effect is heightened by its aural equivalent, the peaceful bird's cry dissolving into silence. Preparation of the soul in this reinvented sense has become a means by which individual anguish can be generalized into a philosophical distance. The pain of impending death is mitigated by the power that the prepared soul gives to see one's true place in that larger scheme.

It is like Yeats to include the death of friends in this consideration of what must be overcome, for it is in that cruel experience that the awareness of the grotesqueness of mortality is most acute. ("Death who takes what man would keep, / Leaves what man would lose" he would say later, through John Kinsella.) This helps us to notice that the image in which the reconciliation is represented is a simile, not a metaphor— "seem but the clouds of the sky"—and the simile always comes with its hinge, the conjunction that silently indicates the gap between fact and desire. The outcome that the image expresses a yearning toward is the overriding or transcendence of ironic self-consciousness. This is reminiscent of Wordsworth in his "Tintern Abbey" mode, but it is finally more scrupulous, as Keats is in "Ode to a Nightingale," where the poet is forced to consider what the kinship between the poet's consciousness and the nightingale's can and cannot be. Not being conscious of being "born for death" is a considerable advantage where the desire for undivided self-presence is the theme, but undivided self-presence cannot be both attained and thought about at the same time, since thinking itself is the problem. The hinge is always there. It may be true that saints or hermits, as in "Meru," achieve the philosophical detachment and reconciliation that Yeats speaks about at the end of "The Tower," but they achieve that detachment at the cost of disassociation from that other world in "The Tower," where libido thrives, symbolized by and affirmed in the "mighty memories" of Red Hanrahan. It is also possible in normal, unascetic life to understand oneself and one's friends as dust that returns to dust, or as a cloud, or as a receding cry in the "deepening shades," and this can be reconciling, too. Even if that thought is painful in its barest form, it can be made less so if transposed into poetry. "Dust thou art and unto dust thou shalt return" does not especially soften or mitigate; nor is it intended to. The last lines of "The Tower" do soften and mitigate by causing nature itself—which, considered rationally, is the problem and not the solution—to seem to become lyrically continuous with human life. The hinge is still there, but the prevailing effect is the illusion—in the supreme fiction of the moment—of reconciliation not just of the individual with his own death and that of others but also of human thought and autonomous nature, which is otherwise thought's impasse. The poet within the poem who, at both levels, has accomplished these reconciliations is a bundle of accident reborn—his soul prepared, for the moment, for death—as an idea. Nature has been made intelligible in order to regenerate and fortify creative power, but this is also so that it not be in place as the unintelligible otherness that negates creative power, or in any case calls creative power into question.

In his memorable analysis of the evolution of "Among School Children," Thomas Parkinson is able to show how being reborn as an idea actually works in the process of composition. Parkinson shows that "Among School Children" started as a straightforward lament for old age and was actually headed in the direction of the bitter and disconsolate resolution that it foreshadows at the start.

> The poem has its germ in a judgment already firmly established in Yeats's mind:
>
> *Topic for poem—school children and the thought that life will waste them, perhaps that no possible life can fulfill their own dreams or even their teacher's hope. Bring in the old thought that life prepares for what never happens.*
>
> The "old thought" had appeared before in the *Autobiography* and *At the Hawk's Well*, and it had come forcibly to his awareness during a Senatorial visit to an elementary school. But in the final poem this notion is only one among many that are folded together in a design of meaning much more complex than this brief statement would suggest. As he contemplated the school children, they became merely a part of the totality of life and death, in fact an occasion for a series of meditative pronouncements on an entire range of antinomies of which age and youth proved to be only a small part. With the poem more fully developed, he wrote to Olivia Shakespear that the poem was a curse upon old age:
>
> *Here is a fragment of my last curse upon old age. It means that even the greatest men are owls, scarecrows, by the time their fame has come. Aristotle, remember, was Alexander's tutor, hence the taws (form of birch).*
>
> > Plato imagined all existence plays
> > Among the ghostly images of things;
> > Solider Aristotle played the taws
> > Upon the bottom of the King of Kings;
> > World famous, golden thighed Pythagoras
> > Fingered upon a fiddle stick, or strings,

What the star sang and careless Muses heard.—
Old coats upon old sticks to scare a bird.

Pythagoras made some measurement of the intervals between notes on a stretched string. It is a poem of seven or eight similar verses. His indeterminacy about the length of the poem is, as we shall shortly see, one of the major forces that compel the final version of the poem to certain ambiguities. I would suggest that Yeats really did at one point intend the poem to be a blend of curse and lament upon old age and that the famous concluding stanza was not part of the poem's intended shape until very late in the process of writing. This accounts for certain very curious qualities in the last two stanzas. "Among School Children" is the ultimate proof of the fact that in Yeats the terms "genesis," "basis," and "final form" are only very distantly related.[7]

What happens instead, in other words, is that Yeats demonstrates to himself in the course of writing that the conventional view of old age is itself a reductive fiction, unless one resigns oneself to it and permits the merely physical reality, and conventional attitudes toward it, to overcome the psychic or intellectual countertruth. In the act of making the poem—because of the concentrated focus of attention necessary to that activity—he overcomes aging in the mind by overcoming his own momentarily morbid preoccupation with it. The idea that he is reborn *as* is not an abstraction at all, or a mask, but an event of understanding. This rebirth enacts the power of the mind to master its own misgivings—or to put it a slightly different way, the power of consciousness to overcome the resistance of what it is conscious of. The poem itself then becomes the formal record of a process of psychic regeneration that has taken place prior to—but because of working toward—its completion.

"The Tower" may be said to display more of this process at work on its surface, but the process and the end result are the same. Indeed—as in "Among School Children"—the decisive action seems again to be the rejection of the prevailing historical reality and the recovery through memory of the power of subjectivity ("the sun's / Under eclipse and the day blotted out"). Though the poem itself is strangely silent on this point, section 3 clearly shows a new energy developed from no other apparent source and moves from there to rally all of Yeats's incantatory

7. Thomas Parkinson, *W. B. Yeats, Self-Critic: A Study of His Early Verse [and] W. B. Yeats: The Later Poetry*, 93–94.

concepts—declaring, mocking, crying, making, rising, dreaming, creating, compelling—and then to making his soul. The poem has worked its course a long way from the demeaning "absurdity" of its origin in the failing body and even from the not-unremarkable capacity to see the physical manifestations of old age as a "caricature" of the true self and inner being. As with "Among School Children," the decisive influence is the value given to the mystery of becoming. Repudiating the conventional attitudes toward old age empowers the poet to overcome the inertia and the conventionality of old age itself. The thinking in "The Tower" is confrontational, and its issue is the willed separation of the unique self from the generic and stereotypical one. However hopelessly others may construe, and decline into, old age, the poet in "The Tower" gradually generates a different idea of himself, a counterfactual one, in effect, who created anarchic Red Hanrahan and who calls upon the "might" of Hanrahan's memories and calls the passional past forward into thinking about what would otherwise be the desolation of the present and impending death.

The attitude is most aggressively condensed, of course, in the epitaph of "Under Ben Bulben"—"*Cast a cold eye / On life, on death. / Horseman, pass by!*" Hugh Kenner has gone so far as to argue that the attitude and the expression of it repudiate not only nature (albeit ironically) but also the very pastoral conventions that had permitted earlier generations to come to terms with it.

Wordsworth had developed "naturally," moving on the stream of nature; and streams run downhill. For the natural man the moment of lowest vitality is the moment of death; in the mid-eighteenth century the image of an untroubled decline into the grave fastened itself upon the imagination of England, and "*Siste viator*" was carved on a thousand tombstones. "Pause, traveler, whoever thou art, and consider thy mortality; as I am, so wilt thou one day be." The traveler came on foot, examined the inscription, and went on his way pondering, his vitality still lower than before. This was one of the odd versions of pastoral sentiment that prepared the way for Wordsworth's career of brilliance and decline; Yeats turns powerfully against it . . . in the epitaph he designed for himself. The last division of his Sacred Book closes with an apocalypse, superhuman forms riding the wintry dawn, Michelangelo electrifying travelers with his Creation of Adam, painters revealing heavens that opened. The directions for his own burial are introduced with a pulsation of drumbeats:

Ún dér báre Bén Búl bén's héad
In DRUMcliff churchyard . . .

The mise en scène is rural and eighteenth century—the churchyard, the ancestral rector, the local stonecutters; but the epitaph flies in the face of traditional invocations to passers-by:

> *Cast a cold eye*
> *On life, on death.*
> *Horseman, pass by!*

Much critical ingenuity has been expended on that horseman. He is simply the designated reader of the inscription, the heroic counterimage of the foot-weary wanderer who was invited to ponder a "*siste viator,*" the only reader Yeats can be bothered to address. And he is not to be weighed down by the realization of his own mortality; he is to defy it.[8]

Aging and death are bad enough in themselves, but for Yeats they also represent the supreme symbol of the unappeasibility of nature. Hence there is no thought of actually overcoming natural processes. There is only the contestation of them in thought, where, while the music lasts, so to speak, natural processes cannot reach. This, put into words, is the faith that he affirms to Dorothy Wellesley: "To me the supreme aim is an act of faith and reason to make one rejoice in the midst of tragedy. An impossible aim; yet I think it true that nothing can injure us."[9] This "us" is the "us" of the mind in those moments when belief and the power of the mind seem supreme.

The familiar story of the Yeats persona's psychosexual development— which is a main narrative line in *Collected Poems*—is a story essentially of the mind's doing what it needs to do to contest whatever the prevailing natural circumstances happen to be at the time. In the youthful poems, sexuality is stylized and dreamy; in the poems of old age, it is raw and explicit. It does not seem very likely in the normal course of human development that one would pass from a languid sexual inertia in young manhood to a condition bordering on satyriasis in one's sixties and seventies. It is apparent, in other words, that in *each* of these cases the poet's sexual identity is a specialized fiction devised from the

8. Kenner, "Sacred Book of the Arts," 18–19.
9. Yeats, *Letters on Poetry,* 13.

subject's need to transcend, in a given moment or phase, the merely material condition of its situation. Normally, in youth, the *real* problem is the indiscriminate energy of the body's capacity and desire; in age, the *real* problem normally is that the body and the body's powers are in decline. Yeats more or less admits to the countertruth of the early poems when he writes to Olivia Shakespear that he had discretely managed to leave out of his autobiographical writings the real vehemence of his youth or when he says elsewhere that, in his old age, he is writing, ironically, for those aged twenty, though he remembers that same period of his own life as being a dreadful time. And yet even when he writes about his early sexual awakenings in the suppressed portion of the autobiographies, he manages to reconstitute from the raw material a portentously formal identity:

> A sexual dream was very rare, I neither then nor at any other time told the woman I loved to come to me [in] such a dream; I think I surrounded her with too great reverence and fear. One night I heard a voice, while I lay on my back, say I would be shown a secret, the secret of life and of death, but I must not speak of it. The room seemed to brighten and as I looked towards the foot of the bed I saw that it was changed into precious stones and yet these stones had a familiar look—they reminded me of the raised glass fruit on the bottles of lime-juice in my childhood. I never associated this growing brightness with sex, until all became suddenly dark and I found I had emitted seed.

In his youth, Yeats's need to stylize his desire in his poems was a reaction formed against the intensity with which his sexual drives asserted themselves. In age, his problem was that his body's resources were in decline at the point where his mind had become most empowered. In the logic of this economy, he therefore achieved a form of transcendence of the real material body by projection into the poems of a libidinous fictional one. The later poems, which are concerned in one way or another with performance anxiety, are, in their energy and candor, decidedly *unimpotent*—that is, they are ostentatiously lurid representations of impotence. These poems emerge in the life story seeming to be about sexual failure, but they are covertly about the forever tumescent libido. Writing for those who are aged twenty is a way of being reborn as aged twenty. It is not really odd that in "The Spur" he equates lust and rage as if they were of the same class of feeling and equally gratifying.

> You think it horrible that lust and rage
> Should dance attention upon my old age;
> They were not such a plague when I was young;
> What else have I to spur me into song?

Both lust and rage are forms of passion, a liberating sacred violence, and therefore a oneness, subjectively, of body, thought, and feeling. Song is the celebration of that release and liberation. Even Eliot was taken in by Yeats's rhetoric and obliged to praise Yeats—albeit fastidiously—for his seeming to grow younger as he grew old.[10] Under the spell of such rhetorical illusions, in which both nature's and the intellect's mechanisms are overridden, the audience is enabled to suspend disbelief and is compensated by a momentary freedom both from moral or ironic scruple and from the morbid, debilitating fear of time.

Once this spell has been cast—in theory, at least—the subjective, erotic world invariably becomes Yeats's appeal from necessity.

POLITICS

> "In our time the destiny of man presents its meaning
> in political terms."—Thomas Mann

> How can I, that girl standing there,
> My attention fix
> On Roman or on Russian
> Or on Spanish politics?
> Yet here's a travelled man that knows
> What he talks about,
> And there's a politician
> That has read and thought,
> And maybe what they say is true
> Of war and war's alarms,
> But O that I were young again
> And held her in my arms!

If we take Yeats at his word, which of course we can't, this moment never took place: "It is not a real incident," he wrote to Dorothy Wellesley,

10. Yeats, *Letters*, 705; W. B. Yeats, *Memoirs [of] W. B. Yeats: Autobiography [and] First Draft Journal*, 127; T. S. Eliot, "The Poetry of W. B. Yeats."

"but a moment of meditation."[11] What is interesting in this context is that he obviously wishes to make it seem actually to have happened and therefore to be taken himself for a haplessly romantic adolescent in an old man's unaccommodating body. The affected self-deprecation—"I am too immature emotionally to care about or to comprehend our political world"—is actually an artful self-aggrandizement, since the larger claim is for the authority of his desire. There *is*, in real life, a sense in which the libido—in its very indiscriminateness, its indifference to individual cases or contexts—is constant and unaging, however imperfectly the body that it inhabits can come to terms with it. So by a rhetorical maneuver, the speaker's identity in "Politics" is disconnected from propriety and from mere historical circumstance and associated instead with a kind of primal eternal verity. The appeal is not from political reality to sexual reality but from real time, as represented by history and politics (and his and the "girl's" ages), to free, subjective time, as represented not only by desire but also by the poem itself, in which pure desire, sequestered, may persist.

When Yeats's John Kinsella grieves for his Mary Moore, he unexpectedly stumbles in his elegiac monologue upon another paradox of the mind-body collaboration. He says: "*What shall I do for pretty girls / Now my old bawd is dead?*" This can only mean that Mary Moore has existed simultaneously in his mind as old and young, as an old bawd and as a pretty girl. Her existing in this indeterminate condition is associated clearly with her having "stories" that are bawdy and transgressive—"not for the priest's ear"—and that therefore "keep the soul of man alive, / Banish age and care." Mary Moore, the "old bawd," is a pretty girl in the world of story, and John Kinsella, by extension, becomes a young man with her. What he considers to be his "soul," which is really his life in desire, is kept alive there. (The "soul" and desire are as often cognate in Yeats as the "soul" and art.) It is like the story in the priest's book, he thinks, about "Eden's Garden," where no man grows old or "girl" grows cold (cold to men's advances, or cold in death). But each of these stories or kinds of stories has a simpler parity in relationship to the other. Kinsella barely knows what the "book" is. His episteme, so to speak, is pagan, and he does know that, in stories, the desire and youth that are subjectively real to him though objectively denied by nature (as by Mary Moore's death) persist unchanged. Stories are a kind of Eden.

11. Yeats, *Letters on Poetry*, 180.

In a similar "story," "The Wild Old Wicked Man," in *his* monologue, can only pity the real girl he is harassing for her not comprehending the transformational magic of words. He therefore bids farewell to her to seek "girls" at the seashore who understand the dark, as he puts it— the subjective libidinal force of life—and have "Bawdy talk for the fishermen." The young girl, naturally, can see the old man only in his material form. He, on the other hand, sees himself alive in a perpetual story: "Because I am mad about women / I am mad about the hills." Stories are narrative transformations of the world in thought, and the libido that lives in stories is the libido that continues to struggle to slip free from nature and time even as nature and time give it—and eventually take away—the only life it can have.

Yeats never seems to have been afflicted with the conventional western compulsion to associate time and death with sin and guilt. This may have been the result of his unorthodox schooling or of his being uncoerced by institutional religious instruction—Protestant or Catholic—or of the liberating influence of his father's cheerful bohemianism, or of any combination of these factors. But he was good at casting out remorse, and he never, in the poems, represents time as a punishment that, because of generic or individual human error, we deserve. He was agreeably unneurotic about guilt or about the association of guilt with the real or symbolic affliction of time. His time, like Dylan Thomas's, is without moral character; it both gives and takes away, and each of those roles in relation to the subjective life is as crucial as the other. Nietzsche exhorted his nineteenth-century European audience to take this simple lesson to heart, and Yeats seems to have done so.

> And now cloud upon cloud rolled over the spirit, until eventually madness preached, "Everything passes away; therefore everything deserves to pass away. And this too is justice, this law of time that it must devour its children." Thus preached madness.[12]

Once time ceases to be thought of as a moral agent, it also ceases to be personal and becomes potentially, instead, a field of play. Once time is not deified—or, really, anthropomorphized—the self is no longer indentured to it by obedience, and the other selves, set free, are at liberty to flourish. Time without moral qualities allows a greater subjective freedom within it. Perhaps we are meant to think of Leo Africanus—

---

12. Nietzsche, *Portable Nietzsche*, 252.

Yeats's "spirit control" in seances from 1912 onward—as symbolizing this freedom of the ego from its own and time's restraints, for Leo after all is, himself, outside of time and of indeterminate aspect, character, and race, standing for not one alter-self but the many that are there in manipulable time, waiting in the wings for the appropriate dialectical moment to struggle forth.

This indeterminate potentiality, the reincarnation of selves, is largely, of course, what *A Vision* is about, but it is helpful not to become too fixated by *A Vision*'s system and, instead, to see Yeats's selves proliferating in the poems in their uncoerced form. It is in the poems, issuing from the same radical understanding of identity formulated in *A Vision*, that the spirit of freedom, rather than of diagram and formula, prevails. This freedom is the affirmation of Nietzsche's eternal recurrence, the free choice to live "this life as you now live it and have lived it . . . innumerable times more."[13]

It is in this spirit that Yeats affirms self-contradiction, allowing antinomies and conflicting points of view to emerge from his thought and claim their own ground rather than being subjugated to a cryptometaphysical authority like consistency or unity of thought. "To hold certain ideas as 'beliefs,'" Richard Ellmann says, "would give them a sort of autonomy; the mind, whose independence Yeats demanded, would become subservient to them, instead of their being necessary expressions of it. Man would be surrounded by a group of mammoth pyramidal conceptions outside his control." Declan Kiberd says that because of his father's influence alone, Yeats was bound to be a skeptic. "He despised the literature of the single point of view, the 'single vision' of a mechanistic psychology which he equated with 'Newton's sleep.' . . . This meant that Yeats could never sponsor one term of an antithesis for long without moving to embrace its opposite; and, even as he sidled away from the original term, he would cast longing glances back in its direction. . . . Ultimately, his guile led him to expose the limitations of either term by fusing both." Kiberd equates this with F. Scott Fitzgerald's famous observation that "the mark of a first-rate mind is its ability to hold opposed ideas while yet retaining the capacity to function."[14]

Skepticism does not seem to be quite the right word for this characteristic in Yeats's case. In the free state of his poetry, it seems more like

13. Nietzsche, *Gay Science*, 273–74.
14. Ellmann, *Identity of Yeats*, 39; Kiberd, *Inventing Ireland*, 317.

an openness to the range of human experience as Ellmann implies—an erotics of the intellect that not only did not restrain his ability to function but also was the only way he *could* function. It seems related directly to what he means when he says that the man of letters, as opposed to the man of politics, dedicates his life and its meaning to "the discovery of reality"—though risk as well as benefit is entailed, since such a mode of understanding is by definition unstable and also isolates those who are driven by it from those—most of the world, Yeats would have thought—who are not.

The poet of "Lapis Lazuli" is contemptuous of "hysterical women" who see war impending and believe that something "must be done" to stop it. All of life is but the same "tragic play" in which we are all actors interpreting a role that has been interpreted many times before by many others. Understanding this helps us to achieve a tragic "gaiety" that transfigures dread. The tragedy cannot grow better or worse; it simply, permanently *is,* and when civilizations fall, they are rebuilt so as to fall again. Aesthetic distance from this spectacle, the poet argues, is the only true consolation—especially, though he does not openly concede this, if one is aged enough not to have a stake in the future. But in "The Man and the Echo"—with no hysterical women to scorn and no postulated audience to parade before—the poet's vision of the individual's relationship to history is quite different:

> All that I have said and done,
> Now that I am old and ill,
> Turns into a question till
> I lie awake night after night
> And never get the answers right.
> Did that play of mine send out
> Certain men the English shot?
> Did words of mine put too great strain
> On that woman's reeling brain?
> Could my spoken words have checked
> That whereby a house lay wrecked?
> And all seems evil until I
> Sleepless would lie down and die.

In these two poems it is as if two separate poetic identities had become two wholly separate persons; no apparent communication has flowed between the two compartmentalized points of view. If what the poet argues in "Lapis Lazuli" is to be taken seriously, then what he broods over in "The Man and the Echo" cannot matter in the long view, and his introspective agonizing itself becomes problematical. The poet in "The Man and the Echo" has not taken to heart the injunctions to transcendence issued by the poet of less than a year earlier. The two are in even less close contact than the self and the soul are in the poem made of a dialogue between those two personae in *The Winding Stair* or than Hic and Ille in "Ego Dominus Tuus," earlier. One sees in this juxtaposition alone why Yeats is so difficult to present steadily in conventional critical discourse—in master readings, for example like this one—except as a turbulence of unresolved contradictions. It is why he is virtually impossible, without misleading editorial selection, to thematize or to fit into any illustrative, historical scheme. Again, think of "The People," where he not only concedes the foolishness of his own reveries and allows Maud Gonne in her own voice to rebuke him for it, but also refuses even to salvage his dignity by taking credit for it: "And yet, because my heart leaped at her words, / I was abashed, and now they come to mind / After nine years, I sink my head abashed." In his own version, like this one, of "negative capability," he imitates by entering life—in its inconsistency and unpredictability—and he makes it his own reconfiguration, which is therefore all the more compelling and credible. This is also what keeps him alive in the imagination of widely divergent readers: if he cannot be adapted to an intellectual scheme he cannot be subsumed into one; in this sense he has outwitted history in yet another way.

A subtler version of this strategy in which different Yeatses flourish may be illustrated by a brief comparison of the two poems for each of his children, Anne and Michael, "A Prayer for My Daughter" and "A Prayer for My Son." This particular pairing of patriarchal personae also illustrates the vagaries of the editorial reconstruction of the Yeats identity. "A Prayer for My Daughter" has become canonical because it nicely fits several different pedagogical schemes for presenting and discussing Yeats (including feminist ones) and because it embodies high seriousness and high style. It appears in anthologies and recurs as a subject of critical discussion. It emerges almost inevitably from the logic of "The Second Coming," as John Unterecker has pointed out, even though the shorter poem was written later and positioned to precede this longer, more personal one. "A Prayer for My Daughter" is grandiose, self-absorbed, apocalyptic, and wistfully retrograde. It is also virtually a paradigm of the human imagination's encounter with the reductiveness of history and nature, of rhetorical, optative incantation opposing itself to the "murderous innocence of the sea." It is not surprising, therefore, that the companion poem has suffered neglect (it does not even appear in Rosenthal's *Selected Poems*). "A Prayer for My Son" might have been written by any number of Christian poets of the seventeenth century or of the twentieth (by Auden, for instance, *mutatis mutandis*); but we do not expect it from Yeats:

> Bid a strong ghost stand at the head
> That my Michael may sleep sound,
> Nor cry, nor turn in the bed
> Till his morning meal come round;
> And may departing twilight keep
> All dread afar till morning's back,
> That his mother may not lack
> Her fill of sleep.
>
> Bid the ghost have sword in fist:
> Some there are, for I avow
> Such devilish things exist,
> Who have planned his murder, for they know
> Of some most haughty deed or thought
> That waits upon his future days,
> And would through hatred of the bays
> Bring that to nought.
>
> Though You can fashion everything
> From nothing every day, and teach
> The morning stars to sing,
> You have lacked articulate speech
> To tell Your simplest want, and known,
> Wailing upon a woman's knee,
> All of that worst ignominy
> Of flesh and bone;
>
> And when through all the town there ran
> The servants of Your enemy,
> A woman and a man,
> Unless the Holy Writings lie,

Hurried through the smooth and rough
And through the fertile and waste,
Protecting, till the danger past,
With human love.

The lyric is simple and complex at the same time, chastened in its style, complicated in its representation of human destiny. The conceit of the devotional strategy wherein God is gently reminded of his own mortal incarnation as the infant Jesus and is called upon to repay with supernatural love and protection the human love that protected him, is witty, tender, and irreverent. The infant Michael is even immodestly compared to the infant Jesus on the grounds that great things would be expected of both. But there is also a formal, traditional quality in the poem's conception and execution that is as much a part of its point as the content itself: bringing Michael within the shelter of tradition—and into poetry—is an added protection. Devotional humility is not a trait that automatically springs to mind when we think of Yeats, but he comes as close to it here as he can, allowing for the slightly patrician tone in addressing his (albeit pro tem) savior. Since Yeats was certainly not in any conventional sense a Christian believer, it seems obvious—from the simple fact of this poem's existence—that he was no more likely to be restrained by his own conventions than he was by anyone else's.

Despite the systematic, intelligent attention that has been devoted to Yeats's theory of masks, it is still easy to underestimate his capacity for spontaneous self-regeneration. And because of its professional interest in unity (a metaphysical principle finally posing as an aesthetic one), academic criticism has failed to appreciate and acknowledge the degree, for Yeats, to which unity itself was coercive. As readers, once absorbed into Yeats's ideologically uncoercive world, we take it for granted that he identifies both with reckless vagrants such as Red Hanrahan or Crazy Jane, on the one hand, and, on the other, with ancestral families who dwell where "all's accustomed, ceremonious," where "traditional sanctity and loveliness" prevail against those who "shift about . . . / Like some poor Arab tribesman and his tent." To be reborn as an idea is to become something "intended, complete" in the respect that *each poem* stylizes and overcomes the incoherence of daily life. But in being reborn *recurrently* as an expression of *different* ideas, from one poem to the next, one becomes complete in the sense of becoming a plenitude, of not remaining partial or bounded, striving to respond to a perceived richness of the possibilities of being.

A quirky version of this enterprise is worked out in Yeats's remarkable correspondence with Lady Dorothy Wellesley. When he wishes to posture as manly—as well he might given the difference between his and Lady Dorothy's ages—he deprecates his own *earlier* poetry as "womanish" and "*un*manly." Yet he confides to her in a different context—reborn, so to speak, as another idea—that her influence upon him and her being lesbian has been to draw out the womanly side of his nature, and he uninhibitedly expresses admiration for the boyishness of her manner and figure.

> What makes your work so good is the masculine element allied to much feminine charm—your lines have the magnificent swing of your boyish body.... Have you noticed that the Greek androginous [*sic*] statue is always the woman in man, never the man in woman? It was made for men who loved men first.[15]

The barely subdued erotic tone of the correspondence between these two is heightened by the tentative polymorphousness of it and by Yeats's willingness to consider, under the influence of yet another intimate friendship—and from the inside out rather than abstractly—the fluidness of sexual identity and the artificiality of gender roles in their form as social practice.

As we have seen, it is in such erogenous zones of the psyche that the poet's interest in self-invention is most animated and complex, and that oppositions are played out and often left unreconciled. "Michael Robartes and the Dancer," for example, with its jovial gender bias on display, seems plain enough as an autonomous rhetorical text; but soon afterwards it is contradicted by a response in "The Hero, the Girl, and the Fool." Robartes argues with his lover that when a knight slays a dragon for a lady he has a right to expect the lady to remain what she seems to be.

> bear in mind your lover's wage
> Is what your looking-glass can show,
> And that he will turn green with rage
> At all that is not pictured there.

15. Yeats, *Letters on Poetry*, 125.

It follows that women must not be too learned lest they also grow too complex, that truly blessed souls are not "composite."

> And that all beautiful women may
> Live in uncomposite blessedness
> And lead us to the like—if they
> Will banish every thought.

If the knight is going to go to the trouble to slay dragons, in short, the lady can at least oblige him by being the proper sort to reflect back to him his own attractive heroism. This particular lady, unimpressed, says simply: "They say such different things at school." Her skepticism keeps the issue here alive and keeps the poem unclosed, so that, in effect, *she* may stay alive for a return engagement. That occasion comes about in the next volume, *The Tower*, in "The Hero, the Girl, and the Fool":

> *The Girl.* I rage at my own image in the glass
> That's so unlike myself that when you praise it
> It is as though you praised another, or even
>
> Mocked me with praise of my mere opposite;
> And when I wake towards morn I dread myself,
> For the heart cries that what deception wins
> Cruelty must keep; therefore be warned and go
> If you have seen that image and not the woman.

She puts this case for the dichotomy between outer and inner being so sensibly and bluntly that the Hero (Michael Robartes here with no name) has had the tables turned and is obliged to concede the logic of her interest in honesty, compared to his previous inclination toward courtly affectation and flattery. He now admits, "I have raged at my own strength because you have loved it." And she points out that if he is no more Strength, in reality, than she is Beauty, then they are both thwarted in a crisis of misunderstanding. The two partners are compelled by their own logic to agree that, as the eavesdropping Fool will put it here, a "faithful love" is therefore impossible in life, and that, as the girl expresses it, "only God has loved us for ourselves." The grim tone of this exchange, especially as it resonates with the faux naïveté of "Michael Robartes and the Dancer," suggests that the poem has been carried by the stages of its own arguments to the edge of an agnostic fatalism. Reflection and honest male-female exchange show them that all personality is artificial, and love is left—as earlier yet in "The Mask"—to have reference only to the invented or socially constructed other and not to the authentic, composite one. It may of course be Yeats's prematurely post-structuralist point that there *is* no reality of the self to be got through to, and that this belief produced, ironically, his decidedly unmodern commitment to a wholly ceremonial and performative concept of heterosexual love. When only God can know us for ourselves, only God can love us for ourselves, and what remains in mere time is passionate but, in the end, necessarily artificial erotic theater.

It may also be argued to follow from this point that Yeats's poems, as they reproduce identities, are meant to be collectively what God alone would see, and they therefore counter the normalizing, reductive social sanction with an existentially open-ended one; and that for this reason, in Yeats's mature reflective work, even small episodes resonate deeply in the genealogical context created by the others. In the *Michael Robartes and the Dancer* volume, for instance, the small, ingratiating poem "Under Saturn" would seem unrelated to the two lovers' dialogue poems, but read in their context it clearly continues to explore and complicate the issue of how social and subjective identity mysteriously remain both intertwined and discontinuous.

> Do not because this day I have grown saturnine
> Imagine that lost love, inseparable from my thought
> Because I have no other youth, can make me pine;
> For how should I forget the wisdom that you brought,
> The comfort that you made? Although my wits have gone
> On a fantastic ride, my horse's flanks are spurred
> By childish memories of an old cross Pollexfen,
> And of a Middleton, whose name you never heard,
> And of a red-haired Yeats whose looks, although he died
> Before my time, seem like a vivid memory.
> You heard that labouring man who had served my people. He said
> Upon the open road, near to the Sligo quay—
> No, no, not said, but cried it out—"You have come again,
> And surely after twenty years it was time to come."
> I am thinking of a child's vow sworn in vain
> Never to leave that valley his fathers called their home.

Here again is the intimation that comes forward of roads not taken, of other lives to have been lived and therefore yet to *be* lived, and of other selves waiting to be called forth when their time comes. Yeats's own past, as represented in this poem, for instance, is made to seem alive with other modes of being, as if its being in the past were more of an odd, exasperating circumstance than an irrevocability. But, of course, even here the issue is more complicated than that. We may assume that the person addressed in "Under Saturn" is Mrs. Yeats, and that the first three lines have reference to a specific (and not frivolous) anxiety of hers of the sort referred to in the poem that precedes this one ("An Image from a Past Life"). His disavowal of claims upon his memory other than that of his child's vow in Sligo may therefore be read as a deliberate repudiation of the fictional self associated in his poems with Maud Gonne or Olivia Shakespear. The ghostly image that Mrs. Yeats has seen in "An Image from a Past Life" is, nicely, not one that Yeats himself any longer sees, though she—the apparition—is remarkably like a projection of Yeats's own erotic dream, of her "arrogant loveliness" loosening "out a tress / Among the starry eddies of her hair / Upon the paleness of a finger." And of course she will never go away, though the Yeats who invented her—who existed only in relation to her in his dream of himself—soon will (no longer wishing to be, or being unable to be the uncomposite knight who slays dragons). In "Under Saturn," the poet tactfully does not claim that lost love and youth are not inseparable from his thought, only that they can no longer make him pine. Here, instead, he is soberly contemplating the aura projected from his male lineage, but Mrs. Yeats is *in*cluded on that account—as the "sweetheart from another life" could not have been—because of the very shrewdness that makes her probe his thoughts and because of the comfort she has made for him and, of course, because of his thoughts of what is now meant by "home." The points of reference in three different periods of time call attention to the effect of Mrs. Yeats's influence having created yet another Yeats who is yet all of the others still.

By the time of *The Tower*, which is the point in the poet's metanarrative at which time begins to be most vividly associated with mortality, a potential for madness has become openly associated in the poems with the very freedom of identity that the poems themselves enable. This outcome is incipient in any such condition of freedom, obviously, and Yeats not only does not fail to acknowledge it, but also seems deliberately to carry his subject forward to that edge. The result of such thought is that we come upon the possibility that truth itself, by ordinary idealist standards of understanding, is mad, or seems like madness when perceived or lived in this disessentializing way from the inside out. This will become clearer in the next volume, when "Crazy Jane" and "Tom the Lunatic" separate themselves out, so to speak, and become freestanding representations of a kind of multiple personality disorder. It is clear enough, meanwhile, in "Owen Aherne and His Dancers," that one way the poet has approached understanding this madness is by failing to follow the safe and sane course in love, which means, in effect, by failing to *be* what, to the outer world, he seems to be or should be.

> I can exchange opinion with any neighbouring mind,
> I have as healthy flesh and blood as any rhymer's had,
> But O! my Heart could bear no more when the upland caught the wind;
> I ran, I ran, from my love's side because my Heart went mad.

The first half of the poem, by comparison with the second half, is an imitation of madness itself in the very act of depicting and decrying that madness; it exhibits a loss of rational control in representing the loss of control.

> The south wind brought it longing, and the east wind despair,
> The west wind made it pitiful, and the north wind afraid.
> It feared to give its love a hurt with all the tempest there;
> It feared the hurt that she could give and therefore it went mad.

The unreasonableness of this surrender of volition, its garbled and aberrant fatalism, is understood in the poem's second half when, ironically, the heart itself turns out to be the voice of common sense and sanity.

> "You have called me mad," it said,
> "Because I made you turn away and run from the young child;
> How could she mate with fifty years that was so wildly bred?
> Let the cage bird and the cage bird mate and the wild bird mate in the wild."

And the heart is the spokesman for sanity, which is addressed at the end as a "murderer." This judgment is not altogether without basis, for sanity does subjugate other selves. The two selves here speak for two different truths and two different modes of existing that are incompatible from the outset. It is the mad self that remains—through no fault of its own—hidden away.

"Speak all your mind," my Heart sang out, "speak all your mind; who cares,
Now that your tongue cannot persuade the child till she mistake
Her childish gratitude for love and match your fifty years?"

Indeed, it becomes an increasingly visible irony in the last decade of Yeats's career that the privileged free play of poetic becoming serves also to make it clear, by comparison, how curtailed identity must be in the monitored environment of real life (where in this case, for example, the "girl" is Iseult Gonne, and the context is the poet's impending marriage to Georgie Hyde Lees), and how, insofar as aging, especially, is concerned, nature and biological process collaborate in that restraint. The girl in "The Wild Old Wicked Man" is indifferent to the old man's rhetoric because she lives in a different story from his and in a story that, unluckily for him, is commonly assumed to be not only the proper story to live in but also the *true* one. The problem from the old man's point of view is not so much that the culture is inflexible as it is that it is unimaginative and unable to be free to invent and live out as many versions of itself as an individual can in the life of the mind. (This full release of identity, rather than patriotic sacrifice with its associated restraints, is the true subject of poems like "September, 1913," where the wildness of the "wild geese" is incomprehensible to the polity of pious mercantilism.) The liberated intensities of personality generate what seems like madness from a normalized perspective, but they may remain under control in the privileged space of poetry, which is therefore plausibly an alternative space and a counterworld.

When the privileged madness of the interior life encounters either a coercive, consensus version of the world or the opposition of mere unappeasable nature, a different form of madness ensues that results from the thwarting of desire. To the degree that the will and the inner life have been creative and spacious to begin with, the constraint and contradiction of it will be of greater violence. This is the theme of Crazy Jane's poems, and her dispute with the Bishop is the clearest allegorical representation of the issues. In her isolation, she not only speaks for Yeats but *is* the Yeats of the inner life that Yeats, in the public world, would not be able to be. The old man who speaks in "A Man Young and Old," Crazy Jane's kinsman in spirit, himself bewitched by the moon and inconsolable, laughs not *at* the characters of old Madge and

Peter in his story but *for* them, because of their uncompromised obedience to the dream of their own life that has driven them mad:

> Laughter not time destroyed my voice
> And put that crack in it,
> And when the moon's pot-bellied
> I get a laughing fit,
> For that old Madge comes down the lane,
> A stone upon her breast,
> And a cloak wrapped about the stone,
> And she can get no rest
> With singing hush and hush-a-bye;
> She that has been wild
> And barren as a breaking wave
> Thinks that the stone's a child.
>
> And Peter that had great affairs
> And was a pushing man
> Shrieks, "I am King of the Peacocks,"
> And perches on a stone;
> And then I laugh till tears run down
> And the heart thumps at my side,
> Remembering that her shriek was love
> And that he shrieks from pride.

And since they are but individual expressions of his and everyone's generalized desire—as they age in Yeats's poetry, the division between individuals becomes less and less distinct—he can absorb their identities into his own. He can become the man and the woman—*if* he could be transported to some atemporal dimension where only the heart and mind rule our reality.

> O bid me mount and sail up there
> Amid the cloudy wrack,
> For Peg and Meg and Paris' love
> That had so straight a back,
> Are gone away, and some that stay
> Have changed their silk for sack.
>
> Were I but there and none to hear
> I'd have a peacock cry,
> For that is natural to a man

That lives in memory,
Being all alone I'd nurse a stone
And sing it lullaby.

The stone that Madge nurses is a version of the empty cup that the man young and old finds:

A crazy man that found a cup,
When all but dead of thirst,
Hardly dared to wet his mouth
Imagining, moon-accursed,
That another mouthful
And his beating heart would burst.
October last I found it too
But found it dry as bone,
And for that reason am I crazed
And my sleep is gone.

Both the cup and the stone are versions of the thorn tree that he and Madge sit beneath to recall old lovers and that suddenly blooms miraculously when brought under the spell of remembered and cherished passion. What is given, in other words, is minimal—a stone, a thorn bush, an empty cup—and what is given in age is only the lowest common denominator of what all of human existence is given to begin with, represented, as it were, by the moon in its unromanticized and merely geological aspect. To make believe that the stone is a child or that the moon is a sailing ship is a form of madness, but it is also a strangely self-destructive wisdom that all of Yeats's personae are at some level compelled to share. The real unmediated world is always just on the other side of their formalizing strategies for evading it. The man young and old grown, suddenly, merely old, concedes the tragic scope of this irony at the end:

Endure what life God gives and ask no longer span;
Cease to remember the delights of youth, travel-wearied aged man;
Delight becomes death-longing if all longing else be vain.

In "Crazy Jane on the Mountain," when Crazy Jane thinks of the murder of the czar and his family, cousins of kings, and of the cruel banality of the coming times, her vision of human possibility abruptly ricochets from the bizarre hallucination of an Irish myth to the finally un-transformable condition of fact:

> There in a two-horsed carriage
> That on two wheels ran
> Great-bladdered Emer sat,
> Her violent man
> Cuchulain sat at her side;
> Thereupon,
> Propped upon my two knees,
> I kissed a stone;
> I lay stretched out in the dirt
> And I cried tears down.

The difference she can see—now that she is old rather than young—is not between the way things used to be and the way they are now, but between the romantically intensified way she has imagined the world to be and the way, unresponding, it always already is.

In "All Souls' Night," which draws *A Vision's* public exposition to a suddenly private closure, Yeats moves his theme of identity in relation-ships away from the world and human discourse altogether into some-thing like a vacuum of reverie. This would be a madness, too, if it were disclosed to the world outside of poems, as he freely acknowledges by calling forth as his audience and eccentric companions in solitude the ghosts of William Thomas Horton, Florence Emery, and Mac Gregor Mathers—all of whom "loved strange thought" and on that account were baffled and maddened by the unstrangeness of the normal world. On their behalf, he imagines a purgation so complete that if they return as ghosts, their "element is so fine / Being sharpened by... death" that they "drink from the wine-breath / While our gross palates drink from the whole wine." For himself in this moment, he wishes a mind isolated wholly from the world, wound in its own pondering "[a]s mummies in the mummy-cloth are wound." The eeriness of this image—though not an uncommon one for Yeats—allows the deep intensity of think-ing to be like a death to the world. This is an odd role for a poet to as-sume, whose trade, after all, is words, and especially coming at the end of a prolonged expository presentation to the world, in *A Vision,* of his entire philosophy of history. But the mummy truths are not for us to hear; they are the mind's own, uncompromised by the mediation of our need to understand: "Such thought, that in it bound / I need no other thing." So we never learn what the mummy truths are. Horton, Florence Emery, Mathers, Yeats—both "the damned who have howled away their hearts" and the blessed who dance—are all together in one place, and we are together in another, identified by our very interest in understanding as trespassers in the secret interior world. Yeats has closed readers out before in this same mood. When "Ille" in "Ego Dominus Tuus" thinks of communion with the mysterious other deep within himself, that other being will, he thinks:

> ...disclose
> All that I seek; and whisper it as though
> He were afraid the birds, who cry aloud
> Their momentary cries before it is dawn,
> Would carry it away to blasphemous men.

The point here is that full self-presence must remain inviolate to be spared the anxiety of the encounter with the world, but of course this also means that it must remain immured. The irony of this is revealing. By declaring, in "All Souls' Night," what it is that he has withheld, the poet indirectly calls attention to the fact that all of the other identities he has generated have been a withholding as well. After all of those rebirths, *because* of their prodigality, there is still no one, irreducible entity there—no man, in other words, who assumes masks, but just masks.

It was partly in the interest of this complex project of self-invention that Yeats was so committed to high art. High art sanctifies a kind of *droit de seigneur* in such existential ventures. Merely ordinary men and women, in his patrician view, could *only* be ordinary and thus hopelessly limited and bounded, mere caricatures of themselves. The various characters from various walks of life that Yeats speaks through all have in common a tendency to present their particular feelings and situations as though they were eternal verities. That is one of the ways we know that Yeats is in them. They would all, rich or poor, despise "the sort now growing up / All out of shape from toe to top." However, those who are "all out of shape" don't simply happen to be that way: they are unformed, as Yeats sees it, because they do not think of themselves as eternal verities, do not appropriate their own higher nature or accept the challenge of being reborn as ideas: "[T]he average man is average because he has not attained to freedom."[16] If Yeats could not

16. Yeats, *Explorations*, 168.

be an aristocrat socially, he eagerly became one existentially. He then struggled to have it both ways by remaining patrician in a democratic country he made of his own poems, ruling over it as a kind of unseen benevolent despot. The most vivid experiences in Yeats's poems are of identities unfolding through permutations that could be ended finally only by death. The process seems to have remained mysterious even to him, but it had to be presented formally as a part of a larger, coherent, but invisible plan. It was, in a sense, the act of rhetoric alone that brought these ghosts to life, as if the solitary activity of writing poetry truly were a séance, and as if the very solitariness of that activity were what made it possible to bring to realization what in the public world would be divided against itself, curtailed, or misunderstood. Poetry, in other words, would be the only condition under which the formation and reformation of identities could safely proceed. The poet, as he said, thus "becomes a part of his own phantasmagoria, and we adore him because nature has grown intelligible, and by so doing a part of our creative power."

5

Six Poems

———— ❧ ————

THE TWO shepherds whose songs (1885, 1886) open the first volume of what would become Yeats's *Collected Poems* exist, unlike Milton's or Virgil's, in a vacuum. They have no spatial or historical context, and for that reason it is all the more obvious that they are not simply mirror images of each other as the titles imply—they are different projections of a single state of mind. The second shepherd is ruled by sorrow, and the first is holding sorrow at bay. The one is the shadow of the other in that he lives the nightmare of the failure of belief. He is not sad because he is alienated from the world; he is alienated from the world because he is sad, because he does not have the self-assurance to extend his own identity into that of nature.

The Sad Shepherd

There was a man whom Sorrow named his friend,
And he, of his high comrade Sorrow dreaming,
Went walking with slow steps along the gleaming
And humming sands, where windy surges wend:
And he called loudly to the stars to bend
From their pale thrones and comfort him, but they
Among themselves laugh on and sing alway:
And then the man whom Sorrow named his friend
Cried out, *Dim Sea, hear my most piteous story!*
The sea swept on and cried her old cry still,
Rolling along in dreams from hill to hill.
He fled the persecution of her glory
And, in a far-off, gentle valley stopping,
Cried all his story to the dewdrops glistening.
But naught they heard, for they are always listening,
The dewdrops, for the sound of their own dropping.

And then the man whom Sorrow named his friend
Sought once again the shore, and found a shell,
And thought, *I will my heavy story tell*
Till my own words, re-echoing, shall send
Their sadness through a hollow, pearly heart;
And my own tale again for me shall sing,
And my own whispering words be comforting,
And lo! my ancient burden may depart.
Then he sang softly nigh the pearly rim;
But the sad dweller by the sea-ways lone
Changed all he sang to inarticulate moan
Among her wildering whirls, forgetting him.

This is an early version of a theme Yeats addressed more than a few times in his life but never—for all the poem's quaintness—as starkly. It is the idealist dilemma of "Dejection: An Ode." Nature cannot restore us to joy because the sources of our feeling are "within," and nature cannot be both itself and ourselves at the same time. Dejection, or sorrow, ensures isolation, since it inhibits the power to override this realization. The power is called "creative" power by Coleridge, and creative power, in this context (if not in all contexts), is the same as Nietzsche's will to illusion. It is that "poetics of will" that the sad shepherd cannot attain.[1] He knows what to wish for, and his imagination achieves the first conventional step: to endow nature with human or, at any rate, sentient, attributes. The sands hum, the stars laugh and sing, the sea cries, the dewdrops listen. But he cannot go beyond that and turn nature—or, say, reality—to his own purpose. And it gets worse: the ironic effect of his conscious attempt is to have the real truth flung back to him in the form of the shell's inarticulate moan. No sooner has his song gone out into the inhuman world—where, in a sense, the transcendent ego should prefer to be, since there it has free range—than it becomes "wildered" and then nothing, and he himself is forgotten. Moreover, nature's self-contained and self-sustaining harmony is disclosed to be unintelligible in human terms. The sad shepherd has wished at the least to have re-expressed to him his own sorrow, for then he could have the consolation of being one with the spirit of things and in this process have his otherwise merely private grief reconstituted as a principle. But he is as alone and as hollow as the shell, an echo

1. Lentricchia, *Gaiety of Language*, 60.

chamber of his own feelings, until he sings out into the world where song is abruptly deconstructed. As things work out, this will be a lesson well learned. Songs are heard by human listeners, not by dewdrops, and this implies association with a community of believers in the necessity of human meaning.

The happy shepherd has a sketchy and agreeably retrograde version of this community to address and exhort, and that, no doubt, is an effect of his being happy—that and his being able to persuade himself that "words alone are certain good":

The Song of the Happy Shepherd

The woods of Arcady are dead,
And over is their antique joy;
Of old the world on dreaming fed;
Grey Truth is now her painted toy;
Yet still she turns her restless head:
But O, sick children of the world,
Of all the many changing things
In dreary dancing past us whirled,
To the cracked tune that Chronos sings,
Words alone are certain good.
Where are now the warring kings,
Word be-mockers?—By the Rood,
Where are now the warring kings?
An idle word is now their glory,
By the stammering schoolboy said,
Reading some entangled story:
The kings of the old time are dead;
The wandering earth herself may be
Only a sudden flaming word,
In clanging space a moment heard,
Troubling the endless reverie.

Then nowise worship dusty deeds,
Nor seek, for this is also sooth,
To hunger fiercely after truth,
Lest all thy toiling only breeds
New dreams, new dreams; there is no truth
Saving in thine own heart. Seek, then,
No learning from the starry men,

Who follow with the optic glass
The whirling ways of stars that pass—
Seek, then, for this is also sooth,
No word of theirs—the cold star-bane
Has cloven and rent their hearts in twain,
And dead is all their human truth.
Go gather by the humming sea
Some twisted, echo-harbouring shell,
And to its lips thy story tell,
And they thy comforters will be,
Rewording in melodious guile
Thy fretful words a little while,
Till they shall singing fade in ruth
And die a pearly brotherhood;
For words alone are certain good:
Sing, then, for this is also sooth.

I must be gone: there is a grave
Where daffodil and lily wave,
And I would please the hapless faun,
Buried under the sleepy ground,
With mirthful songs before the dawn.
His shouting days with mirth were crowned;
And still I dream he treads the lawn,
Walking ghostly in the dew,
Pierced by my glad singing through,
My songs of old earth's dreamy youth:
But ah! she dreams not now; dream thou!
For fair are poppies on the brow:
Dream, dream, for this is also sooth.

The happy shepherd is able to persuade himself that "words alone are certain good" because he is able to transcend "Grey Truth" and the tune that Chronos sings, history itself, evolving into what passes in this setting for modern time. By "Grey Truth" he does not mean a certain kind of truth but Truth, period, whatever is true to the positivist's material world, gray by definition, and in its form as science (the "starry men" with their "optic glass") preemptive of all new dreams, as opposed to those of an ahistorical reverie. Not only, also, are the men of action, the warring kings, rejected; they in turn are associated with the earth itself, the site of action, which is made to seem both an accident and an idea only, an irrelevance in the silent meditation of eternity. The kings had mocked words, and now words mock them and contain all that is left of them; and the earth itself, no longer magically sentient, has become truth as well and, no longer dreaming, must have its dreams dreamed for it. The only meaning is subjective, the truth of "thine own heart." Nothing is important but release, reverie, and intellectual narcosis. Objective reality is admitted to exist, but it is simply rejected. This much of the poem is an unabashed symbolist manifesto, perhaps worked out of Shelley, as Harold Bloom says, but precocious all the same in 1885, considering the way it resonates with the poem it is paired with, and before *symbolisme* even on the continent had become an institution.

The experience of the sad shepherd proves the happy shepherd's point. One broods upon the truth only at the peril of having one's illusions dispersed and with them the untroubled continuity with life that is the pastoral dream. He enjoins the sick children of the world to make song of their sorrow echoed in the shell until the words lose their edge of grief in aesthetic form, though they then die. But the happy shepherd does not do this himself. He undertakes, only half believing, to revive the buried faun, to restore the Arcady and its antique joy that he has already pronounced to be dead and past. This is more of a mission than the mere sublimating of grief in song. So he has not really rejected time at all, nor community, as the sad shepherd appears to have done. His dream is of an ideal of human life, not of a future but of the old utopia restored to the present. His universe turns out to be not, as Harold Bloom says, a purely verbal one but one that implies discourse, words in action in a society among implied hearers where, if anywhere, words may have value, where allied with dance and music they are the surviving trace of the mystic human. The happy shepherd seems to have distinguished himself from the "sick children of the world." And just as the sad shepherd's fate has proved the happy shepherd's point about needing to believe in dreams and words, the happy shepherd has indirectly proved the sad shepherd's about words in isolation. Words alone are "certain good" only if they can be imagined, however hopelessly, to give dreams themselves human utility. The shell is not of much use, it turns out, in either poem, but dreaming in the first poem has not yet, as it threatens to, taken leave of the world.

If all of this seems unreasonably convoluted, it is because Yeats had envisioned all at once, before he was mature enough to have reason to realize it, the basic configuration of issues that would pervade the poems he wrote for the rest of his life. Arcady, obviously, will reappear in many forms, along with the theme of Grey Truth as a materialist (and even colonialist) oppression. Associated with these two themes is the argument about the virtue of words, as representation or as music, as means of engaging with or escaping from experience. The happy shepherd's need to envision some sort of society, however stylized and impractical, motivated Yeats's romantic politics and his belief in art's role as a communal act. At the end of "Lapis Lazuli," there are, after all, three men with glittering eyes, not one, who are revived by the music as together they stare down upon the "tragic scene." The question that haunts both shepherd poems, finally, is whether there is any meaning in the world *but* human meaning, and the answer in each poem, in a different form, is no. That is why there is only Arcady in words or nothing.

In "The Two Trees" (1892), the themes of the two shepherd poems are eroticized, and their associated declarations grow plainer and bolder.

> Beloved, gaze in thine own heart,
> The holy tree is growing there;
> From joy the holy branches start,
> And all the trembling flowers they bear.
> The changing colours of its fruit
> Have dowered the stars with merry light;
> The surety of its hidden root
> Has planted quiet in the night;
> The shaking of its leafy head
> Has given the waves their melody,
> And made my lips and music wed,
> Murmuring a wizard song for thee.
> There the Loves a circle go,
> The flaming circle of our days,
> Gyring, spiring to and fro
> In those great ignorant leafy ways;
> Remembering all that shaken hair
> And how the wingèd sandals dart,
> Thine eyes grow full of tender care:
> Beloved, gaze in thine own heart.
>
> Gaze no more in the bitter glass
> The demons, with their subtle guile,
> Lift up before us when they pass,
> Or only gaze a little while;

For there a fatal image grows
That the stormy night receives,
Roots half hidden under snows,
Broken boughs and blackened leaves.
For all things turn to barrenness
In the dim glass the demons hold,
The glass of outer weariness,
Made when God slept in times of old.
There, through the broken branches, go
The ravens of unresting thought;
Flying, crying, to and fro,
Cruel claw and hungry throat,
Or else they stand and sniff the wind,
And shake their ragged wings; alas!
Thy tender eyes grow all unkind:
Gaze no more in the bitter glass.

Once a lover has entered the scene of the shepherd, Arcady is reimagined and revived within a more intimate composition, and speech and song take on the role of ensuring its sustained life. This Arcady exists within the encompassing zone of Grey Truth, and the zone of Grey Truth impinges upon consciousness because it is visible—because, in other words, neither of these lovers is a shepherd any longer. Yeats never states his case for the authority of consciousness, or, poetically, for the truth of the heart, more plainly than he has here. Joy is a condition of the inner life alone. Not only is it not won from outward forms, as Coleridge had concluded, it is threatened by outward forms, by the truth that is external to the self and the poem. God is within the self as well. God is what is good, and what is good is God. Obedience to the inner reality thus receives divine sanction. Indeed, one must believe in something like this divine sanction in order not to be persuaded by reason to gaze instead into the bitter glass. In the reflection of the bitter glass, one sees not only the outer world but also oneself *in* the outer world, an extension of it, no longer a pure, creating, and self-generating subject but an object in time and materialized space—Grey Truth. Since this is a truth that these lovers cannot but be exposed to, being conscious and aware in spite of themselves, it is a truth that thought must be powerfully restrained from turning toward—and thought, by its nature, is unresting, like the ravens, sniffing the wind. "Man's life is thought,"

Yeats will say later in "Meru," and it cannot help eroding all stable positions, including stable subject positions. Consciousness sows the seeds of its own self-deconstruction and can only fantasize equilibrium. For this reason, the appeal of the first state in "The Two Trees" is precisely its Blakean childishness—something to be "remembered"—and, for all its busy motion, a kind of stasis. The verbs do not seem really to do anything except serve as connectives between charmed objects. Even at that, the connections they do make fall just short of intelligibility, as in a dream: the fruit and blossoms dower the stars with light, the sturdy root plants quiet in the night, the blowing leaves give the waves their melody, and so on. At work here is a naive synaesthesia and an indeterminate logic of cause and effect that is reminiscent of the return to childhood in part 1 of Eliot's "Burnt Norton."

The world reflected in the bitter glass is without doubt that of a fall into knowledge, but that fall is from a state not of pure but of willed innocence, a condition that is susceptible to subversion at every moment by, so to speak, the return of the repressed. This unproductive dialectic is a condition of the ordinary life, of course, as well as of the poem's. And one can see how the reality of the bitter glass would inhibit love and that love, as it always is in Yeats, on the other hand, is an agent against despair. For love must believe in itself for its animating visions to flourish. (The opposite of what Yeats is thinking of here would be nineteenth-century naturalism.) "The Two Trees" is therefore about the poet and his role, as well, since he is the creative agent of this dreamed life and of the element of artifice that makes love possible; he is even the maker of that life. This is what his "wizard song" is for—an enchantment that will lure his beloved into the "flaming circle"—like the wall of flame in which Dante encloses Eden. It achieves that by causing her to remember the presumably enchanted quality of childhood. Since this innocent condition is reinstated but also generated by the poet, it is by definition not public, and it is all the more valued for its shared intimacy and, of course, for its being its own invention. The task of "wizard song" is to sustain both illusion and the sanctity of intimacy, since intimacy by its nature ensures shutting out the world—as represented, that is, in the second part of "The Two Trees."

The poem becomes most interesting, however, at the point where the poet's task begins to seem futile. The realm of the bitter glass is presented so as to seem vaguely three-dimensional in a way that the happy realm of the heart is not. It has depth of field where the other is flat-surfaced. The gaze is drawn to it and away from the other as naturally as one reads toward it in the narrative time of the poem. So when it is clear at the end of the poem that the wizard song has failed— "alas! / Thy tender eyes grow all unkind"—it seems natural that it should have done so. Only two choices have been presented, and given a simple choice between, so to speak, the narcissism of the mirror stage of childhood and the rule of the law, of the symbolic order, the maturing personality is teleologically if not morally coerced to choose the latter. Certainly it is the choice that Yeats himself made in the long run, so his despair at the end here may be sincere, but it cannot be uncomprehending. This little parable is essentially the same as that of "The Stolen Child" but with the ending reversed, and, characteristically, we are meant to understand each of these endings as unhappy ones. "The Two Trees," spoken as if from within the flaming circle, seems to want to predicate that one's identity, and even Being itself, is fictitious and therefore determined by choice. The emphasis on what the beloved gazes upon implies a decisive advantage, as well, to averting the gaze, although as in the real world, averting the gaze does not make what had been gazed upon go away.

In effect, the poet in "The Two Trees" wishes to persuade us and the beloved that what we see is what we get, but we do not get to see very much here, and that, in itself, is the effect of a binary reduction of the scope and the real complexity of experience. The self-declaring artificiality of the poem's style and structure underscores this effect by making artifice and fictionalizing a prominent aspect of its action as well as subject: the poem is acting out what it is speaking of. Moreover, each of these limitations upon what we are allowed to see, and of the idiom that mediates it, implicitly concedes a distrust of the real authority of the mature imagination and its creation, love, by suggesting that they can only flourish under highly specialized circumstances in which the material it works upon is not irresistibly threatening or harsh. Even the mirroredness of the model is restricting, leaving no room for a tertium quid and representing indirectly a mind restrained by its own dualistic predispositions. Essentially, "The Two Trees" is an early dialogue poem in which the tragic view is decisive. This means that in the world that is not under the mind's control nature, time, truth, and death prevail. They prevail in two ways: by denying the poet the control he seeks over reality, and by denying him control over the mind and heart of the person to whom he appeals.

Knowledgeable commentators—Ellmann, Bloom, Parkinson, and Kermode, preeminently—have identified "The Two Trees" with sources in Blake (both philosophical and iconic) and in the Kabbalah. It is common, also, to argue that since the beloved is obviously Maud Gonne, it must be that what the second tree symbolizes is abstraction and politics and other perils associated with commitment to the public realm. But none of this is self-evident in the poem that we have, however vividly it may have been in Yeats's head at the time and however relevant it may be to certain kinds of presentations of the poem. The poem is plainer than that. It is about a contest between two different ways of looking at the world—one that appropriates, internalizes, and stylizes, and the other that faces the cold truths of the laws of time and nature without mediation. It may indeed imply a little story about Yeats and Maud Gonne, but irreducibly it is a paradigm of consciousness itself—of anyone's consciousness—and, on a broadly simplified scale, the accommodations that consciousness is compelled to make in its moment-to-moment negotiations with the exterior world.

In *The Identity of Yeats*, Richard Ellmann calls attention to a recurring aspect of Yeats's style that acts as a trace of the conflict in his thinking between the romantic desire that saves experience from inconsequence and the corrective signals that come from "unresting thought." "In the end," Ellmann says, "his rhetoric is made up of both firm assertiveness and subtle, complex qualifications," and Ellmann cites instances that seem to accumulate into a characteristically Yeatsian rhetoric of self-subversion.[2] Behind the scenes in "The Two Trees," however, and in the two shepherd poems, is a desire to keep awareness simple and, in effect, inorganic. The willed artificiality of "The Two Trees" is no accident. When we speak of Yeats's mature poetry, we are describing a condition of mind in which the compartmentalized worlds of "The Two Trees" have infiltrated each other so that the one view is scrutinizing the other from the inside out. The "heart" still cries against "necessity," but necessity has been recharacterized as a worthy adversary, not as a demon of childhood. This change can be read as not so much a philosophical issue as one of strategy, since it permits the poet

2. Ellmann, *Identity of Yeats*, 144.

to depict in the frame of the poems his shrewd and unflagging conflict with the unintended and therefore unpoetical world. When this contest is not opened up discursively, as in "The Tower" or "Sailing to Byzantium," it is likely to be disguised by irony in a way that permits him to express both points of view at once—and hence to strengthen the theoretical role of, and necessity for, the artifact, the poem, within which (and only within which) opposing functions may be reconciled.

In "A Memory of Youth" (1912), the emphasis is on a knowing artifice associated with remembering and an innocent artifice associated with callow and self-important infatuation. Within the poem, the dramatic action is one of artifice in the dialogues of courtship itself.

> The moments passed as at a play;
> I had the wisdom love brings forth;
> I had my share of mother-wit,
> And yet for all that I could say,
> And though I had her praise for it,
> A cloud blown from the cut-throat North
> Suddenly hid Love's moon away.
>
> Believing every word I said,
> I praised her body and her mind
> Till pride had made her eyes grow bright,
> And pleasure made her cheeks grow red,
> And vanity her footfall light,
> Yet we, for all that praise, could find
> Nothing but darkness overhead.
>
> We sat as silent as a stone,
> We knew, though she'd not said a word,
> That even the best of love must die,
> And had been savagely undone
> Were it not that Love upon the cry
> Of a most ridiculous little bird
> Tore from the clouds his marvellous moon.

Clearly the older and wiser speaker is meant to be seen here as latent in the younger one. This dual perspective is part of the story, the young man seeming to look over his shoulder at the evidence around him of the very reverse of his own glib and merely verbal self-mastery—the "cut-throat North" he calls it, as if to tame it by giving it a metaphorical name. "A Memory of Youth" is a shrewd story about the full, underside implications of the pathetic fallacy and how easy and natural it is for youth's exuberant eroticism to override them. The worst part about the obscured moon and the darkness overhead is that the setting does not suitably enhance the drama of the lovers' heightened sense of themselves and the occasion. Except for nature's not collaborating, the occasion is like a play, in that the two lovers agreeably generate fictional identities for each other. The praiser has all the wisdom love brings forth, he says, but what evidently seemed like a solemn fact at the time now seems more like a pompous delusion. His wit in language transforms the praised one, recreates her in her own idealized image of herself. She verges upon becoming unearthly and apart from nature, a person in a play—or in a poem. It all makes sense at the time, as love's illusions ordinarily do. What does not make sense in this vale of sense-making—created by vanity, wisdom, and mother-wit—is nature's not corroborating their enhanced stature. This missing piece of the idealized coherence causes them to doubt the coherence itself. "Savagely undone" must then imply not just decreated, but decreated and returned to the condition of nature. So deep is this fear that when the moon reappears from behind the clouds, as it randomly will, the event is read into the script as an intentionality that Love as an agent guarantees for the world, whereas in reality it is only love as a reorganizing human feeling that tears the clouds from the moon—that is, causes the clouds to be interpreted as having been torn from the moon. The decisive factor here is the random little bird who is assimilated into the story, as well, and in the same way, only because he happens to cry out at the right time in the right place. A cow here or a fox would have been assimilated, too.

In other words, the poem is not only a memory of youth—a recollection, that is, of what youth was like—but also a self-referential judgment on the poet's part of one aspect of his own nature, which, in diminished form, has survived into maturity. It seems clear that the poet of the present regards his youthful reincarnation with an amused and ironic skepticism: "And yet for all that I could say... / A cloud blown from the cut-throat North / Suddenly hid Love's moon away." It cannot be so easy now to think of nature as an extension of one's desire. The poet of the present has seen implications in the story that the youthful version of himself could not quite comprehend or bring himself to face. By comparison with Wordsworth's credulous vision of children sporting on the shore, this analogous story is decidedly agnostic. And yet the poet's will to believe in the power of desire is still there, implicit in the goodwill projected back through time toward the youthful lovers—who seem to inhabit the present as well as the past—and in the very ambiguity with which their story is portrayed: it still remains possible to read the poem unironically, as if Yeats were again using the venue of poetry as a means of having a real-life human dilemma both ways. By calling the moment forward, the poet carries forward with it the innocence of outlook that will make other such visions of reality possible in different contexts. In that transaction, the poem moves from being a poem about love to being a poem about a victory of artifice over time, but also about the transience of such victories in the larger scheme of temporal experience.[3]

It may be said to follow from such realizations (emerging from the earlier poems) that when authentic time and the material body within it move into the foreground of Yeats's poems—in the form of what Lentricchia calls "existential immersion"—a new structure of thinking moves with them. Poems like "The Tower," which one would expect to be overdetermined intellectually, commanded by the mature authority of consciousness, pass through phases of organization that show that authority of will to be subvertible, and rhetorical defenses to be subject to sudden and unpredictable penetration by the arational. "Vacillation" (1932) represents the most sophisticated point in this development, and it enshrines at an appropriately late point in Yeats's life all of the paradoxes that he himself has allowed to be called up in his argument with the dispiriting implications of his own thought.

3. The clever rhyme scheme of "A Memory of Youth" replicates the poem's story in its sound pattern. In each seven-line stanza, the rhymes move forward in a rising, expectant action *(a b c)* then repeat the first *a* rhyme, then reverse themselves in a falling action *(c b a)* which is suitable to the mood of thwarted hopes expressed in the content of the last line of each of the first two stanzas: "Suddenly hid love's moon away" and "Nothing but darkness overhead"—as if a door were closing. But then in the third and last stanza, when the mood lifts slightly (for whatever reason), the rhyme scheme changes slightly, too. The precise *a* rhymes that had given the first two stanzas their enclosing effect *(play, say, away* and *said, read, head)* become less confining slant rhymes *(stone, done, moon)*. Even though the pattern itself remains the same, there is an appropriate aural illusion of opening outward and release.

I

Between extremities
Man runs his course;
A brand, or flaming breath,
Comes to destroy
All those antinomies
Of day and night;
The body calls it death,
The heart remorse.
But if these be right
What is joy?

II

A tree there is that from its topmost bough
Is half all glittering flame and half all green
Abounding foliage moistened with the dew;
And half is half and yet is all the scene;
And half and half consume what they renew,
And he that Attis' image hangs between
That staring fury and the blind lush leaf
May know not what he knows, but knows not grief.

III

Get all the gold and silver that you can,
Satisfy ambition, animate
The trivial days and ram them with the sun,
And yet upon these maxims meditate:
All women dote upon an idle man
Although their children need a rich estate;
No man has ever lived that had enough
Of children's gratitude or woman's love.

No longer in Lethean foliage caught
Begin the preparation for your death
And from the fortieth winter by that thought
Test every work of intellect or faith,
And everything that your own hands have wrought,
And call those works extravagance of breath
That are not suited for such men as come
Proud, open-eyed and laughing to the tomb.

IV

My fiftieth year had come and gone,
I sat, a solitary man,
In a crowded London shop,
An open book and empty cup
On the marble table-top.

While on the shop and street I gazed
My body of a sudden blazed;
And twenty minutes more or less
It seemed, so great my happiness,
That I was blessèd and could bless.

V

Although the summer sunlight gild
Cloudy leafage of the sky,
Or wintry moonlight sink the field
In storm-scattered intricacy,
I cannot look thereon,
Responsibility so weighs me down.

Things said or done long years ago,
Or things I did not do or say
But thought that I might say or do,
Weigh me down, and not a day
But something is recalled,
My conscience or my vanity appalled.

VI

A rivery field spread out below,
An odour of the new-mown hay
In his nostrils, the great lord of Chou
Cried, casting off the mountain snow,
"Let all things pass away."

Wheels by milk-white asses drawn
Where Babylon or Nineveh
Rose; some conqueror drew rein
And cried to battle-weary men,
"Let all things pass away."

From man's blood-sodden heart are sprung
Those branches of the night and day
Where the gaudy moon is hung.
What's the meaning of all song?
"Let all things pass away."

VII

The Soul. Seek out reality, leave things that seem.
The Heart. What, be a singer born and lack a theme?
The Soul. Isaiah's coal, what more can man desire?
The Heart. Struck dumb in the simplicity of fire!
The Soul. Look on that fire, salvation walks within.
The Heart. What theme had Homer but original sin?

VIII

Must we part, Von Hügel, though much alike, for we
Accept the miracles of the saints and honour sanctity?
The body of Saint Teresa lies undecayed in tomb,
Bathed in miraculous oil, sweet odours from it come,
Healing from its lettered slab. Those self-same hands perchance
Eternalised the body of a modern saint that once
Had scooped out Pharoah's mummy. I—though heart might find relief
Did I become a Christian man and choose for my belief
What seems most welcome in the tomb—play a predestined part.
Homer is my example and his unchristened heart.
The lion and the honeycomb, what has Scripture said?
So get you gone, Von Hügel, though with blessings on your head.

The poem is unusually associative, and this quality of its structure expresses not so much a loss of rigor in Yeats's thinking—it is also excruciatingly introspective—as a willingness to approach understanding by surrendering control over the processes of regulated thinking. The term *vacillation*, in this respect, connotes indecisiveness and wavering and therefore a form of meditative suggestibility rather than a deliberate shifting from one binary position to the other. The title is given its definition by the text generated from it. That text describes and considers the inability to master one's life (and the difference between life and poems) or even one's own emotional condition. In this regard, it inscribes a movement back toward a primal aspect of reality, toward the pre-rational authority of the random and what is given—the body of fate, so to speak. The dialectic between unreflective, generative nature on the one hand and the idealism of human intellect on the other is tumultuous and disruptive and is so described in the violent imagery of the first two sections.

These eighteen lines of "Vacillation" are among the most cryptic in Yeats's work, and it is difficult to find any single explanation of them wholly satisfying. Together, however, they do describe for the poem its necessarily indefinite subject—a primordial unchanged and unchangeable condition in which men live between extremities without the possibility of escaping *into* one of the extremities or the other of them or without possibility of resolution. The point here is the same as that of the interlocking gyres of *A Vision*. The end of this running of the course comes only with death. For the body, which does not think or foreknow this end, it is merely death; for the heart, it can only be remorse, for the heart and its desire—"sick with desire and fastened to a dying animal"—can then never be fulfilled, for the running of the course is over. The sense, then, of the question, "what is joy?" is that, given the pitiless authority of this arrangement, what could "joy" really be said to be, assuming that it is achievable in some form in the first place? The answer in the poem will turn out to be that there is no answer—that, except in sweetly transient moments, joy, grief, and pain, and what Thomas Parkinson describes as "deathful knowledge," are so inextricably interwoven that there is no word that describes the state that the word *joy* is otherwise taken to refer to.

The poem's first full stanza ends with the extremity "joy," and the poem's second full stanza ends with the extremity "grief." There is a logical connection in this parallel. In its pure form, "joy" cannot be known (and, as we will learn in the course of the poem, therefore does not repay pursuing); on the other hand, it is within the possibilities of being fully human that one might at least transcend grief. Thus man runs—or may run—*between* these extremities. In the second stanza, Yeats reworks his central trope of antinomies by inventing what is made to seem ("A tree there is") an ancient icon. It is important to realize of this stanza that the tree, half flame and half abounding foliage, came into the poem's composition first—before, that is, the symbol of Attis was added to it. Attis seems to have been an afterthought cooked up by association with the magical tree. However, this divided tree—the idea of which Yeats apparently had found years before in an enigmatic reference in the *Mabinogion* (which features, in some tales, a Welsh version of Cuchulain)—is nothing like the sacred pine of the Attis rituals of Frazer's accounts upon which the effigy of this famous dying and resurrected god was said to have been suspended. We can piece this compositional process together from Thomas Parkinson's reproduction and analysis of Yeats's compositional notes. An early stage of this stanza gives us the key to understanding how the icon of the tree and the icon of Attis work together:

> There is a tree
> > that from its topmost bough

and then eventually

> > Is one half glittering flame, the other green
> > Abounding foliage moistened with the dew
> > > They that
>
> > And some let Attys image hang between
> > Consuming flame and lush abounding leaf
> > Know not what they know but know not grief

Yeats then tried an additional line, "The tree of knowledge and of life and scene"; then, later, this line becomes: "Knowledge and life made one for in the scene." As Parkinson says (surmising of course): "Hence he corrected his earlier notation, and in filling out the line to maintain his momentum and consider the possibilities implied by 'scene,' he learned what his tree would be. Knowledge and life, flame and dew— these were set." Other versions of this explanatory line in the poem were "Knowledge and life made one for in the scene"; "wisdom displays all death but in the scene"; "wisdom has summoned death but in the scene"; and then, for his last eventually rejected version, a line that follows: "what it destroys the foliage must renew."[4]

This evolving notion of thought and life engaged in a perpetual dialectical process is evidently what brought the idea of Attis into the pattern, Attis being perhaps the most famous of the vegetation gods and an archetype of perpetual renewal. We may suppose, then, that

---

4. Parkinson, *W. B. Yeats, Self-Critic: A Study of His Early Verse [and] W. B. Yeats: The Later Poetry*, 220–28.

nothing else about the Attis story or about the self-emasculating cele-
brants of the Attis cults much matters to this primary allusion to rebirth,
including the frenzy of their ceremonies and their indirect if drastic
obeisance to the forbidding earth mother, Cybele. Attis, in other words,
is appropriate here as a symbol for eternal renewal, and it is fitting to
hang his image there between the fire of intellect and thought on the
one hand and the insentient power of life outside of thought, of nature,
on the other. Doing so is to affirm a belief in the productive inter-
dependence between intellect and body, mind and nature, flame and
foliage—the one "staring" and the other "blind"—and to take the burden of this knowledge on. To say "half is half and yet is all the scene"
would then mean that the two halves complement and complete each
other but also that this dialectic is what *is* and is *all* there is. Here again
is a mythical form of understanding, like the conflict of antithetical
and primary forces in *A Vision*, or like the Apollonian and Dionysian
tragic modes. It is not a philosophy and is not susceptible to discursive
abstraction—hence "he . . . may know not what he knows"; as this
understanding affirms life on its own terms and disaffirms teleology or
promise, it is beyond grief just as it is beyond good and evil. It is
beyond grief because in its very form of understanding it repudiates
the Grey Truth of Enlightenment thought. The conceit is also an iconic
condensation of what "Vacillation" is about.

What is shown in "Vacillation" is a course man runs between extremities, and that course is depicted as random and unpredictable rather
than as guided by purpose and conscious determination. The poem's
highly associative, almost paratactic structure reflects this intention,
and this structure, in turn, implies both a yielding to and an immersion
in the unregulated processes of life beyond thought. Yeats writes in this
poem of the authority of consciousness and of the will from within the
limits of an ironically acknowledged unfreedom. The exchanges in experience represented here are wholly blind transactions, and the will can
be trusted, therefore, only as a symbolic agent of intransitive desire.

This is the point of poem III: no matter how decisive and resolute a
man may be in making something of himself, he will discover sooner
or later that, both literally and metaphorically, what women will truly
care about is not success but idleness—literally in the sense that this
is often in fact the case; figuratively in the sense that such dissonance
between expectation (thought) and outcome (fact) is always the case.
This is either not as misogynist as it seems or more so, since the poem

then goes on to state, as another "maxim," that women are disposed in this way even against their own best interest, since they and their children require supporting and therefore, were reason to prevail, they should prefer the accomplished man with "gold and silver." So both men and women, insofar as conventional courtship strategies and their associated life courses are concerned, end up irrationally at odds with their own better judgment. Since one cannot know what, so to speak, to pray for in these respects, all that is left is the disinterested—albeit male— energy that is symbolized in the verbs themselves *(get, satisfy, animate, ram)* and then the stoic detachment from the uncertain fortunes of the world that is so cogently expressed in the authority of the next, self-consciously masterful, single-sentence, ottava rima stanza ("No longer in Lethean foliage caught," and so on). The authority of these lines is rhetorical posturing, of course. Nothing very specific can be attached to the language of the stanza other than the refusal to know not what one knows. But with Yeats, rhetoric and attitude are powerful agents because they are what *can* be controlled, and they become the condition—and existential attitude—where the making of poetry and of a life come closest to coinciding. Any of the more tangible outcomes are beyond one's foretelling or grasp. Not to see this point is to be caught in "Lethean foliage," subsumed into "primary" obliviousness or evasion.

In case we have missed this point, it is reconfigured in the next two poems (IV and V) in two incidents that call even the existential posture into question as itself being a folly that assumes more about our command over attitude and feeling than actual experience will confirm. The beauty and mystery of the first of these events—his body improbably blazing in a sudden access of blessedness—is that it is causeless (the scene being a crowded shop in a London street) and that poetically, it ought, by rights, be associated with the natural setting of the second poem (about despair) rather than with its own congested, urban one. This irony is one that Coleridge—whose "Dejection" is pointedly restated in IV—would appreciate, and it may be taken even as anti-romantic, if Wordsworth and his version of the pathetic fallacy were to be taken as the norm. For it not only suggests a dissociation between setting and feeling, and thus relegates, or brackets, romantic nature in yet another way; it also dissociates the will of the human subject from either. Will, on the one hand, and feeling, on the other—just a dozen lines earlier united in existential assurance—are abruptly left to fend for themselves. The authority of consciousness, for the moment—one in which the poet is visited unwittingly by the modern psychoanalytical era—is overcome wholly by the irrationality of feeling. The irresistible depression of IV causes the thoughts about responsibility and failure that deepen the depression; the thoughts do not induce the feeling. The loose organization of "Vacillation" has permitted this insight, since the insight's point is that it comes unbidden and yet becomes the decisive factor in the poet's evaluation of the course of his own relation to nature and time. The epiphany contradicts the very theme of his own created existence and therefore has the persuasive character of the other that truth-in-itself—behind thought—invariably has: the sublime, in other words, in its modern, ego-opposing, least-prepossessing form.

Human intelligence may contain that otherness only by bearing witness to and affirming it. This is the thesis hidden in the three parables of poem VI. Even human power depends in some sense upon the awareness of its own ultimate limitations. The "great lord of Chou" responds to the event of change—to the rich odor of the freshly cut hay that makes a "river" before his gaze—even though this process in the world, extended, will also carry him and his empire away. The conqueror of the second stanza seems to acknowledge that even conquest is conquered in time—that, ironically, conquest *is* change. Otherwise new worlds to be conquered, and the conquerors themselves, could not come into being. And so it is, the third stanza implies, for the poet himself—the third of these three assumed masters of their worlds: let all things pass away so that song may continue to be. Richard Ellmann has written of this stanza:

> [M]an, who creates everything, both the antinomies and their reconciling image (night and day, and the "gaudy moon"), wills the extinction of his own monuments.... Yeats may have had in mind an unpublished note for *A Vision:* "Homer was wrong in saying 'Would that strife might perish from among gods and men.' He did not see that he was praying for the destruction of the universe; for if his prayers were heard all things would pass away...." But here he takes Homer's part.[5]

Uncharacteristically for Ellmann, this, too, seems wrong. The poet is not taking Homer's part but is affirming the perpetualness of change so as to ensure the identity and sanctity of song, which is about all things passing away. The contrast in the emblematic lines of this stanza

5. Ellmann, *Identity of Yeats*, 273–74.

("from man's blood-sodden heart are sprung / Those branches of the night and day / Where the gaudy moon is hung") between "blood-sodden heart" and "gaudy moon" gives weight—and supremacy in the diction—to the mortal and to nature, while the epithet "gaudy" faintly trivializes what would otherwise be a symbol (the moon) of immutable excellence. "Gaudy" implies meretriciousness and illusion. So insofar as the "hung" moon and created song could be said to be equivalent here, they are cautiously qualified as human agents against despair. Norman Jeffares has suggested that this entire poem VI could have been influenced, in spirit at least, by the "Ode" by Arthur O'Shaugnessy in his *Music and Limelight,* which celebrates the bardic tradition and "the poets of the ages."[6] If this is the case, the operative lines of O'Shaugnessy's "Ode" would seem to be these: "For each age is a dream that is dying, / Or one that is coming to birth."

In poem VII, then, the Soul (as usual) comes upon the scene, offering to rescue the poet from the odd paradox of the conditions of his being. "Seek out reality, leave things that seem," it says. Significantly, though, it is "The Heart" that not only speaks for the poet (the "blood-sodden heart" of the previous stanza cleaned up for dialogue), but also *is* the poet. This poet, as he has said from the beginning, may know not what he knows, but he knows not grief. He also knows enough to understand that to walk over wholly out of the antinomies of fire and foliage into the salvation that the soul claims the fire to be would be to know nothing at all, to be "Struck dumb in the simplicity of fire." To be struck dumb and to know nothing would be to cease to exist. Moreover, to be a "singer born" means, in effect, to have no choice in the matter, and since both the cause and the meaning of all song is that all things pass away, the poet, like the conqueror, owes his very existence to eternal mutability. Salvation by transcendence, which the soul urges, is thus a negation of existential identity, and just as the poet Homer had only original sin for his theme—salvation not having been accessible or even an issue in his time—so for this poet, psychologically Homer's analogue, there is no middle way. Being a singer born is yet one other ironic aspect of his life over which he has no control: "I . . . play a predestined part," he will say in the next section. "Homer is my example and his unchristened heart."

6. Jeffares, *New Commentary,* 246. See also Phillip Marcus's informative discussion of O'Shaugnessy in *Yeats and Artistic Power,* 35ff.

In poem VIII, when Von Hügel takes up the Soul's part, it becomes clearer that the poet is at the mercy finally of his own nature—as the ironic epiphanies of IV and V already have shown. It makes sense, the poet says, to choose belief, since then his "heart might find relief." But this point sets up an interesting crisis in which his better judgment and, so to speak, his whole being are at odds with each other. It is clear, too, that the issue is not one of invidiously modern skepticism. That is why he goes to such elaborate lengths to credit the miracles of Saint Teresa's exhumation: it raises the question of why—if he accepts the miracles and honors sanctity—he cannot, as well, go on to walk with salvation within the fire. For all the bravura tone of these last lines, he is still left oddly volitionless, choosing in the end only the condition over which he has no choice. Shrewdly, though, he has salvaged a supportive metaphor from the Saint Teresa miracle, for that story may be taken also as a story of the unsuppressibility of life, of creation succeeding and therefore, in a sense, defying and being one with decay. It is made to be a version of the story of the lion and the honeycomb: out of the death of the strong shall come forth the sweet. In turn, this famous riddle of Samson's, in the last lines of the poem, becomes a metaphor for an even deeper riddle, which, for Yeats, is embedded in our being. It is not just that out of the strong shall come forth the sweet, but that out of death and our foreknowledge of it comes the mysterious counterlife of song, and with it everything—desire, affirmation, overcoming—which, in the existential environment of Yeats's poem, song symbolizes.

Yeats's last great confrontation with his own vision of a created life, with his own mission in effect, was "The Man and the Echo" (1939). It appeared with "The Circus Animals' Desertion" (written earlier) in the *Atlantic Monthly* and the *London Mercury* in the month that he died. In it the metaphor of the seashell from "The Sad Shepherd" has come full circle. The seashell has become Alt.

MAN

In a cleft that's christened Alt
Under broken stone I halt
At the bottom of a pit
That broad noon has never lit,
And shout a secret to the stone.
All that I have said and done,

Now that I am old and ill,
Turns into a question till
I lie awake night after night
And never get the answers right.
Did that play of mine send out
Certain men the English shot?
Did words of mine put too great strain
On that woman's reeling brain?
Could my spoken words have checked
That whereby a house lay wrecked?
And all seems evil until I
Sleepless would lie down and die.

ECHO

Lie down and die.

MAN

That were to shirk
The spiritual intellect's great work,
And shirk it in vain. There is no release
In a bodkin or disease,
Nor can there be work so great
As that which cleans man's dirty slate.
While man can still his body keep
Wine or love drug him to sleep,
Waking he thanks the Lord that he
Has body and its stupidity,
But body gone he sleeps no more,
And till his intellect grows sure
That all's arranged in one clear view,
Pursues the thoughts that I pursue,
Then stands in judgment on his soul,
And, all work done, dismisses all
Out of intellect and sight
And sinks at last into the night.

ECHO

Into the night.

MAN

O Rocky Voice,
Shall we in that great night rejoice?
What do we know but that we face

One another in this place?
But hush, for I have lost the theme,
Its joy or night seem but a dream;
Up there some hawk or owl has struck,
Dropping out of sky or rock,
A stricken rabbit is crying out,
And its cry distracts my thought.

The sad shepherd's seashell is now less quaint and no longer portable. It requires being met in its own place on its own terms. It is also now otherness itself—Alt—given a mediating name but still implacable and unappeasable, the unspeaking earth in its most unresponsive inhuman form. The counsel that echoes from it (for it cannot speak) is appropriately the counsel of despair, because it embodies all that calls constructed human reality into question. The echo speaks for the poet's awareness of his own nonbeing, so this is a secret communion and not, like "Under Ben Bulben," a proclamation. Its scene is therefore one of truth-telling, and in this moment of truth-telling, the poet has stumbled again across the realization that "words alone are certain good" only to the degree that they can be imagined to give dreams a human utility. It is in the nature of the truth that the poet inhabits in this moment—in the cave christened Alt, where there is no interpreting human society and where there is only unreceptive incognition—that all outcomes of human action are unpredictable. Whatever may be the motive of words intended to achieve certain good, some wholly other result will be the real effect of them. The intended cause-and-effect continuity of human action and discourse is only a projected fiction of consciousness, a totalization only in the theater of the mind. The poet's waking nightmare is his realization that there is no entitled control over human events, only instead the ironic corollary, effects upon them. He does not overstate the condition when he describes it as seeming evil. There is no way to know, since reality takes its own course, and in this poem's nonhuman setting, reality has taken the poet himself into its autonomous course. He is conscious of that irony's being the cause of his own now-relentless self-doubt: "All that I have said and done . . . / Turns into a question." Being old and ill brings him closer to the stone and carries him farther from Arcady.

But even at this extremity (or especially at this extremity) his being conscious not only of the theoretically random and destructive consequences of his own words but of *why* he has had this suddenly dreadful encounter with the truth—his being old and ill and isolated from the reassuring context of human society—is his only imaginable redemption. He at least remains, as an act of will, sleepless—unwilling not to know what he knows. After Echo says "Lie down and die," the word MAN seems suddenly to stand out on the page as a claim upon human worth. Whether he can get the answers right or not, he will lie awake trying to. Any other course would be unmanly.

This, of course, becomes the "theme" of the next sequence in this essentially declarative meditation—not shirking the "spiritual intellect's" great work. Death cannot be a chosen release so long as the answers have not been got right—it cannot *be* an answer. Of course for us, if not for the stubborn visionary in the poem peering intently past where human thought can take him, this means that there is no release at all—that in these terms, appalling as the thought may be, death cannot be made acceptable to consciousness. Consciousness, not the body, is death's opposite; consciousness is what is not death and not other. The body's only merit at this point is its role in staying alive in order to keep the spiritual intellect viable. And the obvious futility of the task set for the spiritual intellect is not even entertained as a possibility. One simply dies too soon. Were the body and its stupidity only able to hang on a bit longer, the answers could be got right and, not only that, all could be "arranged in one clear view."

There are two challenges at stake in this somehow simultaneously depressed and manic ambition. The first is to get the answers right, to think one's way through the discontinuities of cause and effect. The other is, having achieved that clarity of understanding, to stand in judgment upon one's own soul. The distinction is nice and ironic: the second achievement can only follow from the first. One cannot transcend one's own particular life, even for purposes of judgment, without transcending all life. Implicitly, this is a way of conceding the entanglement of one's own will and destiny with that of others. Yet as hopeless as such a project might seem to anyone less aggressive toward the conditions of human life, the speech act of its uttering achieves an almost plausible rhetoric. Once again, the complexity of Yeats's syntax—an expression of the intimacy of the relationship of each part of this thought to the other parts—exhibits a command of the structure of language, which in turn affirms the supremacy of thought. Not to appear amateurish, Yeats has not only compressed this convoluted thought into one twelve-line sentence but also held it firmly anchored as it progresses with a responsibly constrained couplet rhyme scheme. Thought and discipline are inscribed on the page, a model of the intellect's work, which, in the end, however, must remain only symbolic and formal, deflected in the end by the condition of unknowing that is the poem's theme. "What do we know," he says, "but that we face / One another in this place"—the self and the unspeaking other, Alt—which is mediated only by becoming an echo of a single component of the self's thought. Only that illusion of an echo saves the cavern's voice from being, like the sad shepherd's seashell, "inarticulate moan." The moment of understanding not only bluntly subverts the logic of the prior assertion, which was not very secure in the first place; it also subverts the logic of the poet's life. The stalemate is absolute. The authority of consciousness is deflected against stone, against Alt, unknowable and unsubduable.

The "theme" in any given Yeats poem, as in this one, is the mind's reorganization, its formalizing, of the data it receives from the world. To lose that theme is to allow the world to recede back into its primal, inchoate condition. The knowledge of this is itself a kind of death, an effacement of self to the degree that self is identical to conceptualization. So "theme" and "dream" are linked conceptually as well as in rhyme. The rhyme—for a last tragic time in Yeats's career—calls thought itself into question. Thought contrives a theme—whether of joy or "night"— especially in the face of impending death, and even a theme of despair remains a theme and therefore mental action and control. Either could be a merely creative falsehood, with no more ontological status than a fantasy. James Pethica points out that in the last four lines of the poem, the previously tightly structured couplet rhyme scheme suddenly loosens into four off-rhymes, a shift that "brilliantly counterpoints the rising distress the Man experiences."[7] It signifies suddenly the loss of his grip upon his theme. But in the last line, the tetrameter metrical regularity collapses, too, with the same coded meaning—as at the end of "The People"—into something that sounds bleakly like prose.

> But hush, for I have lost the theme,
> Its joy or night seem but a dream;
> Up there some hawk or owl has struck,

7. Pethica, in Yeats, *Last Poems*, xi.

> Dropping out of sky or rock,
> A stricken rabbit is crying out,
> And its cry distracts my thought.

This abrupt, disruptive intervention of the ongoing, outside world, as the poet of all people must pay the price of knowing, is symbolic only in its not symbolizing anything. It is murderous innocence again fitted into a poem and domesticated by reflection but finally of its own being, beyond human forms and categories. This is the antithesis of theme, where human consciousness stops and everything else (nature, life, death) goes its own way, where something else—something other— begins.

Epilogue

WHATEVER that something other may be said to be, it was always
bringing pressure upon Yeats's thought from somewhere behind
it, and the challenge of facing it squarely is what caused his formalism
to become ideological. From the beginning, it echoes in the Sad Shepherd's seashell, which reduced "all he sang into inarticulate moan." It is
there—perhaps—as the stone "in the midst of all" in "Easter 1916." It
drives the unrelenting cycle of procreation and death in the country
that is not for old men. It is incarnated in the frog spawn of a blind
man's ditch in "Dialogue of Self and Soul," which the poet concedes
that life—behind thought—could be reduced to but which he nevertheless affirms. (He reminds us what is at stake here with a revisionist
metrical echo: "unless / Soul clap its hands and sing, and louder sing";
"I am content to live it all again / and yet again.") It engenders the
thought that the folly of what we consider romantic love may only be a
kind of psychoanalytical "superstructure" for the "base" of mere natural
selection—"that most fecund ditch of all." (This would be reason
enough in itself in "The Two Trees" for lovers not to gaze in the bitter
glass.) This other is in the "place of excrement" where, for Crazy Jane,
Love must "pitch his mansion," whether we like it or whether we care
to think about it or not. Indeed in some sense it *is* the place of excrement where the imagination and sexual desire are decoupled. It is the
appalling irrationality of the forces of history in "Meditations in Time
of Civil War" and "Nineteen Hundred and Nineteen"—the "it," as Hillis
Miller calls it, from which politics cannot rescue us. It is the rough
beast of "The Second Coming," the unknowable and unknown, latent
in all civilizations, biding its time. The wheel of *A Vision* itself moves
out of this primal, preconscious state of being and then inexorably back
into it. This embedded *absence* of the human underlying and enclosing
human life is what caused Yeats to revere what he identified as enclaves

174

of civilization (Coole Park among them) that were bulwarks against the unknown and other—and to underacknowledge the compassionless social and economic forces in history that made them possible. It sent him (allowing for liberties with his metaphor), like a last courtier into gypsy campsites—rather than into salons, or public houses, or lecture halls—to babble of fallen majesty.

And yet, paradoxically, as his being in a gypsy campsite to begin with implies, what was outside his thought pressing in was also inside his thought pressing out—as he knew: it is seductive as well as fearsome. Hence the inevitable confrontation at the end of his life with Alt. It had found one expression in the implicit primitivism of the Celtic revival. When Oisin repudiates St. Patrick and Christian redemption in favor not only of his Fenian comrades but also of their great hounds, he is repudiating both the Church and, along with it, a whole course of a western history in which an idea of the human has evolved.

There are many conventional arguments about the emergence of primitivism in this form as a dominant mode in modernist literature and art: that it emerged from the growing awareness, under imperialism, of exotic cultures and alternative, non-Western modes of thought; that anthropologists like Frazer had shown ancient cultures to have a coherence in mysteries and ritual that the enlightened modern West had lost touch with; that modern industrial and commercial life had become regimented and empty of passion; that the abstracting forces of reason had prevailed through its agent the machine. All of these arguments apply as certainly to Yeats as they had, say, to D. H. Lawrence. Yeats, however, had the good fortune to have had ready to hand in the Celtic mythologies—like the stories of Oisin and the Fenians—a cultural countersymbol to set against the modern world, which did not require him to condescend to other races and to other peoples by appropriating them as symbols (nor to the other gender, for that matter, since the sagas and the heroic in them are largely gender neutral). He was also able to present the prehistoric (and therefore, of course, conveniently unfalsifiable) cultural values that he and Lady Gregory became spokesmen for as a vision of anticolonial nativism—Irish negritude, so to speak. This Celticizing presented itself as a nationalist political agenda and in doing so provided respectable cover for the otherwise deviant and transgressive energies of both a modernist and a primitivist subtext. "Hound Voice," with its gentrified setting crashing open at the end into not only an ancient but even prehuman violence (again, with the hounds), could be thought of as metonymy for this larger representational pattern.

As William Barrett has pointed out (and he is not the first to do so, obviously), the primitive remains buried within us all—behind thought, so to speak—and does not get left behind as societies advance or even as societies advance their understanding of the influence of such ancestral survivals.[1] Indeed, the discontinuity between the hard-wired, unconscious influences in us of what biologists call "the environment of evolutionary adaptation" and the actual enlightened world we inhabit now— what Freud called "civilization"—becomes more apparent as the external advances of modern reason and technology become more spectacular, "emissaries of light" though we continue to imagine ourselves to be.

Interestingly, in this context, Yeats's investment in the myths of Cuchulain seems in practice to have been cautious and tentative, and his representations of Cuchulain seem correspondingly stylized and abstract, considering what Cuchulain, the protobarbaric Celtic mercenary, must have been, so to speak, in real life—that is, before the first stages of his romanticization in the earliest sagas. Cuchulain may have been, as it is said, the Irish Achilles, but in Yeats's presentations of him, he exhibits in action nothing remotely akin to Achilles's vividly described surges of rage and exuberant cruelty. A primitive warrior mediated through the rigorous ceremoniality of the Noh drama is more of an allusion to the primitive than a representation of it. Yeats fell victim in this case (as Lawrence had in a different way—and as Homer had not) to the irony of discursive abstraction's being required in order to repudiate abstraction, in order to represent and commend the preabstract. But Yeats had good reason to hold Cuchulain as an alter ego at arm's length, just as he had had good reason to ask of himself, "Did that play of mine send out / Certain men the English shot?" He understood the seductive single-mindedness, the un-self-dividedness of rage:

> You that Mitchel's prayer have heard
> "Send war in our time, O Lord!"
> Know that when all words are said
> And a man is fighting mad,
> Something drops from the eyes long blind

---

1. William Barrett, *Time of Need: Forms of Imagination in the Twentieth Century*, 338.

He completes his partial mind,
For an instant stands at ease.
("Under Ben Bulben")

He may also have known—since he knew almost everything else about
himself and his own illusions—that if the spirit of Cuchulain had lived
on at all in Ireland, it had lived on not in the stylized form of myth and
poetry but in the murderous insouciance of the Provisional IRA and its
splinter groups. If, indeed, Pearse, on the day of the Easter Rising, "summoned Cuchulain to his side," as the poet imagines in "The Statues,"
what answered and "stalked through the Post Office" does not seem in
retrospect to have been "intellect, calculation, number [and] measurement" but self-perpetuating internecine violence and terrorism. It is
hard to guess why Yeats thought that intellect, calculation, number, and
measurement could even remain in play once Cuchulain's ghost was
summoned. The spirit of Cuchulain has, instead, had a great deal of
pointless carnage to answer for since the Easter Rising, both on Irish
soil and elsewhere.

In the end, the logic of formalism—Pythagorean in origin in "The
Statues"—and the logic, or illogic, of primitivism move the mind in
opposite directions. Primitivism, moreover, has the advantage of having nature on its side and therefore the final word. The conjunction in
modernist art of the archaic with the modern, Peter Nicholls has said,
"led to the encoding of the archaic within the modern not merely as a
binary 'other' to be dialectically assimilated to Western modes, but as a
network of desires capable of deforming representation from within."
The "primitive," he adds, "could function as the correlative of experiences and emotions which were felt to lie beyond representation, to
resist sanctioned Western modes of expression."[2] In those terms, admit-
ting the "primitive" into ideologically formalist representation, even, as
with Cuchulain, only by metonymy, admits into the text a deconstructive agent that always points back and inside to where process, behav-
ior, and survival are all there is, to what Nietzsche called nature "on
which as yet no knowledge has been at work." This would be the point
at the farthest end of the ladder of being from what "The Circus Animals' Desertion" calls "pure mind." The hermits of "Meru" are the per-
sonifications of this spirit, "primitivists" themselves (that is, modernists

2. Nicholls, *Modernisms*, 118.

disguised as ancients), in that they are outside of Enlightenment history and undeluded by its orthodoxies; they can see directly into the unmediated "desolation of reality" that persists underneath. The "ravening, raging, and uprooting" that are said to bring man to this place are themselves expressions of a primal energy, actions of thought in the poem but primordial in a way that transforms thought simply into an epiphenomenon.

The young Nietzsche—mediating Kant through Schopenhauer—considered that he had discovered his own "something other" in the unchanging, primordial ground of being that he called the Dionysian. Apollonian representation was an epiphenomenon, a symbolic dream picture that reconfigured the terrible encounter with the core of things, with the destructive processes of universal history and the cruelty of nature. For Yeats, the impulse of primitivism was not a stylistic affectation, or a cultural misappropriation, but a sign (a not very subtly coded representation) of this Dionysian recognition of primordial unity, always just beneath the surface of his thought—the Eternal in the ironic, material form of what Nietzsche liked to call "inverted Platonism." The "pictures" of the thus-enlightened lyrist, Nietzsche said, "are nothing but his very self and, as it were, only different projections of himself, on account of which he as the moving center of this world [is entitled] to say 'I': of course, this self is not the same as the waking, empirically real man, but the only truly existent and eternal self resting at the basis of things, through whose images the lyric genius sees this very basis."[3]

Everywhere—not just in poems, or in Yeats's poems—the projects of formalist ideologies are threatened to be undermined by the unreflecting force of Nietzsche's nature out of which in Apollonian resistance they arise; they are the "caverns measureless to man" in Coleridge's version of this story. Indisputably, what Yeats and Plotinus would have called his "soul" was fitfully restless and not at home in this world—"unappeased and peregrine" as his shade is made to express it in "Little Gidding." But grounded as it necessarily was in the post-Darwinian, post-Nietzschean world of "Primordial Unity," the force of eros, of desire, that drove it could only be intransitive. It was therefore compelled to create for itself—as at the end of "The Tower," out of the bits and pieces of the self's experience in the phenomenal world, recycled rags and bones—the "home" that Plotinus imagined the soul to long

3. Nietzsche, *Birth of Tragedy*, 50.

toward. Meditating in 1930, in his provocative way, upon our human need for despair, Yeats wrote in his diary, "When the image of despair departed with poetical tragedy the others could not survive, for the lover and the sage cannot survive without that despair which is a form of joy and has certainly no place in the modern psychological study of suffering." He explains himself: "When I say the lover I mean all that heroic casuistry, all that assertion of the eternity of what Nature declares ephemeral." Formalism was this kind of casuistry for Yeats, and it was heroic for both the poet and the lover because it was always one of contradiction and crisis. Its point was contradiction.[4]

4. Yeats, *Explorations*, 295–96.

Bibliographical Note

───────── ఈ⁄ ─────────

THERE ARE, OF course, as many different strategies for explaining Yeats's poetry as a whole as there are (often contradictory) Yeatses in the poems to be explained. There are numerous expositions of his interest in occult and mystical philosophy and magic, the cornerstones of which now are the translations and analyses of the *Vision* papers and what are known as the "spirit notebooks" by George Mills Harper and his team of editors. There are the essential studies of his identification with Irish history and culture and his evolving political philosophy. In recent years, these have edged Yeats over into the field of postcolonial studies. There are major studies of the surprisingly complicated subject of Yeats and gender issues. The influences upon Yeats's thought from earlier writers and literary traditions—his kinship relations, both Irish and non-Irish—have been a major focus in Yeats studies from the very beginning. Since Richard Ellmann's essential *Yeats: The Man and the Masks* (1948, 1979), biographical contextualizations of the poems have become increasingly more sophisticated as more evidence has emerged. Interest in Yeats's life has intensified over the last fifteen years because of Roy Foster's monumental two-volume biography and because of the extraordinary editions of Yeats's letters produced in *The Collected Letters* project directed by John Kelly. Even the three volumes of *The Collected Letters* published so far—scrupulously edited and annotated by Eric Domville, Ronald Schuchard, Warwick Gould, and Deirdre Toomey— have added invaluable nuance to the life that Foster has narrated in such comprehensive detail. An entirely new Yeats has arisen from these two projects alone.

Since Richard Finneran's (as it turned out) controversial edition of Yeats's poems in 1983 for Macmillan and then the lapse of the non-U.S. copyright in 1990 that resulted in competing editions in the United Kingdom, textual editing itself has become a major scholarly field within

Yeats studies. The emerging monument of this enterprise is the Cornell Yeats, which projects a reproduction, much of it in facsimile, of all of the extant manuscripts of Yeats's published poems and plays edited and annotated by distinguished Yeats scholars from around the world. The disputes that have arisen in this period—not only over the appropriate arrangement of Yeats's poems in their various editions (a matter about which Yeats seems to have been both scrupulous and indecisive) but also over the definitiveness of the printed texts of the poems themselves—have tended to defamiliarize even Yeats the poet (never mind the man) whom we had become accustomed to. This effect is especially visible in the relatively new work of textual theorists who have resourcefully grounded meanings of Yeats's poems in the material circumstances of their publication, in what has come to be known as their "bibliographical codes."

The uninitiated can track all of these different (and often competing) manifestations of Yeats's identity over roughly the last quarter of a century in the *Yeats Annual,* edited by Warwick Gould in the United Kingdom, and in *Yeats: An Annual of Critical and Textual Studies,* edited by Richard Finneran in the United States.

The present volume is aligned with a tradition of Yeats criticism in which the poems, supplemented by his critical writings and other prose, are understood as creating the context for themselves—the poems, in other words, as they may be shown to be accessible to the common reader. The landmark in this tradition is, of course, Richard Ellmann's *The Identity of Yeats,* first published in 1954. Since Ellmann's critical study, everything else in this tradition can only be understood as variations on the rich configuration of themes that Yeats has put before us. Some of these studies are more streamlined than others in the sense of being dis-historicized. Streamlining in this sense is a limitation in that it reduces the poems (and the critical writings as well) to what textual theorists refer to as their merely linguistic code—the poems as they appear on the page—and tends to separate them from biography and from the material conditions of their publication and organization (and republication and reorganization) in different editions and different kinds of editions in specific times and places.

Textual theory is perhaps the most intriguing and promising field in Yeats studies to have emerged over the last fifteen years. But textual theory is by nature both conservative, in the best scholarly sense, and empirical, and it limits itself to the material evidence available at a

given time. (Thus James Pethica, for example, supercedes Curtis Bradford. See below.) Textual evidence, like the historian's, is always subject
to reevaluation, pending the emergence of new material. Even the nature
of the material evidence is subject to dispute, as the post-Finneran debates among highly qualified Yeats scholars have shown. (Aesthetic
judgments on the poet's behalf often determine textual decisions.) Textual theory also works best when it contextualizes single poems or
plays, or single editions, the constant bibliographical recodings of which
can be traced over a long period of time. At present, at least, it is plainly
impossible to achieve an overview of Yeats's work by means of even the
simplest of bibliographical decodings—say, a study of only the parts of
Yeats's work whose production he personally supervised. Any overview
of Yeats, any argument like this one about Yeats's work as a whole,
must necessarily proceed within the limitations of the linguistic code.
Considering Yeats's lifelong and largely unwavering dedication to the
supremacy of art and his constant, only somewhat disingenuous, effort
to disengage his work from politics—from the material circumstances
of time and space—this procedure does not seem as much of an infrac-
tion as one's fascination with bibliographical grounding would have
one believe.

Even Richard Finneran—not because of the controversies but as an
outcome of his own work—has conceded that there may never be a
definitive edition of Yeats's poems. Moreover, it seems to be an article
of faith among textual theorists that there can be no definitive version
of a text since each new material presentation adds new bibliographical
codes, which, in turn, change what George Bornstein (adapting Ben-
jamin) has called the "aura" of the poem's context, which, in turn,
inevitably changes, however slightly, the poem's "meanings." Under
the circumstances, I have based my readings of Yeats's poems upon the
original gold standard, *The Variorum Edition of the Poems of W. B. Yeats,*
ed. Peter Allt and Russell K. Alspach (New York: Macmillan, 1957) in
its second printing in 1965.

Because there is a well-established canon of Yeats scholarship and
criticism, much of which I have drawn upon and cite in my own work,
I will only cite here the relatively recent examples of work in the above-
mentioned subfields of Yeats studies. George Mills Harper's editions
of *Yeats's Vision Papers* (London: Macmillan, 1992) are as follows: volume 1, *The Automatic Script: 5 November 1917–18 June 1918,* ed. Steve L.
Adams, Barbara J. Frieling, and Sandra L. Sprayberry; volume 2, *The*

Automatic Script: 25 June 1918–29 March 1920, ed. Steve L. Adams, Barbara J. Frieling, and Sandra L. Sprayberry; and volume 3, *Sleep and Dream Notebooks, Vision Notebooks 1 and 2, Card File,* ed. Robert Anthony Martinich and Margaret Mills Harper. Margaret Mills Harper has an instructive essay on the use of such materials in explicating Yeats's poetry: "Yeats's Religion," *Yeats: An Annual of Critical and Textual Studies* 8 (1995): 48–71. Kathleen Raine's lifelong interest in religion and poetry, in the sacred books of the East, and in Neoplatonism found expression in two books on Yeats in the last years of her life: *Yeats the Initiate* (Dublin: Dolmen Press, 1986) and *W. B. Yeats and the Learning of the Imagination* (Ipswich, U.K.: Golgonooza Press, 1999). For those who would resist materialist readings of Yeats, the latter, much shorter book is a lucid primer, as is Graham Hough's *The Mystery Religion of W. B. Yeats* (Brighton, U.K.: Harvester Press, 1984). The most recent of the many important studies of Yeats and the *Vision* system is Hazard Adams's *The Book of Yeats's Vision: Romantic Modernism and Antithetical Tradition* (Ann Arbor: University of Michigan Press, 1995).

Jonathan Allison's *Yeats's Political Identities: Selected Essays* (Ann Arbor: University of Michigan Press, 1996) with its valuable introduction and bibliography and wide range of contributors and points of view is an excellent compendium of the most important discussions to date of Yeats's political attitudes and their relation to his aesthetic practices. Edward Said's "Yeats and Decolonization," in his *Culture and Imperialism* (New York: Vintage, 1993), is another essential essay but is not included in Allison's volume. Phillip Marcus's *Yeats and Artistic Power* (New York: New York University Press, 1992)—extending the subject of his earlier *Yeats and the Beginning of the Irish Renaissance* (Ithaca: Cornell University Press, 1970)—systematically traces Yeats's fluctuating belief (and the influences upon his belief) in the power of the artist, through his art, to effect political and social change. Declan Kiberd's discussions of Yeats in *Inventing Ireland* (London: Jonathan Cape, 1995) address essentially this same issue in the context of Yeats as a colonial subject. A related argument by David Lloyd from his *Anomalous States: Irish Writing and the Postcolonial Moment* (Durham: Duke University Press, 1993) is excerpted in *Yeats's Political Identities* as "The Poetics of Politics: Yeats and the Founding of the State." Deborah Fleming has edited a collection of essays on the subject, *W. B. Yeats and Postcolonialism* (West Cornwall, Conn.: Locust Hill Press,

2001). Paul Scott Stanfield's *Yeats and Politics in the 1930's* (New York: St. Martin's Press, 1988) and Elizabeth Cullingford's *Yeats, Ireland, and Fascism* (London: Macmillan, 1981) are both knowledgeable and dispassionate evaluations of Yeats's political views.

Elizabeth Cullingford's *Gender and History in Yeats's Love Poetry* (Cambridge: Cambridge University Press, 1993) is a comprehensive analysis of many different kinds of gender issues in Yeats's poetry from a variety of angles, and it also has the merit of summarizing virtually all of the gender-related scholarship on Yeats up to the time of its publication. Brenda Maddox's controversial *George's Ghosts: A New Life of W. B. Yeats* (London: Picador, 1999) focuses on Yeats's sexual identity and his relations with the women in his life, especially his wife (as mediated by the Automatic Script); Maddox considers the poems mainly as data for a psychoanalytical profile of Yeats. Marjorie Elizabeth Howes's *Yeats's Nations: Gender, Class, and Irishness* (Cambridge: Cambridge University Press, 1996) considers Yeats's evolving notions of Irishness and nationhood within the context of competing gender discourses: a representative excerpt appears in *Yeats's Political Identities*. Deirdre Toomey's *Yeats and Women* (New York: St. Martin's Press, 1997) is an updated reissue of her special number of the *Yeats Annual* (1992) and comprises essays dealing largely with the influence of specific women in Yeats's life.

Influence studies since those of Hazard Adams, Harold Bloom, George Bornstein, and others, which focused mainly upon Yeats in the Romantic tradition, have broadened in instructive ways and include James Longenbach's *Stone Cottage: Pound, Yeats, and Modernism* (New York: Oxford University Press, 1988); Patrick J. Keane's *Yeats's Interactions with Tradition* (Columbia: University of Missouri Press, 1987); Wayne K. Chapman's *Yeats and English Renaissance Literature* (New York: St. Martin's Press, 1991); and Jahan Ramazani's study of Yeats as a modernist adapter of classical genres, *Yeats and the Poetry of Death: Elegy, Self-Elegy, and the Sublime* (New Haven: Yale University Press, 1990).

The first three volumes of *The Collected Letters*—vol. 1, 1865–1895, ed. John Kelly and Eric Domville; vol. 2, 1896–1900, ed. John Kelly, Warwick Gould, and Deirdre Toomey; and vol. 3, 1901–1904, ed. John Kelly and Ronald Schuchard (Oxford: Clarendon Press, 1986–1997)— as well as R. F. Foster's *W. B. Yeats: A Life*, vol. 1, *The Apprentice Mage*, and vol. 2, *The Arch-Poet* (Oxford: Oxford University Press, 1997, 2003) have no doubt surprised more than one student of Yeats with their evidence of Yeats as an imposing, industrious, and inexhaustibly worldly presence in his own times. In the poems, Yeats is a disconcertingly different personality, but the two presences are being drawn closer together. Foster's second volume, for example, devotes considerably more attention to the poems than the first. This subgenre of biographical readings of the poems is represented also, for example, by Ronald Schuchard's "Hawk and Butterfly: The Double Vision of *The Wild Swans at Coole* (1917, 1919)," *Yeats Annual* 10 (1993): 111–34; and by Lea Baechler, "Beauty Is So Difficult: W. B. Yeats and 'Upon a Dying Lady,'" *Yeats: An Annual of Critical and Textual Studies* 10 (1992): 259–80. Terence Brown's biography, *The Life of W. B. Yeats* (Oxford: Blackwell, 1999), appearing in the interval between Foster's two volumes, was conceived and executed specifically for the purpose of reinstating the authority of a biographical grounding of readings of Yeats's work. Ann Saddlemyer's *Becoming George: The Life of Mrs. W. B. Yeats* (New York: Oxford University Press, 2002) must now, with its fresh perspective and insights, be considered an essential text in the Yeats biographical canon.

George Bornstein's *Material Modernism: The Politics of the Page* (Cambridge: Cambridge University Press, 2001) is a cogent introduction to the new textual theory and a demonstration of its applications to Yeats as well as to other poets. See also his "What Is a Text of a Poem by Yeats?" in *Palimpsest: Editorial Theory in the Humanities,* ed. George Bornstein and Ralph Williams (Ann Arbor: University of Michigan Press, 1993). This new mode of editing began to take its current ideological shape with Jerome McGann's *The Textual Condition* (Princeton: Princeton University Press, 1991). David Holdeman's *Much Labouring: The Texts and Authors of Yeats's First Modernist Books* (Ann Arbor: University of Michigan Press, 1997) is the first book-length application of these editorial theories and practices to Yeats's work (focusing upon the evolutions of *In the Seven Woods*). In the Cornell Yeats, James Pethica's edition of *Last Poems: Manuscript Materials* (Ithaca: Cornell University Press, 1997) is a model of how modern editorial scholarship with its analysis of publication history and manuscript revisions—building upon the seminal work by Curtis Bradford, Thomas Parkinson, and Jon Stallworthy—has been able to show how problematical and complicated determining what used to be called "the author's intentions" can be.

Among the now more or less standard presentations of Yeats's work considered primarily as a "linguistic code"—by Richard Ellmann, T. R. Henn, Giorgio Melchiori, Amy Stock, Thomas Whitaker, Edward Engleberg, Marjorie Perloff, Denis Donoghue, Harold Bloom, Alex Zwerdling, Benamin Reid, Hazard Adams, and Robert Snukal—should be included more recent works by David Lynch, *Yeats: The Poetics of the Self* (Chicago: University of Chicago Press, 1979); Joseph Adams, *Yeats and the Masks of Syntax* (New York: Columbia University Press, 1984); Larry Brunner, *Tragic Victory: The Doctrine of Subjective Salvation in the Poetry of W. B. Yeats* (Troy, N.Y.: Whitson, 1987); M. L. Rosenthal, *Running to Paradise: Yeats's Poetic Art* (New York: Oxford University Press, 1994); Edward Larrisey, *Yeats the Poet: The Measure of Difference* (New York: Harvester Wheatloaf, 1994); and Helen Vendler's essays "Yeats and Ottava Rima," *Yeats Annual* 11 (1995): 26–44, and "Technique in the Earlier Poems of Yeats," *Yeats Annual* 8 (1991): 26–44. These anticipate a larger forthcoming study by Vendler analyzing Yeats's formal strategies as a poet.

Bibliography

———— ❧ ————

Adorno, Theodor W. *Minima Moralia: Reflections from a Damaged Life.* Trans. E. F. N. Jephcott. London: Verso, 1978.

Altieri, Charles. "From a Comic to a Tragic Sense of Language in Yeats's Mature Poetry." *Modern Language Quarterly* 33, no. 2 (June 1972): 156–71.

Archibald, Douglas. *Yeats.* Syracuse, N.Y.: Syracuse University Press, 1983.

Barrett, William. *Time of Need: Forms of Imagination in the Twentieth Century.* New York: Harper and Row, 1972.

Baudelaire, Charles. *Baudelaire: Selected Writings on Art and Literature.* Trans. P. E. Charvet. New York: Penguin Books, 1972.

Bell, Vereen, and Laurence Lerner, eds. *On Modern Poetry: Essays Presented to Donald Davie.* Nashville, Tenn.: Vanderbilt University Press, 1988.

Bloom, Harold, ed. *William Butler Yeats.* New York: Chelsea House Publishers, 1986.

Bohlmann, Otto. *Yeats and Nietzsche: An Exploration of Major Nietzschean Echoes in the Writings of William Butler Yeats.* Totowa, N.J.: Barnes and Noble Books, 1982.

Bornstein, George. "Remaking Himself: Yeats's Revisions of His Early Canon." *Text* 5 (1991): 339–58.

———. *Transformations of Romanticism in Yeats, Eliot, and Stevens.* Chicago: University of Chicago Press, 1976.

Bornstein, George, ed. *Romantic and Modern: Revaluations of Literary Tradition.* Pittsburgh: University of Pittsburgh Press, 1977.

Bornstein, George, and Ralph G. Williams, eds. *Palimpsest: Editorial Theory in the Humanities.* Ann Arbor: University of Michigan Press, 1993.

Brown, Terence. *Ireland's Literature: Selected Essays.* Totowa, N.J.: Barnes and Noble Books, 1988.

Cullingford, Elizabeth. *Yeats, Ireland, and Fascism.* London: Macmillan, 1981.

Davie, Donald. *Ezra Pound: Poet as Sculptor.* New York: Oxford University Press, 1964.

Deane, Seamus. *Celtic Revivals: Essays in Modern Irish Literature, 1880–1980.* London: Faber and Faber, 1985.

de Man, Paul. *Blindness and Insight.* Minneapolis: University of Minnesota Press, 1983.

Donoghue, Denis. *William Butler Yeats.* New York: Viking Press, 1971.

Eliot, T. S. *On Poetry and Poets.* New York: Farrar, Straus and Cudahy, 1957.

———. "The Poetry of W. B. Yeats." *Southern Review* 7, no. 3 (winter 1942): 442–54.

Ellmann, Richard. *Eminent Domain: Yeats among Wilde, Joyce, Pound, Eliot, and Auden.* New York: Oxford University Press, 1967.

———. *The Identity of Yeats.* New York: Oxford University Press, 1964.

———. "Joyce and Yeats." *Kenyon Review* 12 (autumn 1950): 618–38.

———. "Yeats without Analogues." *Kenyon Review* 26, no. 1 (winter 1964): 30–47.

Engelberg, Edward. *The Vast Design: Patterns in W. B. Yeats's Aesthetic.* Washington, D.C.: Catholic University of America Press, 1988.

Finneran, Richard J., ed. *Critical Essays on W. B. Yeats.* Boston: G. K. Hall, 1986.

Foster, Roy F. *W. B. Yeats: A Life.* Vol. 1, *The Apprentice Mage, 1865–1914.* Oxford: Oxford University Press, 1997.

———. *W. B. Yeats: A Life.* Vol. 2, *The Arch-Poet, 1915–1939.* Oxford: Oxford University Press, 2003.

Frank, Joseph. *The Widening Gyre: Crisis and Mastery in Modern Literature.* New Brunswick, N.J.: Rutgers University Press, 1963.

Gentile, Giovanni. *The Theory of Mind as Pure Act.* Trans. W. Wildon Carr. London: Macmillan, 1922.

Harrison, John R. *The Reactionaries: A Study of the Anti-Democratic Intelligentsia.* New York: Schocken Books, 1967.

Holloway, John. "Style and World in *The Tower*." In Donoghue, *An Honoured Guest: New Essays on W. B. Yeats,* ed. Denis Donoghue and J. R. Murloyne, 88–105. New York: St. Martin's Press, 1966.

Jeffares, A. Norman. *A New Commentary on the Poems of W. B. Yeats.* Stanford, Calif.: Stanford University Press, 1984.

Joyce, James. *A Portrait of the Artist as a Young Man.* New York: Viking Press, 1964.

Kaufmann, Walter. *Nietzsche: Philosopher, Psychologist, Antichrist.* Princeton: Princeton University Press, 1974.

Keane, Patrick J. *Yeats's Interactions with Tradition.* Columbia: University of Missouri Press, 1987.

Keats, John. *The Letters of John Keats, 1814–1821.* Ed. Hyder Edward Rollins. Cambridge: Harvard University Press, 1958.

Kenner, Hugh. "The Sacred Book of the Arts." In Finneran, *Critical Essays on W. B. Yeats,* 9–19.

Kermode, Frank. *Romantic Image.* London: Routledge and Paul, 1957.

———. *The Sense of an Ending: Studies in the Theory of Fiction.* New York: Oxford University Press, 1967.

Kiberd, Declan. *Inventing Ireland: The Literature of the Modern Nation.* London: Jonathan Cape, 1995.

Lange, Friedrich. *The History of Materialism and Criticism of Its Present Importance.* 3d ed., trans. Ernest Chester Thomas. New York: Humanities Press, 1950.

Lentricchia, Frank. *The Gaiety of Language: An Essay on the Radical Poetics of W. B. Yeats and Wallace Stevens.* Berkeley: University of California Press, 1968.

Marcus, Phillip L. *Yeats and Artistic Power.* New York: New York University Press, 1992.

Miller, J. Hillis. "Yeats: The Linguistic Moment." In Bloom, *William Butler Yeats,* 189–210.

Nicholls, Peter. *Modernisms: A Literary Guide.* Berkeley: University of California Press, 1995.

Nietzsche, Friedrich. *Beyond Good and Evil: Prelude to a Philosophy of the Future.* Trans. Walter Kaufmann. New York: Vintage Books, 1966.

———. *"The Birth of Tragedy" and "The Case of Wagner."* Trans. Walter Kaufmann. New York: Vintage Books, 1967.

———. *"The Gay Science" with "A Prelude in Rhymes" and an Appendix of Songs.* Trans. Walter Kaufmann. New York: Vintage Books, 1974.

———. *"On the Genealogy of Morals" and "Ecce Homo."* Ed. Walter Kaufmann, trans. R. J. Hollingdale and Walter Kaufmann. New York: Vintage Books, 1969.

————. *The Portable Nietzsche.* Trans. Walter Kaufmann. New York: Viking Press, 1954.

————. *The Will to Power.* Ed. Walter Kaufmann, trans. R. J. Hollingdale and Walter Kaufmann. New York: Vintage Books, 1968.

Olney, James, ed. *Autobiography: Essays Theoretical and Critical.* Princeton: Princeton University Press, 1980.

Oppel, Frances Nesbitt. *Mask and Tragedy: Yeats and Nietzsche, 1902–10.* Charlottesville: University Press of Virginia, 1987.

Parkinson, Thomas. *W. B. Yeats, Self-Critic: A Study of His Early Verse [and] W. B. Yeats: The Later Poetry.* 2 vols. in 1. Berkeley: University of California Press, 1971.

Perloff, Marjorie. "'The Tradition of Myself': The Autobiographical Mode of Yeats." *Journal of Modern Literature* 4, no. 3 (February 1975): 529–73.

Plato. *The Republic.* Trans. Desmond Lee. 2d ed., revised. New York: Penguin, 1987.

Raine, Kathleen. *Yeats the Initiate: Essays on Certain Themes in the Work of W. B. Yeats.* London: Allen and Unwin, 1986.

Said, Edward W. *Yeats and Decolonization.* In *Culture and Imperialism.* New York: Vintage, 1993.

Sasso, James. *The Role of Consciousness in the Thought of Nietzsche.* Washington, D.C.: University Press of America, 1977.

Seiden, Morton Irving. *William Butler Yeats: The Poet as a Mythmaker, 1865–1939.* New York: Cooper Square Publishers, 1975.

Shelley, Percy Bysshe. "A Defence of Poetry." In *Shelley's Prose, or The Trumpet of a Prophecy,* ed. David Lee Clark, 275–97. New York: New Amsterdam, 1988.

Snukal, Robert. *High Talk: The Philosophical Poetry of W. B. Yeats.* Cambridge: Cambridge University Press, 1973.

Stanfield, Paul Scott. *Yeats and Politics in the 1930s.* New York: St. Martin's Press, 1988.

Steiner, George. *After Babel: Aspects of Language and Translation.* New York: Oxford University Press, 1975.

Stock, A. G. *W. B. Yeats: His Poetry and Thought.* Cambridge: Cambridge University Press, 1961.

Taylor, John. "Bloom's Day: Hanging Out with the Reigning Genius of Lit Crit." *New York Times Magazine,* November 5, 1990, 55.

Thatcher, David S. *Nietzsche in England, 1890–1914: The Growth of a Reputation.* Toronto: University of Toronto Press, 1970.

Tóibín, Colm. "Erasures." *London Review of Books* 20, no. 15 (July 30, 1998): 17–23.

Vendler, Helen. *Wallace Stevens: Words Chosen out of Desire.* Knoxville: University of Tennessee Press, 1984.

Whitaker, Thomas R. *Swan and Shadow: Yeats's Dialogue with History.* Chapel Hill: University of North Carolina Press, 1964.

Wilde, Oscar. *Complete Works of Oscar Wilde.* New York: Harper Perennial, 1989.

Wilson, F. A. C. *W. B. Yeats and Tradition.* New York: Macmillan, 1958.

Yeats, John Butler. *Letters to His Son W. B. Yeats and Others, 1869–1922.* Ed. Joseph Hone. London: Secker and Warburg, 1983.

Yeats, W. B. *Autobiographies.* London: Macmillan, 1955.

———. *The Collected Letters of W. B. Yeats.* 3 vols. Ed. John Kelly. Oxford: Clarendon Press, 1986–1997.

———. *The Collected Poems of W. B. Yeats.* 2d ed. London: Macmillan, 1982.

———. *The Collected Works of W. B. Yeats.* Vol. 1, *The Poems.* Ed. Richard J. Finneran. New York: Macmillan, 1989.

———. *Essays and Introductions.* New York: Macmillan, 1961.

———. *Explorations.* New York: Macmillan, 1962.

———. *Last Poems: Manuscript Materials.* Ed. James Pethica. Ithaca: Cornell University Press, 1997.

———. *The Letters of W. B. Yeats.* Ed. Allan Wade. London: R. Hart-Davis, 1954.

———. *Letters on Poetry from W. B. Yeats to Dorothy Wellesley.* New York: Oxford University Press, 1940.

———. *Memoirs [of] W. B. Yeats: Autobiography [and] First Draft Journal.* Ed. Denis Donoghue. London: Macmillan, 1972.

———. *Mythologies.* New York: Macmillan, 1959.

———. *Uncollected Prose.* Ed. John P. Frayne and Colton Johnson. 2 vols. New York: Columbia University Press, 1970–1976.

———. *A Vision.* London: Macmillan, 1937.

———. *Wheels and Butterflies.* New York: Macmillan, 1935.

Yeats, W. B., ed. *The Oxford Book of Modern Verse, 1892–1935.* New York: Oxford University Press, 1936.

Yeats, W. B., and T. Sturge Moore. *W. B. Yeats and T. Sturge Moore: Their Correspondence, 1901–1937.* Ed. Ursula Bridge. New York: Oxford University Press, 1953.

Young, Dudley. *Out of Ireland: A Reading of Yeats' Poetry.* Cheadle,
     England: Carcanet Press, 1975.
Zwerdling, Alex. *Yeats and the Heroic Ideal.* New York: New York Uni-
     versity Press, 1965.

Index

Credits

Acknowledgment is made as follows for permission to quote from copyrighted material:

Passages from the poems of William Butler Yeats under copyright are reprinted with the permission of A P Watt Ltd. on behalf of Michael B. Yeats, and with the permission of Scribner, an imprint of Simon & Schuster Adult Publishing Group, from *The Collected Works of W.B. Yeats, Volume 1: The Poems, Revised,* edited by Richard J. Finneran. Copyright © 1983, 1989 by Anne Yeats. Copyright © 1928 by The Macmillan Company; copyright renewed © 1956 by Georgie Yeats. Copyright © 1933 by The Macmillan Company; copyright renewed © 1961 by Bertha Georgie Yeats. Copyright © 1934 by The Macmillan Company; copyright renewed © 1962 by Bertha Georgie Yeats. Copyright © 1940 by Georgie Yeats; copyright renewed © 1968 by Bertha Georgie Yeats, Michael Butler Yeats, and Anne Yeats.